Books should be returned on or before the
last date stamped below.

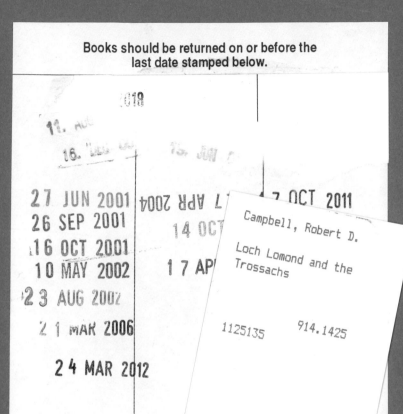

LOCH LOMOND AND THE TROSSACHS

Loch Lomond and the Trossachs

Robert D. Campbell

MAINSTREAM
PUBLISHING

EDINBURGH AND LONDON

First published in Great Britain in 1999 by
MAINSTREAM PUBLISHING COMPANY (EDINBURGH) LTD
7 Albany Street
Edinburgh EH1 3UG

ISBN 1 84018 189 3

Cover illustration: Ben Lomond from Culag, north of Luss (© Argyll, The Isles,
Loch Lomond, Stirling and Trossachs Tourist Board)

A catalogue record for this book is available from the British Library

Typeset in Garamond and Gill Sans
Printed and bound in Finland by WSOY

Contents

Acknowledgements

First, I have to thank my good friend Duncan MacDonald of Alexandria for providing news and information about the region over many years. Thanks are also due to the staff of the excellent Local History Section at Dumbarton Public Library. In particular, I would mention Graham Hopner and Arthur Jones (both authors of excellent local histories), whose researches into the history of West Dunbartonshire have been made readily available to others, and Rhoda MacLeod, for efficiently retrieving items. Also, to Stirling Council Countryside Rangers and the Argyll, The Isles, Loch Lomond, Stirling and Trossachs Tourist Board for assistance with illustrations. Acknowledgement must also be made to the work of those authors of historical and descriptive works about the region, to which reference has been made in the preparation of this publication.

 I would like to place on record my appreciation of the work of the Scottish Record Office, Edinburgh; the National Library, Edinburgh; the Scottish Library at Edinburgh Public Library; the Royal Commission on Ancient & Historic Monuments of Scotland Library, Edinburgh, and the Mitchell Library, Glasgow, in preserving Scotland's history in word and picture. Finally, I pay tribute to the sterling efforts of the Argyll, The Isles, Loch Lomond, Stirling and Trossachs Tourist Board and Forest Enterprise, a division of the Forestry Commission, in compiling much valuable information about this beautiful region and in actively promoting its manifold attractions. Forest Enterprise deserve a particular vote of thanks for having done much over the years to encourage public access and in providing excellent facilities for visitors throughout the region.

Loch Lomond and The Trossachs

Introduction

The unsurpassed beauty of the region embracing Loch Lomond, The Trossachs and Breadalbane is world-famous and ranks among Scotland's leading scenic attractions. With increasing numbers of visitors converging on the region every year, it is now hard to imagine that before the mid-eighteenth century few had ever gazed upon these lovely scenes, other than the war-like Highlanders who inhabited the mountainous clan lands beyond the Highland boundary.

It was the breakdown of the old clan system following the ill-fated Jacobite Rising of 1745–6 and the progressive improvement of road, rail and water communications over the next two and a half centuries that opened up this scenic paradise to the world. And it was Sir Walter Scott's historical romances, *The Lady of the Lake* (1810) and *Rob Roy* (1817) that brought its attractions before a wider public and placed it firmly on the tourist map. In more recent times, the success of the Hollywood 'block-buster' movies *Rob Roy*, starring Liam Neeson and Jessica Lange, and *Braveheart*, starring Mel Gibson as Scotland's revered patriot-hero Sir William Wallace, has brought a further influx of visitors to explore the real country of these legendary figures.

This irresistible mix of stirring history and spectacular scenery has ensured that tourism has remained paramount in the region's economy for many years now, but it has assumed particular importance on Loch Lomondside during the twentieth century with the breaking-up of the great landed estates, owned by a few wealthy owners, and the development of facilities for visitors. It has recently been estimated that around two million people now visit Loch Lomond each year, while another three million pass through the district en route to and from the Western Highlands.

Multi-million-pound hotel, marina, golf course and other recreational developments have sprung up along the south-western shores of the bonnie banks in recent times and world-famous stars of stage, screen and sport are now regular visitors. Good road and rail links, greatly improved in recent years, have helped to make Loch Lomond the most accessible natural playground within easy reach of the city of Glasgow and central Scotland. Balloch, at the loch's southern end, has historically been regarded as being 'the gateway to Loch

Lomond', but Luss, Tarbet and Ardlui, on the loch's western shore, and Gartocharn, Drymen, Balmaha, Rowardennan and Inversnaid on the quieter eastern side, also cater for visitors. In the summer months, cruising and pleasure boats thread their way among the loch's emerald islands; thousands tramp the scenic West Highland Way on the eastern shore, climb mighty Ben Lomond and other hills, or just stop by the lochside to camp or picnic and enjoy the magnificent scenery.

To the west of the district, the famous Three Lochs Tour will take you from Glasgow to Tarbet on Loch Lomondside and then south by way of Arrochar on the shores of fiord-like Loch Long, the gentler scenery of the Gare Loch, and on to Helensburgh at the entrance to the glorious Firth of Clyde, or the route may be reversed. To the east, the magnificent lochs, bens and glens of The Trossachs and Breadalbane districts also lie within easy reach of Glasgow, while Stirling, Callander, Aberfoyle, Strathyre, Lochearnhead, Killin and Crianlarich all provide good touring bases. Loch Katrine's silver waters lie at the heart of The Trossachs and Rob Roy Country, but there are many more beautiful lochs sprinkled among the hills and glens, each with a unique atmosphere of its own. Further north and accessed from the pretty village of Killin, Loch Tay is the pride of the fair district of Breadalbane, which extends westward from Killin by Glen Dochart and Strath Fillan to Tyndrum.

More has probably been written about the Loch Lomond, Trossachs and Breadalbane districts than of any others in Scotland. Yet, considering all that has been written, the wealth of scenic beauty and history associated with the region and the vast numbers of visitors that arrive each year, it is remarkable that no comprehensive guide to the entire region has existed until now. Therefore, by bringing together in this guide much diverse information about this beautiful region, it is hoped that it will prove useful to many visitors in years to come. It also coincides with a most important development, for in September 1997, the Secretary of State for Scotland announced that Loch Lomond and The Trossachs are to form Scotland's first National Park, thus ensuring conservation of the region's rugged beauty for the benefit of future generations.

GENERAL NOTES

Points of Interest

The letters (R) and (L) in the text indicate points of interest to the right (R) and to the left (L) for road routes and walks, according to the direction of travel described. In the few cases where a feature is common to more than one route, the description of it is usually repeated, thus avoiding the necessity of having to refer back to another page.

Some interesting circular tours can be undertaken by combining routes in whole or in part. (See general map.) The location of public toilets (T) and parking areas (P) is also indicated in the text. (See also the introductory chapter on Visitor Services, Sport and Leisure Facilities, Public Transport and Accommodation.)

1 km = 0.621371 miles	1 mile = 1.60934 km
1 m = 3.28084 feet	1 foot = 0.304800 m

Distances, Heights, etc.

Metric measurements are shown throughout, in kilometres (km) and metres (m). The relevant conversions to and from the old Imperial System are as follows:

Place-names

The possible derivations of some of the principal place-names are noted in the text as a matter of interest, mainly based on John Irving's *Place-names of Dunbartonshire* (1928) and James B. Johnstone's *The Place-names of Stirlingshire* (2nd ed. 1904) and *Place-names of Scotland* (1934). The latter two works were edited and reprinted by Stirling District Libraries in 1987 as *Place-names of Stirling District*. Another useful reference is W.J. Watson's *The Celtic Place-names of Scotland* (1926, since reprinted).

However, it will be appreciated that the interpretation of place-names is an inexact science! Since Gaelic names predominate throughout the region, a note on the historical background to their origin and a glossary of Gaelic words commonly used in place-names and geographical features is given in an appendix.

Natural History and Geology

A Natural History of Loch Lomond (University of Glasgow Press 1974, since reprinted by Loch Lomond Park Authority) provides an introduction to the geology, botany, birdlife, mammals, aquatic plants, animals, fish, archaeology and land use of the Loch Lomond district. *Central Scotland – Land, Wildlife, People* (The Forth Naturalist and Historian, Stirling University 1993) covers the Stirling, Trossachs and Breadalbane districts. See also the *Queen Elizabeth Forest Park Guide* (Forest Enterprise 1990) and the booklet, *An Introduction to the Wildlife of The Trossachs* (Stirling District Council Countryside Ranger Service 1995). The geology of the region is described (in full colour) in *Loch Lomond to Stirling: A Landscape Fashioned by Geology* (British Geological Survey and Scottish Natural Heritage 1995). *The Loch Lomond Story* (Loch Lomond Park Authority 1996) provides a general introduction to Loch Lomond.

History

Many historical works about the district have long been out of print and are often available for consultation only at reference libraries. Some of the more recent works include *A Short History of Dunbartonshire* by I.M.M. MacPhail (1962, since reprinted); *Loch Lomond, Loch Katrine and The Trossachs* by George Eyre-Todd (c1946); *Loch Lomond, The Trossachs and Loch Katrine* by W.D. Cocker (c1952); *The Islands of Loch Lomond* by Clair Calder and Lynn Lindsay (1997); *The Trossachs and the Rob Roy Country* by Campbell Nairne (1961); *In Famed Breadalbane* by William A. Gillies (1930, rep. 1980); *The Braes o' Balquhidder* by Elizabeth Beauchamp (4th ed. 1993) and *Rob Roy MacGregor: His Life and Times* by W.H. Murray (1982, since reprinted).

Maps

Ordnance Survey
- Outdoor Leisure Map 39, Loch Lomond*
- Explorer Leisure Map 11, The Trossachs and Queen Elizabeth Forest Park*
- Landranger Series, 1:50 000, Sheets 50, 51, 56, 57, 63, 64
- Pathfinder Series, 1:25 000, Sheets 334, 347, 357, 368, 370, 380, 381, 382, 390, 391, 402, 403*

* The Outdoor Leisure and Explorer Leisure maps cover much of the area formerly covered by the Pathfinder Series, 1:25 000. Where the area of a Pathfinder map is wholly covered by an Outdoor Leisure or Explorer Leisure map, the Pathfinder map will no longer be available.

Harvey's Maps
- 1:40,000, Arrochar Alps
- 1:40,000, West Highland Way

- 1:40,000, Trossachs East
- 1:40,000, Ben Lawers
- 1:100,000, Loch Lomond and Trossachs Tourist Map
- 1:100,000, Stirling and District Map and Street Plans

Other Maps
- Official Tourist Map: Argyll, The Isles & Trossachs (No. 191) (Estate Publications)
- Footprint Map Guide to the West Highland Way
- Footprint Map of National Cycle Network: Map 7C, Glasgow to Inverness

GETTING THERE

By Car
From the south and west follow M6, A74, M74, M73 then take M8, M898 (Erskine Bridge), A82 for Loch Lomond or M73, A80, M80, M9 for Stirling. From the south and east follow A1 to the outskirts of Edinburgh, take A720 (Edinburgh City By-Pass), then M8, M898 (Erskine Bridge), A82 for Loch Lomond and the west or M8, M9 for Stirling.

By Coach
National Express coach services (0990 808080) operate from London Victoria Coach Station to Stirling Bus Station, Glasgow Buchanan Street Bus Station and Edinburgh St Andrew Square Bus Station, to link with regular local services. Several tour companies operate coach tours to the area.

By Rail
Regular express services link London Euston with Glasgow Central and Edinburgh Waverley by the West Coast Route, to link with regular local services. On the East Coast Route, services link London King's Cross with Edinburgh Waverley and Glasgow Central. On both routes some services continue on to Inverness (via Stirling) and Aberdeen (via Fife and Dundee). The Caledonian Sleepers (a division of ScotRail) provide overnight sleeping-car services from London Euston to Glasgow, Edinburgh, Inverness (via Stirling), Aberdeen (via Fife and Dundee) and Fort William (via Gare Loch, Loch Long and Loch Lomond stations). Contact your local station for details of services and fares, including cheap Apex and other advance purchase fares.

By Air
Frequent services operate to Glasgow and Edinburgh Airports from London, English regional, Scottish internal and many

European airports. Glasgow also has regular scheduled and charter flights direct from the East Coast of North America.

VISITOR SERVICES, SPORT AND LEISURE FACILITIES, PUBLIC TRANSPORT AND ACCOMMODATION

Particulars of local public transport services are shown at the beginning of each route. Information regarding visitor services and facilities in towns and villages is shown within separate panels at the conclusion of the relevant entry. Only the principal accommodation (generally larger establishments listed in the local Tourist Board's Accommodation Guide) is shown. A detailed accommodation list, a series of district Visitor Guides showing services, and *What's On* guides to events, are published annually by the Argyll, The Isles, Loch Lomond, Stirling and Trossachs Tourist Board and may be obtained free of charge from the Board's Tourist Information Centres, where an accommodation booking service is also available.
  Services and facilities are, of course, subject to change and information regarding the current position may be obtained from Tourist Information Centres. While every effort has been made to ensure the accuracy of information contained in this guide, no responsibility can be accepted for errors or omissions.

Public Transport Operators
The principal rail and road operators in the district are:
- ScotRail (on behalf of Strathclyde Passenger Transport in the west of the district): Glasgow to Balloch, Helensburgh, and West Highland Line stations to Oban, Fort William and Mallaig; Glasgow and Edinburgh to Stirling, Perth, Dundee, Aberdeen and Inverness. (0345 484950)
- Scottish Citylink Coaches (operating in association with Skye-Ways Express Coaches and West Coast Motor Co.): Glasgow to Campbeltown, Oban, Fort William and Uig (Skye) via the west side of Loch Lomond; Glasgow to Stirling, Perth, Dundee, Aberdeen and Inverness; Edinburgh to Fort William via Callander and Crianlarich. (0990 505050)
- First Glasgow: Local services, Clydebank, Dumbarton and Helensburgh* to Balloch. Dumbarton to Helensburgh. (*From Helensburgh, Sundays only). (0141 636 3195)
- McColls Coaches (on behalf of Strathclyde Passenger Transport): Alexandria/Balloch to Luss. (01389 754321)
- Weir's Tourlink and P J Travel (on behalf of Argyll and Bute Council and Strathclyde Passenger Transport): Clydebank and Helensburgh to Luss, Arrochar, Lochgoilhead and

Carrick Castle. (Weir's Tourlink 0141 941 2843; P J Travel 0141 942 4377)

- Wilson's of Rhu and Garelochhead Minibuses: Helensburgh to Garelochhead, Kilcreggan and Coulport. (Wilson's 01436 820300; Garelochhead Minibuses 01436 810200)
- First Midland Bluebird: extensive local services throughout the district, including Glasgow to Drymen, Balfron, Aberfoyle and Stirling; Alexandria/Balloch to Drymen and Balmaha or Stirling, and Stirling to Callander, Killin and Tyndrum. (01324 613777)
- Royal Mail Post Buses. Aberfoyle to Kinlochard; Aberfoyle to Inversnaid; Callander to Trossachs Pier and Aberfoyle; Killin to Ardeonaig and Callander, and Crianlarich to Killin and Callander, or Tyndrum. (Customer Services 0345 740740)
- Martin's Coaches: Glasgow to Fort William via the west side of Loch Lomond. (01397 712579/772042)

Note: Certain bus services are operated under contract to local authorities and operators and routes are liable to change.

Timetables for rail, bus and ferry/cruise services are available from Tourist Information Centres (addresses follow), Travel Information Centres or from transport operators. Rail timetables can also be obtained from staffed rail stations. Royal Mail Post Bus timetables are available from local Post Offices. In Glasgow, Strathclyde Passenger Transport Travel Information Centres at Buchanan Bus Station (0141 332 7133); St Enoch Square (0141 226 4826); Glasgow Airport (UK Arrivals) (0141 848 4330); and Hillhead Underground Station, Byres Road (0141 333 3673), sell local tickets (not St Enoch Square), take long-distance coach bookings, day and extended tour bookings and deal with timetable enquiries. Strathclyde Passenger Transport offer reduced-rate Day Tripper and Rural Daycard Tickets within the region (ask for leaflets).

Stirling Council's Travel Information Centre at Stirling Bus Station provides information and sells coach and bus tickets. The Council also operates a Public Transport Helpline for all services within Stirling District (01786 442707).

Cheap Day Return tickets are available on most rail services, subject to advertised restrictions (leaflet available). First Midland Bluebird have a Heart of Scotland Explorer ticket which covers much of the district. There are two useful Rover tickets. A Stirling Day Rover gives unlimited travel for one day on all First Midland Bluebird journeys between Stirling and Callander and on all Trossachs Trundler services. Enquire at Stirling Bus Station Travel Centre. An Aberfoyle/Callander Day Rover gives unlimited travel for one day on all Trossachs Trundler journeys round the Callander–Trossachs–Aberfoyle–Callander circle and may be obtained on the bus.

Tourist Information Centres

Tourist Information Centres, operated by the Argyll, The Isles, Loch Lomond, Stirling and Trossachs Tourist Board, are located at the following places within the district:

ABERFOYLE: Trossachs Discovery Centre, Main Street 01877 382352 (April to October and weekends only November to March)
ARDGARTAN: Glen Croe 01301 702432 (April to October)
BALLOCH: Balloch Road 01389 753533 (April to October)
CALLANDER: Rob Roy and Trossachs Visitor Centre, Ancaster Square 01877 330342 (March to December and weekends only in January and February)
DRYMEN: Drymen Library, The Square 01360 660068 (May to September)
DUMBARTON: (Milton) A82 Northbound 01389 742306 (All Year)
DUNBLANE: Stirling Road 01786 824428 (May to September)
HELENSBURGH: Clock Tower, The Pier 01436 672642 (April to October)
KILLIN: Breadalbane Folk Centre, Falls of Dochart 01567 820254 (March to November and weekends only during February)
STIRLING: 41 Dumbarton Road 01786 475019 (All Year) M9/M80 Junction 9: Motorway Service Area 01786 814111 (April to October)
Royal Burgh of Stirling Visitor Centre, Castle Esplanade 01786 479901 (All Year)
TARBET (LOCH LOMOND): Main Street 01301 702260 (April to October)
TYNDRUM: Main Street 01838 400246 (April to October)
ADVANCE BOOKING SERVICE: 01631 566606

Ranger and Information Services
Loch Lomond Park Authority
The Loch Lomond Park Authority's headquarters is at the Old Station (opposite Balloch Railway Station), Balloch Road, Balloch, G83 8SS (01389 753311), and there are Visitor Centres at Balloch Castle, Luss and Balmaha. For details and Ranger Service events call 01389 758216.

Queen Elizabeth Forest Park
The Queen Elizabeth Forest Park Visitor Centre is at Aberfoyle, just off the Duke's Pass road (A821) which links Aberfoyle with The Trossachs (01877 382258, open March to Christmas). At other times, information about the Park can be obtained from: Forestry Commission, Forest Enterprise, Aberfoyle, FK8 3UX (01877 382383).

Argyll Forest Park
The Forestry Commission's Cowal District Office, which administers the forests around Arrochar, is at Kilmun, By Dunoon, Argyll, PA23 8SE (01369 840666).

Stirling Council Countryside Ranger Service
The Countryside Ranger Service headquarters is at Stirling Council Offices, Environmental Services, Viewforth, Stirling, FK8 2ET. For information and Ranger Service events call 01786 442875, or see Ranger Service brochure.

National Trust for Scotland Ben Lomond Nature Reserve
The Trust's Ranger can be contacted at Ardess Lodge, Rowardennan, By Drymen, Stirling District, G63 0AR (01360 870224).

National Trust for Scotland Ben Lawers Nature Reserve
For information contact N.T.S. Office, Lynedoch, Main Street, Killin, Stirling District, FK21 8UW (01567 820988).

Leven Valley Initiative
For information contact the Initiative's office at 147 High Street, Dumbarton, G82 (01389 742544).

Weather Forecasts
The local weather is notoriously unreliable and in winter near-Arctic conditions often prevail on the hills in the Highland region. Before heading for the hills obtain an up-to-date weather forecast. Telephone the Met. Office's Mountaincall Forecast for the West of Scotland (0891 500441), or check the TV or radio forecasts.

Events and Festivals
The following are just some of the popular annual events which are held in the district. See the local Tourist Board's free seasonal *What's On* guide to events and entertainments for dates and venues. Approximate dates are shown thus, for the relevant month: Early; Mid; Late.

May
Late – Doune and Dunblane Fling
Late – Drymen Agricultural Show

June
Early/Mid – Stirling Agricultural Show
Mid – Killin Traditional Music and Dance Festival
Mid/Late – Clyde Regatta

July
Early – Doune and Dunblane Agricultural Show
Early – Loch Lomond World Invitational Golf Tournament, Luss (date may vary)
Mid – Stirling Highland Games
Mid – Balloch Highland Games
Mid – Rosneath and Clynder Highland Games
Mid/Late – Luss Highland Games
Mid/Late – Trossachs Highland Festival
Late – Balquhidder, Strathyre and Lochearnhead Highland Games, Lochearnhead
Late – Callander International Highland Games

August
Early – Killin Highland Games (may be late July)
Early – Bridge of Allan Highland Games
Mid – Killin Agricultural Show

Local Newspapers
Local newspapers also provide information on forthcoming events and services, as well as providing a valuable insight into local life. The *Dumbarton and Vale of Leven Reporter* (Wednesday), the *Helensburgh Advertiser* (Thursday) and the *Lennox Herald* (Friday), all published weekly, cover the western part of the district around Dumbarton, Loch Lomond, Helensburgh and the Gare Loch. The *Stirling Observer*, published twice weekly (Wednesday and Friday), covers the eastern part, including eastern Loch Lomond, Menteith, The Trossachs and Stirling. The *Stirling News* (Wednesday) also covers the Stirling area.

Key to Abbreviations

Visitor Services

B	Bus Service
Bk	Bank
C	Caravan Site (may not be open all year)
CC	Caravan and Camping Site (may not be open all year)
Ch	Church
Cr	Cruises
D	Doctor (GP)
F	Ferry Service (Pedestrian, may not operate all year)
G	Garage/Filling Station
H	Hospital with Casualty Facilities (may not be open 24 hours)
I	Tourist Information Centre (may not be open all year)
MR	Mountain Rescue Post
P	Parking
PO	Post Office
PS	Police Station (may not be continuously staffed)
PT	Public Telephone (may be in hotel)
R	Rail Service
SA	Serviced Accommodation
SC	Self-Catering Accommodation
T	Toilets (may not be open all year)
YH	Youth Hostel (may not be open all year)

Sport and Leisure Facilities

A	Art Gallery (Retail)
Bw	Bowling
Cf	Crafts
CP	Country Park
Cy	Cycling
Fi	Fishing
FP	Forest Park
Go	Golf
HB	Historic Building or Monument
L	Library
M	Museum/Art Gallery (Public)
PB	Public Bar (may be in hotel)
Pu	Putting
RC	Restaurant/Cafe (may be in hotel)

Ri	Riding/Trekking
S	Shopping
SB	Sailing/Boat Hire
Sk	Skiing
SL	Sports and Leisure Centre
SP	Swimming Pool
TC	Tennis Court
VC	Visitor/Interpretive Centre (may not be open all year)
W	Walking
Wa	Watersports

Follow the Country Code

Enjoy the countryside and respect its life and work

Guard against all risk of fire

Fasten all gates

Keep your dogs under close control

Keep to the public paths across farmland

Use gates and stiles to cross fences, hedges and walls

Leave livestock, crops and machinery alone

Take your litter home

Help to keep all water clean

Protect wildlife, plants and trees

Take special care on country roads

Make no unnecessary noise

ROUTE 1. 'TAKING THE HIGH ROAD' TO LOCH LOMOND

Glasgow to Balloch by the A82 or M8/A82

Glasgow to Balloch and Loch Lomond's Western Shore by Public Transport

Rail
A frequent electric train service operates from Glasgow (Queen St and Central Low Level Stations) to Balloch and Helensburgh. When travelling from Glasgow Central change at Partick. On Sundays most Balloch services operate through Glasgow Central. West Highland Line trains to Fort William, Mallaig and Oban, which run via the Gare Loch, Loch Long and along Loch Lomondside between Arrochar and Tarbet and Ardlui, usually leave from Glasgow Queen Street (High Level).

Bus and Coach
Coaches from Glasgow Buchanan Bus Station serve Inveraray, Campbeltown, Oban, Fort William and Uig (Skye), via Loch Lomond's western shore, calling at Balloch (A82 roundabout), Luss, Inverbeg and Tarbet. Beyond Tarbet, the Inveraray, Campbeltown and Oban services cross to Arrochar on Loch Long, while the Fort William and Skye service continues along Loch Lomondside to Ardlui and Crianlarich.

An infrequent bus service operates from Clydebank (Dock Street) to Lochgoilhead and Carrick Castle via Dumbarton, Helensburgh, Luss, Tarbet and Arrochar. Bus services between Clydebank (Bus Station) and Dumbarton, Balloch and Helensburgh cater mainly for local journeys.

Cruises and Ferries
Cruises on Loch Lomond operate from Balloch, Luss and Tarbet. Ferries operate from Mid-Ross (near Arden) to Inchmurrin Island; Inverbeg to Rowardennan; Tarbet and Inverbeg to Rowardennan and Inversnaid; Inveruglas to Inversnaid, and Ardlui to Ardleish (for the West Highland Way).

GLASGOW

The city of Glasgow (pop. 616,340), Scotland's largest and most populous city, offers visitors a wide range of accommodation, services, entertainments and attractions, as well as being a key focal point for road, rail and air routes. This vibrant city has long been a main departure point for exploring Scotland's magnificent Western Highlands and is particularly well located for undertaking day – or longer – expeditions to the Loch Lomond and Trossachs districts, which lie virtually on Glasgow's doorstep. In fact, from the summit of Ruchill Park, in the city's north-western suburbs and just three kilometres from the city centre, you may discern the outline of Ben Lomond, 'Glasgow's mountain', which is climbed by hundreds of city-dwellers every year. In few other places is it possible to be transported from the bustling streets of a great city to some of the finest scenery in the world within the space of half an hour!

Glasgow was an important ecclesiastical centre, modestly engaging in commerce, long before it became famous as a great commercial and industrial centre. In 543AD the Celtic missionary St Kentigern, or Mungo, founded a little church here on the banks of the Molendinar Burn and some six centuries later, in 1136, the first cathedral was built on the sacred site. Within a few years this building was destroyed by fire, a second one completed in 1197 shared a similar fate and the present cathedral was started in the early thirteenth century.

The Union of the Scottish and English Parliaments in 1707 marked a crucial turning-point in Glasgow's fortunes, for it meant that Scottish merchants could now trade freely with the American and West Indian colonies. Over the next two and a half centuries, the capacity of the city's merchants for innovation, their ability to adapt to changing circumstances and the improvement of the Clyde into a canal-like waterway capable of floating all but the largest ships, laid the foundations of the city's greatness.

In the latter decades of the eighteenth century, tobacco and sugar were imported from the Americas and West Indies in exchange for all manner of goods, ranging from locally manufactured linen goods and glassware to nails and pots and pans. In the nineteenth century, cotton manufacturing and then shipbuilding and marine and general engineering emerged as the city's staple industries. By the close of the nineteenth century, Glasgow, proudly boasting that it was 'Second City of the Empire', had flourished into being the world's greatest shipbuilding and engineering centre, a leading port and a great commercial centre.

Alas, increased overseas competition and world recession led to the decline of shipbuilding after the First World War, until at the present day only two yards remain in business on the upper Clyde. The development of road transport and containerisation of cargoes, with services concentrated on a few ports, have also served to divert traffic from the city's docks. The electronics industry, services and tourism now predominate in the regional economy.

Glasgow has shaken off its industrial image in recent years and the city's wide range of shopping facilities, unrivalled museums and art galleries, sylvan parklands and dynamic nightlife are now enjoyed by ever-increasing numbers of visitors each year. Shopping, centred on Sauchiehall, Buchanan and Argyle Streets, ranges from leading department stores to colourful open-air markets, while the sparkling new St Enoch Centre is Europe's largest glass-covered mall. The magnificent Buchanan Galleries shopping complex occupies an entire block near the Glasgow Royal Concert Hall at the top of Buchanan Street. Unrivalled art galleries and museums include the world-famous Burrell Collection; Kelvingrove Art Gallery and Museum; the Museum of Transport; the People's Palace social history museum; the St Mungo Museum of Religious Life and Art; the Gallery of Modern Art; and the Hunterian Museum at the University of Glasgow. The city's many fine parks include the Botanic Gardens, Kelvingrove Park, Glasgow Green and Pollok Country Park, where the Burrell Collection is housed.

The city contains a wealth of historic buildings, dating mainly from the height of Glasgow's greatness in the nineteenth century, which range from elegant terraces, mansions and churches to ornate office blocks. Much of early Glasgow fell to the demolisher's hammer in the course of various improvement schemes, but survivors include Glasgow Cathedral (early thirteenth century onwards); Provand's Lordship (1471), the city's oldest house (opposite the cathedral); the Tolbooth Steeple (1626) at Glasgow Cross; the Tron Steeple (1630–6) in Trongate; and the Merchant's Steeple (1665) in Bridgegate. Prominent among later buildings is the opulent City Chambers (1888) in George Square, which reflects Glasgow's greatness in the Victorian era.

After dark, entertainment ranges from cinema, theatre, symphony concerts, opera and ballet to folk, jazz, ceilidh dances, nightclubs and pubs. Glasgow has also become a favourite venue for concerts, exhibitions and conferences since the completion of the Scottish Exhibition and Conference Centre, just to the west of the city centre. Best of all, Glasgow is noted for the friendliness and unpretentious nature of its people!

The city's fascinating history and numerous visitor attractions have been touched upon only briefly here. However, further information can be gleaned from the numerous guide books and historical works about the city which are currently available.

GLASGOW

Visitor Services
B Bk CC Ch Cr D G H I P PO PS PT R SA SC T YH

Sport and Leisure
A Bw Cf CP Cy Go HB L M PB Pu RC S SB SL SP TC W

Public Transport
Rail
Glasgow Central Station (enter from Union, Gordon, Hope or Argyle Streets) for destinations south of the Clyde, in southern Lanarkshire, on North Clydeside suburban lines and in England via the West and East Coast Routes. Glasgow Queen Street Station (enter from West George, Dundas or North Hanover Streets), for destinations north of the Clyde and to Edinburgh and the Lothians. A Station Link Bus Service (Service 398) connects the two railway stations (Gordon Street to N Hanover Street) and also Buchanan Bus Station (stance 1) daily.

Bus and Coach
Buchanan Bus Station (in Killermont Street, off the north end of West Nile Street) for local and national destinations. Other local services pass through the city centre.

Air
Glasgow International Airport (flight enquiries, 0141 887 1111), at Abbotsinch, Paisley, approx. 13km west of the city centre, just off M8 Motorway Junctions 28 or 29, for destinations in Scotland and England, Europe and North America. Glasgow Airport Link bus service to and from Glasgow Buchanan Bus Station and city centre stops.

Tourist Information and Accommodation
A free Visitor and Accommodation Guide is available from Greater Glasgow and Clyde Valley Tourist Board, 11 George Square, Glasgow, G2 1DY (0141 204 4400), open Mon – Sat all year. An Accommodation Reservation Service is also available (0141 221 0049, Fax 0141 221 3524). In addition, the Tourist Board also has a Tourist Information Desk at Glasgow Airport (0141 848 4440), open seven days all year. Glasgow Youth

Hostel is located at 7/8 Park Terrace, in the West End about 2km west of the city centre, and is open all year (0141 332 3004). There are also independent backpackers' hostels.

GLASGOW–DUMBARTON

'O, ye'll tak the high road, and I'll tak the low road, And I'll be in Scotland afore ye,' runs the opening verse of the world-famous song 'Loch Lomond'. According to legend, the song refers to the last meeting between a Jacobite soldier, who was about to be executed at Carlisle, and his sweetheart who had come from Loch Lomondside to bid farewell to her beloved. The girl would return home to the bonnie banks of Loch Lomond by the 'high road', but the condemned man would take the 'low road' to the grave.

These days, by far the busiest 'high road' to the bonnie banks is the A82, which begins at St George's Cross in Glasgow's West End as Great Western Road, and continues as a dual carriageway beyond Anniesland as it traverses the city's sprawling western suburbs, before descending to the north bank of the world-famous River Clyde at Old Kilpatrick. The dual carriageway section, known locally as 'The Boulevard' after the wide Parisian highways, was pushed through hitherto pleasant, open countryside as far as Bowling in the depressed years of the late 1920s to relieve chronic unemployment on Clydeside.

However, motorists can now follow an alternative route for this initial stage, by the westbound M8 Motorway, which avoids the busy suburban streets and is of particular benefit to those entering Glasgow from Edinburgh by the M8, approaching from the south by the M74/M73/M8 or starting from Glasgow Airport south of the Clyde. The M8 crosses the Clyde at Glasgow by the Kingston Bridge, opened in 1970, and follows the south side of the river to Erskine. When starting from Glasgow Airport, the M8 is joined at Junctions 28 or 29. Leaving the M8 at Junction 30 at Erskine, the Clyde is crossed again on the Erskine Bridge (toll payable) to join the A82 at Old Kilpatrick.

As 'The Boulevard' descends past Old Kilpatrick, a splendid vista of the widening estuary of the River Clyde unfolds, with the volcanic plug of Dumbarton Rock standing sentinel. The Erskine Bridge can be seen (L) just beyond the bridge approach/exit road (A898). This 1,230-metre-long bridge, of undistinguished cable-stayed steel box-girder design, was opened by Princess Anne in 1971 to replace the old Erskine Ferry. It was closed for several weeks in 1996 after having been struck by an oil rig mounted on a barge which was being towed downriver!

Old Kilpatrick (L), one of several reputed birthplaces of St Patrick (b.373AD), the patron saint of Ireland, also boasts the site of the terminal fort on the Antonine Wall, which was built right across Scotland by the Roman legions in 142AD to keep the wild Caledonians of the north at bay. Erskine House, which appears on the south bank of the Clyde, was erected in 1828 to designs by Robert Smirke, architect of the British Museum, for Lord Blantyre. Since 1916 it has been occupied by the Princess Louise Scottish Hospital for Limbless Sailors and Soldiers.

The village of Bowling (L), which is by-passed, was the busy western terminal of the Forth and Clyde Canal, which opened throughout from Grangemouth to Bowling in 1790. Closed in 1962, it is to be reopened following completion of the Millenium Link Project, which is due for completion in the year 2000. Shipbuilding and distilling were also carried on until recent times. In the early years of the nineteenth century the Kilpatrick Hills behind the village were the haunt of illicit whisky-distillers and smugglers, owing to the imposition of heavy duties on spirits at that time.

At Dunglass roundabout, the picturesque ruin of Dunglass Castle and the Henry Bell Monument may be glimpsed (L). The castle was built around 1380 by the Colquhouns, who became important landowners on Loch Lomondside by marriage as far back as the fourteenth century. Dunglass was fortified by King James IV in 1489, while his army besieged Dumbarton Castle, which was held by the rebel Earl of Lennox. In 1603 the Colquhouns were massacred by the MacGregors at the battle of Glen Fruin and the depositions of witnesses to the battle were taken within the castle. This was to lead to the proscription of the MacGregor name and tartan for many years thereafter. The Covenanters, in their struggles with Charles I in the 1640s, seized Dumbarton and Dunglass Castles and provisioned them against possible attack by Montrose, who was trying to rally the northern clans to the royal standard. The castle fell to Cromwell's Ironsides during the ensuing Commonwealth era and they left it in a ruinous state.

A more modern wing of the castle, built around 1592, was home to the noted graphic artist Talwin Morris in the 1890s, at which time the famous Glasgow architect Charles Rennie Mackintosh was a frequent visitor. Dunglass was subsequently purchased by Mackintosh's future father-in-law (he married

Margaret MacDonald in 1899), who commissioned him to re-design the interior in his unique style. Alas, this historic building is now in a shamefully ruinous state and surrounded by an abandoned oil depot.

The Henry Bell Monument was erected there in 1838 to commemorate Henry Bell, owner of the *Comet*, the first successful sea-going steamship in Europe, which was built at Port Glasgow in 1812 for service on the Clyde. This marked the beginning of the Clyde's rise to fame as one of the world's greatest shipbuilding and engineering centres. A right-of-way exists to the castle and monument, but access arrangements are uncertain at present, following abandonment of the adjacent oil depot.

Entering Milton, the Dumbarton Tourist Information Centre (01389 742306, open all year) is on the left, by the filling station and restaurant. The village was formerly known as Milton of Colquhoun, for the Colquhouns once had their ancient stronghold on the hill behind the village, where Middleton Farm now stands. A cotton-mill established on the Milton Burn in the late eighteenth century (part of which remains) housed the first power-loom in Scotland. The mill-owner's residence, Milton House, a fine Georgian mansion, can be seen on the lower slopes of Dumbuck, a prominent volcanic plug which has been sadly marred by quarrying. Tradition relates that in the late thirteenth century Scotland's revered patriot Sir William Wallace ('Braveheart') watched the English garrison in Dumbarton Castle from Wallace's Cave on Dumbuck, before attacking and burning the houses of the English in the town. Milton Brae (R) leads to Overtoun House and estate, where some beautiful walks in the foothills of the Kilpatricks may be enjoyed. (A brochure may be available from the Tourist Information Centre.)

The A82 continues straight ahead at Dumbuck, while the A814 branches left for Dumbarton and Helensburgh (Route 3). Dumbuck was the lowest fording-point on the Clyde in the years before the river was deepened. Prehistoric canoes have been discovered in the river upstream from here and in 1898, a crannog (a man-made island homestead dating from the Iron Age and later) was discovered on the Dumbuck foreshore. In more recent times, Jackie Stewart, the World Champion racing driver, lived here as a youth when his father owned the Dumbuck Garage.

DUMBARTON

The town of Dumbarton (pop. c24,000), capital of the ancient Kingdom of Strathclyde in the Dark Ages, was created a Royal

Burgh by Alexander II in 1222, thus conferring trading and other privileges. The town, which short-sightedly refused the opportunity of becoming Glasgow's port in the late eighteenth century, later redeemed itself by acquiring a world-wide reputation for excellence and innovation in shipbuilding. It is now Scotland's 'whisky capital', with a distillery and extensive bonding, blending and bottling facilities located around the town.

Dumbarton's main attraction is historic Dumbarton Castle, precariously perched on 74-metre-high Dumbarton Rock, the basaltic vent of an ancient volcano. Panoramic views of the Clyde estuary, the Vale of Leven and the Highland hills may be enjoyed from the Rock's summit. In the Dark Ages, which followed the departure of the Roman invaders, Dumbarton Rock was the seat of the Britons of Strathclyde, whose kingdom extended all the way from Glen Falloch, beyond the head of Loch Lomond, southwards to Morecambe Bay. They were also connected with the Britons of what is now Wales.

Dumbarton Castle was made a Royal fortress in 1222 by Alexander II, for the purpose of securing peace in the regions bordering the wild Highlands. The Earls of Lennox, all-powerful territorial magnates in the region, were intimately involved in the castle's turbulent history over the centuries. A dazzling array of famous historical figures feature in the history of Dumbarton Rock and its castle, including Arthur, war-leader of the Britons, (the legendary 'King' Arthur) and the wizard Merlin; Sir William Wallace; King Robert the Bruce; King James IV, who built and assembled his navy at Dumbarton; and the young Mary, Queen of Scots, who sailed from Dumbarton Castle in 1548 for her arranged marriage to Francis, Dauphin of France. Wallace's huge sword was guarded within the castle for several centuries, until it was unfortunately removed to the Wallace Monument at Stirling in 1889. The oldest part of the castle is the Portcullis Arch, which dates back to the fourteenth century, although most of the present buildings date only from the eighteenth and nineteenth centuries. (01389 732167. Open all year, Apr-Sept Mon-Sat 0930-1830, Sun 1400–1830; Oct-Mar Mon-Sat 0930-1630, Sun 1400-1630. Closed Thurs p.m. and Fridays. Admission charge.)

The castle is reached from Dumbuck by taking the A814 to just beyond the rail bridge at Dumbarton East Station (where rail travellers should alight for the castle). Go second left into Victoria Street and continue ahead on Castle Road to the castle car park. The Dumbarton Foreshore Walk, to Milton, starts from the car park. To rejoin the A82, return to the A814 (Glasgow Road) and go left, passing the Denny Tank Museum

(L). Continue on to the roundabout near Dumbarton Central Station (R) and take the third exit, Townend Road, which passes under the railway and joins the A82 at Barloan roundabout.

Among other places of interest in Dumbarton, the Denny Tank Museum in Castle Street is a ship model experimental tank, once attached to the world-renowned shipbuilding yard of William Denny and Bros., but now administered by the Scottish Maritime Museum (01389 763444. Open all year. Check opening times. Cafeteria. Admission charge). Nearby is the enormous red brick whisky distillery of Allied Distillers, which was the largest in Europe when it was built in 1938.

The ornate French Gothic Revival style Burgh Hall in Church Street (off High Street, opposite Riverside Church), built in 1865 and sadly now derelict, is a fine example of the work of the noted Glasgow architect William Leiper. Originally completed as the Burgh Academy and Town Hall, its most famous pupil was A.J. Cronin (1896-1981), the immensely popular novelist and creator of the *Doctor Finlay's Casebook* television series. Several of his best-selling works were made into films and television and radio plays. Some of them, notably his pioneer work *Hatters Castle*, are actually set in Dumbarton, disguised as the town of 'Levenford'.

Dumbarton Public Library in Strathleven Place, near the Central Railway Station, has a small museum and an excellent local history collection covering the Dumbarton, Vale of Leven, Loch Lomond and Helensburgh districts. (01389 763129. Open Mon-Sat all year, except public holidays.)

The adjacent red sandstone Municipal Buildings (James Thomson Jun. (1903)) provide a good example of Scots Baronial architecture. The College Bow Arch, within the grounds, is all that remains of the Collegiate Church of St Mary, built around 1450 by Isabella, Countess of Lennox, on the site now occupied by the railway station. The Meadow Sports and Leisure Centre in Meadow Road (R), beyond the railway bridge, caters for a wide range of family activities and includes a leisure pool and aqua slide, sports hall, gymnasium, sunbed suite, a bar and diner, and a creche (01389 734094. Check opening times).

The Glencairn 'Greit House' (1623), half way along High Street (L), the main shopping centre, was the house of the Earls of Glencairn and later of the Dukes of Argyll. It is now the oldest surviving example of Scottish domestic architecture in the town. (P at Riverside (L) and Risk Street (R); T at Quay Street (L)).

Crossing the River Leven by Dumbarton Bridge (1765 with later additions), Levengrove Park (T) in Clydeshore Road (L), once the grounds of Levengrove House, was presented to the town in 1885 by local shipbuilders Peter Denny and John MacMillan. The park, which contains the ruins of the ancient Parish Church of Cardross, affords impressive views of Dumbarton Rock, while a bracing promenade leads westward along the Clyde shore. In the summer months recreational activities include bowling, tennis, putting, crazy golf and a children's bouncy castle. Dumbarton Golf Course is located at Broadmeadow, off Overburn Avenue, north of the town (01389 732830).

DUMBARTON

Visitor Services
B Bk Ch D G I (Milton) P PO PS PT R SA T

Sport and Leisure
Bw Cf Cy Fi Go HB L M PB Pu RC S SL SP TC W

Public Transport
Rail
Dumbarton Central Station for Denny Tank Museum and Meadow Leisure Centre; Dumbarton East Station for Dumbarton Castle; Dalreoch Station for Levengrove Park. Services to Glasgow, Balloch, Helensburgh and West Highland line stations to Fort William, Mallaig and Oban. West Highland Line trains call only at Central.

Bus and Coach
High Street for Clydebank, Balloch, Helensburgh and infrequent service to Lochgoilhead and Carrick Castle. Stop on A82 road east of Barloan roundabout for Campbeltown, Oban, Fort William and Uig (Skye) via Loch Lomondside.

Accommodation
Hotels
The Abbotsford, Stirling Road (A82) 01389 733304
Dumbuck, Glasgow Road (A814) 01389 734336
Milton Inn, Dumbarton Road, Milton (A82) 01389 761401

Tourist Information
A82 Northbound, Milton (3.5km east of Town Centre) 01389 742306 (All Year).

DUMBARTON–ALEXANDRIA AND BALLOCH

Leaving Dumbarton, the A82 crosses to the west side of the Vale of Leven, with lofty Ben Lomond dominating the northern skyline. Extensive bonded warehouses (L) and Allied Distillers' modern blending and bottling plant (R) provide evidence of Dumbarton's status as Scotland's 'whisky capital'. This is truly King Robert the Bruce country, for the manor house where the famous patriot king (1274–1329) spent his final years is believed to have stood at Mains of Cardross, on the west bank of the River Leven, just south of the A82 bridge over the river (L).

The towns of Renton and Alexandria (population with Balloch c21,000), which are by-passed, began as busy textile-dyeing and printing villages in the late eighteenth century, using the pure waters of Loch Lomond extracted from the Leven. Calicoe and Turkey Red cloths were exported to India, the Far East and the South Pacific, among other places. Alas, the industry declined after the First World War, owing to increased competition and the development of new processes, and the last factory in the Vale closed in 1980. The Smollett Monument, an obelisk commemorating Tobias Smollett, the pioneer novelist (1721–1771), stands in Renton's Main Street, near his birthplace at Dalquhurn House, which was demolished many years ago. This Tuscan column, erected in 1774 by his cousin James Smollett of Bonhill, boasts an inscription to which the redoubtable Dr Samuel Johnson contributed some lines.

At Balloch roundabout the A82 continues ahead, by Loch Lomond's bonnie western banks, for Crianlarich (Route 2) and the Three Lochs tour (Route 3). Go right here on A811 for Alexandria, Balloch, Drymen, Loch Lomond's eastern shore, Aberfoyle and The Trossachs (Routes 5 to 7).

ALEXANDRIA

At a second roundabout on A811, keep straight ahead for Drymen, the east side of Loch Lomond and The Trossachs. Go right for Alexandria, where the Vale of Leven Swimming Pool is in Main Street (L) (01389 756931, open daily, all year), and also for the Antartex Village Visitor Centre, a complex of mill/factory shops retailing knitwear, woollens, tartans, gifts and souvenirs, with a craft centre. Follow the signposted route to Lomond Industrial Estate, off Heather Avenue (third exit left). (01389 752393. Open daily. Coffee shop, free admission and parking.)

Another major new retail facility, Loch Lomond Factory Outlets, offering end-of-range and other discounted lines, together with a Scottish Motoring Heritage Museum, now occupies the magnificently palatial former Argyll Motor Co. Factory in Main Street, just beyond Heather Avenue (L). This splendid red sandstone building, featuring an Italian marble main staircase which has been recreated, was erected in 1905–6. The Argyll Co. produced excellent, much-sought-after cars there until 1914, when the firm went into liquidation for the second time. The early death of the firm's dynamic founder from food-poisoning, an expensive legal case and the £250,000 cost of erecting this grand factory all contributed to the firm's demise. The factory was later used for manufacturing munitions and then by the Admiralty for making torpedoes. (01389 710077. Open daily except Christmas Day, 1 and 2 January; cafe; free admission and parking; admission fee for Motoring Museum.)

Continue along Main Street for Alexandria shopping centre, which is just beyond The Fountain, at the junction of Main and Bank Streets. This ornate (but sadly non-functioning!) memorial fountain was erected in 1870 to commemorate local laird and county MP Alexander Smollett, who lived at Cameron House on Loch Lomondside. It was an earlier Alexander Smollett MP, killed at the Battle of Alkmaer in Holland in 1799, who gave his name to the infant town, which until then had been known as 'The Grocery'! (P off Main and Bank Streets. T in Bank Street.)

There is a small museum at the Public Library in Gilmour Street (R). Vale of Leven Golf Club, a moorland course giving scenic views of Loch Lomond, is located at Northfield Road, Bonhill, on the east side of the Vale beyond the Bonhill Bridge over the River Leven (01389 752351).

ALEXANDRIA

Visitor Services
B Bk Ch D G H P PO PS PT R T

Sport and Leisure
A Bw Cf Cy Fi Go HB L M PB Pu RC S SP TC W

BALLOCH

Balloch, 'the gateway to Loch Lomond' and long a favourite destination for day-trippers from central Scotland, is entered by leaving the A82 at Balloch roundabout, going left at the A811 roundabout and then right, on Balloch Road. Improved road and rail links with Glasgow in recent years have transformed what was once a small rural village into a township which is the largest settlement by far around the bonnie banks (population with Alexandria and Renton c21,000).

Here you may enjoy a cruise on Loch Lomond, cast a fishing line in the loch or the River Leven (by permit), participate in water sports, cycle on the Glasgow–Loch Lomond–Killin cycle route or walk amid some of the finest scenery in all Scotland. Accommodation is available to suit all tastes between here and Duck Bay (on the loch shore, 3km north), ranging from a prestigious hotel and country club and other hotels, to cabin accommodation, a caravan and camping park, a Youth Hostel occupying a grand mansion house and bed and breakfast houses.

Heading down Balloch Road, the Loch Lomond Project, a multi-million-pound visitor centre which is one of Scotland's most significant tourism developments, is being developed by Dunbartonshire Enterprise on a large site on the left. This was formerly the site of the British Silk Dyeing Co.'s factory, the last textile-dyeing factory to be built in the Vale of Leven and the last to close (1930–1980).

Just beyond the Lomond Park Hotel (R), Pier Road (L) leads to Balloch Pier, where there is a car park and picnic area. The fine paddle steamer *Maid of the Loch*, which sailed on the loch from 1953 until 1981, is undergoing restoration at the pier following several years of disuse. Her successor, the *Countess Fiona*, which sailed until 1988, is drawn up on the slipway.

The Tourist Information Centre (01389 753533, open April to October) occupies the attractive old railway station building, which dates from the opening of the railway in 1850. The old steam trains, heavily-laden with day-trippers, once puffed on to Balloch Pier to connect with the Loch Lomond steamers. The new Balloch Railway Station is directly opposite. A walking path leads from beside the Tourist Information Centre to Balloch Pier and the Glasgow–Loch Lomond Cycleway and Leven Valley Heritage Trail also terminates nearby, down by the River Leven under Balloch Bridge.

Opposite the Tourist Centre, note the Tullichewan Hotel, designed in unusual 'English Cottage' style and first erected in 1889 as a temperance (alcohol prohibited) hotel for James Campbell of nearby Tullichewan Castle, who owned most of the land to the west of the River Leven. The hotel was rebuilt in 1893 following a fire. Campbell's father William had amassed the family fortune, in partnership with his brother James, as a wholesale draper in Glasgow. The hotel is no longer a temperance establishment!

Crowds arrive at Balloch by train in 1991 for a Runrig concert at Balloch Castle Country Park, attended by 40,000 fans (© Robert D. Campbell)

The River Leven, the second-fastest-flowing river in Scotland after the Spey, is crossed by Balloch Bridge, erected in 1887. The view from the bridge, looking towards Loch Lomond and the Luss Hills, presents a scene of great activity on fine summer days. At such times it resembles scenes on the Thames, as cruisers sail up and down-river past tree-clad Balloch Isle (known locally as 'Monkey Island') in mid-stream. Cruises to the southern reaches of Loch Lomond leave from both ends of the bridge. Houseboats and small craft once crowded the river about here, making it a favourite haunt in the 1920s of George Leslie Hunter (1879–1931), one of the famous 'Scottish Colourist' school of artists. The Balloch Hotel (L) features in one of Hunter's best-known Scottish paintings. The Empress Eugenie of France actually spent a night there when visiting Loch Lomond in 1860 and her visit is commemorated by a plaque at the main (riverside) entrance.

Moss o' Balloch Park (L), which has a car park, lies beyond the hotel and St Kessog's R.C. Church. Opposite are some shops, restaurants and bars. The park was formerly the site of the annual Balloch Fair, an ancient horse-market held in September which brought buyers and sellers from near and far. Textile workers from the printworks in the Vale of Leven and Highlanders from

Loch Lomondside came to enjoy the side-shows and liquor booths, before staggering homewards much the worse for wear.

The main pedestrian entrance to Balloch Castle Country Park (L), at the heart of which stands Balloch Castle, is opposite the bus stance (with toilets) and car park at Carrochan Road. Before setting out to enjoy a walk in this beautiful park, pause briefly to reflect on some local history and the crucial role that Balloch and its castle played in the governance and development of the huge region known as the Lennox.

People have lived around these southern shores of Loch Lomond since prehistoric times. Large stone-built burial cairns dating from the Neolithic period of the Stone Age still stand in the surrounding hills, while numerous Bronze Age burial sites have been unearthed over the years in the Vale of Leven and just to the north of Balloch. The remains of Iron Age forts and homesteads crown the summits of nearby hills, while crannogs dot the southern reaches of Loch Lomond.

Balloch was a place of great strategic importance during the early mediaeval period, for it was here, at the point where the River Leven empties from Loch Lomond, that the ancient Balloch Castle was built in 1238. In fact, the name Balloch comes from the Gaelic 'bealach', meaning 'a pass or gorge' or 'the mouth of the loch', and it was from this key location, commanding access to the countryside around Loch Lomond and the passage down the River Leven to the Clyde, that the powerful Earls of Lennox ruled over their huge fiefdom and granted lands to lesser magnates, such as the local clan chiefs, by charter. Known as the Lennox, their territory eventually reached all the way from beyond the head of Loch Lomond almost to Glasgow, and from the eastern shore of Loch Long as far east as the upper River Forth, Fintry and Kirkintilloch. The name Lennox is said to come from Levenach or Levenax, meaning 'smooth' (a term which is certainly applicable to the river or the loch, which was once called Loch Leven), although some say it means 'place abounding in elm trees'.

The Lennox Earls often featured prominently in national affairs and were always intimately involved in the fortunes of the nearby royal fortress of Dumbarton Castle. Malcolm, the 5th Earl, was a strong supporter of the patriotic cause in the Wars of Scottish Independence of the late thirteenth and early fourteenth centuries. Scotland's great national heroes Sir William Wallace and King Robert the Bruce were both active in the district and so it seems likely that they would have been entertained at Balloch Castle.

In 1485 Duncan, the 8th Earl, paid a high price for his family's prominent position in national affairs. His eldest daughter

Isabella married Murdoch, Duke of Albany and a cousin of King James I, who had acted as Regent during James's long exile as a prisoner in England. However, Albany's rule had incurred the king's displeasure and, following his release from captivity, James had Murdoch, his two sons and Duncan, Earl of Lennox, tried and executed on the Heading Hill at Stirling.

Later in the fifteenth century the Earldom was partitioned between Sir John Stewart of Darnley (who acquired the title Earl of Lennox), John Napier of Merchiston and Sir John Haldane of Gleneagles, descendants of Duncan's daughters Elizabeth and Margaret. The Earldom was subsequently raised to a Dukedom. The Lennox dynasty's long and turbulent association with Balloch finally ended in 1652, when the Duke of Lennox sold the Balloch estate to the Colquhouns of Luss.

There was a ferry and ford at Balloch from very early times, as it was the first crossing-place below Loch Lomond on the main track from the south-west to Stirling and the central Highlands. Great droves of black cattle being driven from the West Highlands to the Falkirk tryst, or south into England, would cross the Leven here, or at Bonhill ford downriver. As late as the nineteenth century, salmon netted from the Leven were still being despatched to Glasgow, Edinburgh and Perth, where the fish fetched high prices.

Publication of Scott's romances *The Lady of the Lake* (1810) and *Rob Roy* (1817) brought the first rush of tourists to the district and from 1818 the steamboat *Marion* sailed on the loch from Balloch. A suspension bridge replaced the ancient Balloch Ferry in 1841. Then, when the railway opened in 1850, Balloch became a popular destination virtually overnight for tourists and day-trippers from near and far and many famous people passed through *en route* to Loch Lomond. When the southern reaches of Loch Lomond froze over during the bitter winter of 1894-5 a shuttle service of special trains brought huge crowds from Glasgow to skate and participate in games of cricket, curling, etc. on the ice.

However, the local lairds (landowners) jealously guarded their privacy and so access to the loch remained difficult and development slow until as late as 1915, when Balloch Castle and Estate were purchased by Glasgow Corporation for use as a public park. The new Loch Lomond Park quickly became a favourite destination for day-trippers and large organised outings from Glasgow. Trains, tramcars (from 1908) and later buses disgorged huge crowds of trippers bound for the park in the summer months. This beautiful lochside retreat, now known as Balloch Castle Country Park and administered by West Dunbartonshire

Council, remains as popular as ever at the present day. The site of the ancient thirteenth century Balloch Castle is now included within the park. The present castle, a country house built for John Buchanan of Ardoch in 1808, stands in a commanding situation on the hillside above and houses a Visitor Centre and tea room.

Industry came to the bonnie banks in 1930, when a large textile dye-works was built by a Swiss firm at Balloch. The plant used the clear waters of Loch Lomond to dye silk, and later synthetic fabrics, until closure in 1980. A multi-million-pound Visitor Centre is now being developed on part of the site.

Improved road and rail links with Glasgow have helped promote tourism and residential development in recent years. Alas, the popular Loch Lomond steamer service ceased in 1988, although it is proposed to resume sailings. A sail on the well-appointed paddle steamer *Maid of the Loch* was by far the best way of viewing the whole loch in comfort. Nevertheless, Balloch's proximity to Glasgow and other populous districts, the wide range of leisure and recreational facilities which can be enjoyed and the new Visitor Centre, mean that it will always remain the principal 'gateway to Loch Lomond' and a popular venue for visitors to the bonnie banks.

A WALK IN BALLOCH CASTLE COUNTRY PARK (4.25km r)

The sylvan trails in Balloch Castle Country Park, one of the most popular walking venues on Loch Lomondside, lead to fine vistas over the southern end of Loch Lomond. Enter by the main pedestrian entrance, opposite the car park and bus stance at Carrochan Road, or drive to Balloch Castle car park by way of Drymen and Mollanbowie Roads (signposted from Balloch) and the North Lodge entrance. There is also pedestrian access from the riverbank beyond the Balloch Hotel and from Moss o' Balloch Park.

Walking up the Main Drive from Balloch, you will see many unusual exotic trees, planted by former owners of the Balloch Castle Estate. A short diversion can be made (L) to the Walled Garden, which once supplied the castle with fruit, vegetables and flowers and now offers a profusion of blooms in spring and summer. Return to the Main Drive, or you can continue on beyond the garden and cross the Picnic Lawns to Balloch Castle.

Balloch Castle, enjoying a commanding situation with fine views over the southern end of Loch Lomond, was built in 1808 as Ardoch Castle, to a Castle Gothic design by English architect

Robert Lugar, for John Buchanan of Ardoch. Buchanan's father Thomas had made the family fortune as owner of the biggest hat factory in Glasgow and as a co-founder of the second Glasgow Ship Bank. His son John succeeded him as a partner in the Ship Bank and was a Member of Parliament. Sir Walter Scott once visited John's grand castle in order to view Rob Roy's great two-handed sword, which the famous outlaw had presented to his father in recognition of some service rendered. The next owner, Gibson Stott (1830–1851), was a leading promoter of the Balloch railway. The estate was then purchased by A.J. Dennistoun Brown J.P. (1851–1890), whose widow and daughters continued living there for some years after his death.

As day-trippers from Glasgow had no means of access to the shores of Loch Lomond at Balloch, the 812-acre Balloch Estate was purchased by Glasgow Corporation in 1915 for £30,000 and opened to the public as Loch Lomond Park. In the summer months, trains, trams and buses brought huge crowds of day-trippers to visit the park and the castle was used as a popular tea room. The park is now leased by West Dunbartonshire Council and administered by the Loch Lomond Park Authority. There is a Visitor Centre in the castle, with an interpretative display and slide presentation, a tea room and a public shelter with vending machines and toilets. (01389 758216. Visitor Centre open daily, 10 a.m. to 6 p.m. Easter to October.)

The Picnic Lawns, fronting the castle, have long been a popular venue for large organised outings such as Sunday School picnics and, more recently, pop concerts. In 1996 Oasis attracted no fewer than 80,000 fans! The Tree Trail beyond the castle (leaflet from Visitor Centre) features many types of common and rare trees and contains the grave of Bran (1883), one of the Dennistoun Browns' pet dogs.

The path beyond the castle soon descends to the Fairy Glen, where the Burn of Balloch tumbles down to the loch through the pretty Horsehouse Wood. This sylvan glade was the reputed haunt of the fairies of Balloch in more superstitious times.

The return to Balloch, or the castle car park, is by a pleasant woodland path which wanders along the loch shore and then beside the River Leven (a favourite haunt of the artist George Leslie Hunter) towards Balloch Bridge. A water-logged moat and grassy mound (L) opposite the mouth of the River Leven are all that remain to mark the site of the ancient Balloch Castle, built in 1238 as the principal seat of the Earls of Lennox, powerful regional territorial magnates. When King James IV dined at the castle in 1507 he lost 16 shillings while playing cards afterwards! Balloch

Castle appears to have been abandoned soon after this, in favour of Lennox Castle on the island of Inchmurrin. From 1652, the lands of Balloch were held by the Colquhouns of Luss, until they were gradually acquired by John Buchanan of Ardoch in 1794–9.

If returning to the castle car park, take the path (L) which leads past the Walled Garden to the Main Drive and go left again to reach the castle and car park. Otherwise, continue ahead by the path near the river to Balloch Bridge and Balloch Road.

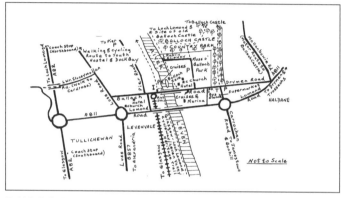

BALLOCH

Visitor Services
B Bk CC Ch Cr G I P PO PT R SA SC T YH (3km N)

Sport and Leisure
Cf CP Cy Fi Go HB L PB Pu RC S SB TC VC W Wa
Note: Includes Balloch, Duck Bay and Arden.

Public Transport
Rail
Balloch Station for services to Dumbarton, Clydebank and Glasgow. Change at Dalreoch for Helensburgh Central. Change at Dumbarton Central for West Highland Line.

Bus and Coach
Bus stance (junction Balloch and Carrochan Roads) for Luss, Drymen, Balmaha, Stirling, Helensburgh (Sundays), Alexandria and Clydebank.* Balloch roundabout (A82 road) for Glasgow to Inveraray, Campbeltown, Oban, Fort William and Skye, via Loch Lomondside.

* Layby north of roundabout northbound and south of roundabout southbound, 1.5km from Balloch. Not recommended for passengers with luggage.

Cruises
Balloch Bridge (either side) for southern end of Loch Lomond.
Mullen's Cruises, 01389 751481; Sweeney's Cruises Loch
Lomond, 01389 752376.

Accommodation
Hotels
Balloch, Balloch Road 01389 752579
Cameron House Hotel and Country Estate, off A82, 3km N of
  Balloch 01389 755565
Dalvait Loch Lomond, Dalvait Gardens, Balloch 01389 606000
Duck Bay Hotel and Marina, off A82, 3km N of Balloch 01389
  751234
Inchmurrin, Inchmurrin Island (Ferry from Midross, 6km N of
  Balloch) 01389 850245
Lomond Park, Balloch Road 01389 752494
Tullichewan, Balloch Road 01389 752052

Caravan and Camping Park
Tullichewan Holiday Park, Old Luss Road 01389 759475

Self-Catering
Loch Lomond Castle Lodges, Arden, off A82, 4km N of Balloch
  01389 850215
Cameron House Hotel and Country Estate (Lodges), off A82,
  3km N of Balloch 01389 755625

Youth Hostel
Loch Lomond Youth Hostel, Arden, off A82, 3km N of Balloch
01389 850226. (Walking or cycling from Balloch, head south
on Balloch Road and turn right into Old Luss Road, which leads
to the A82 near the Duck Bay road junction. Cross A82 (with
care), just beyond the junction, to the Youth Hostel access road.)

Tourist Information
Old Station, Balloch Road 01389 753533 (April to October)

ROUTE 1A. THE GLASGOW–LOCH LOMOND CYCLEWAY

Glasgow to Balloch by the Cycleway

The 34-kilometre-long Glasgow–Loch Lomond Cycleway, opened in 1989, starts from the footbridge over the Clydeside Expressway at the west end of the car park at the Scottish Exhibition and Conference Centre, which opened in 1985 and is located 2km west of the city centre. There is a railway station (Exhibition Centre) nearby. The Cycleway runs more or less parallel to the River Clyde and the Glasgow–Balloch railway as far as Dumbarton. The track-bed of an old railway is followed from Partick to Clydebank; then the towpath of the Forth and Clyde Canal as far as Bowling, and the route then continues, mainly on old railways, to Dumbarton. Crossing the town from Dumbarton Central Station to Dumbarton Bridge, the Cycleway turns inland to follow the west bank of the River Leven, through the Vale of Leven, to terminate at Balloch Bridge. An approved cycle route continues to Aberfoyle, the Trossachs, Callander and Killin. As a free map/guide to the cycleway is available and a description of it is also given in several cycling guides, it is not proposed to describe the route in detail here.

The Glasgow–Loch Lomond Cycleway follows an old railway line at Bowling. The ornamental tunnel supported the drive leading to Auchentorlie House (© Robert D. Campbell)

43

ROUTE 2. THE COLQUHOUN
AND MACFARLANE COUNTRY

Balloch to Crianlarich by the A82

Loch Lomond's Western Shore by Public Transport
See Route 1 for particulars of public transport services.

The drive from Balloch to Tarbet or Ardlui along Loch Lomond's lovely western shore must rank as one of the finest in all Scotland. This scenically magnificent highway whisks travellers from the softly contoured Lowlands to the ruggedly mountainous Highlands, as it passes through the gateway to the Highlands around Arden, in little more than the proverbial twinkling of an eye. Whether you decide to make the round of the Three Lochs returning by way of Arrochar, Loch Long, the Gare Loch and Helensburgh (Route 3), or the Six Lochs, returning by Crianlarich, Killin, Strathyre and Callander (Route 8), you may be assured that the exquisite vistas of mountain, moor and loch will linger long in the memory.

  Improvements made to the busy A82 road as far north as Tarbet in recent years mean that 'taking the high road' to the bonnie banks has never been easier. This has also benefited walkers, for a good footpath now extends all the way from Balloch to Tarbet (although maintenance has been poor in the vicinity of Inverbeg!).

LOCH LOMOND
Renowned for its natural beauty the world over, Loch Lomond's sweet-sounding name is so well known that it is surprising to discover that its origins are lost in the mists of time. The early ninth century chronicler Nennius called it 'Stagnum Lumonoy' and some say this is connected with Ben Lomond's name, allegedly derived from the Brythonic (language of the local Britons) 'llumon', 'a beacon' – hence 'beacon mountain'. However, land charters granted by the Earls of Lennox in the thirteenth and fourteenth centuries show variously 'Lochlomne',

'Loch Leven' (the name of the river flowing from the loch) and 'Louchlommid', the suggested derivations including the Gaelic 'leamhan', 'elm river or loch'; the Brythonic 'llevn', 'smooth loch or river'; or the Gaelic 'lomnochd', meaning 'bare'.

The writer Christopher North once exclaimed, 'Loch Lomond is a sea!' This veritable 'sea' is 34km (21 miles) long and varies in width from about 7km (4.5 miles) towards its southern end, measured from near Rossdhu to the Aber shore on the eastern side, before narrowing to less than a kilometre (0.5 miles), towards its mountainous northern end, above Inveruglas and Inversnaid. The dark waters reach a maximum depth of 191m (630ft) between Tarbet and Inveruglas, where the loch occupies a deep, glacier-carved trench. As the mean surface level is only about 7.92m (26ft) above sea level, it will therefore be appreciated that this part of the loch lies well below sea level. Indeed, it is deeper than the Atlantic Ocean is for a hundred miles off the West Coast, until the Continental Shelf is reached. In the immediate Post-Glacial period (some 7,000 to 5,500 years ago), when the sea level rose, the loch actually became a sea loch connected to the Firth of Clyde by the Vale of Leven for a time, before the sea level finally receded.

With a surface area covering about 7,123ha (17,600a.), Loch Lomond is the largest fresh-water lake in Great Britain. Its catchment area also covers a huge area of around 76,893ha (190,000a.), with a further 2,185ha (5,400a.) being contributed through the Loch Sloy catchment. Long, deep and wide it may be, but Loch Lomond holds no records in the 'longest and deepest fresh-water loch in Scotland' contest, for it is only the third longest and third deepest. Loch Awe is longest; Loch Morar is deepest; and Loch Ness second longest and deepest.

South of a line drawn from Inverbeg to Rowardennan, where glacial action was lessened as Ice Age glaciers spread out along and beyond the Highland margin, the loch shallows progressively and nowhere does it exceed about 64m (210ft). Levels can vary considerably, owing to heavy rainfall and snow melting on the hills in winter and spring, or droughts in summer. As recently as March 1990 and January 1993, record levels of over 3m (10ft) above normal surface level were recorded. High levels sometimes cause serious flooding and in the nineteenth century the loch steamer sometimes had to tow a rowing boat behind to land its passengers, owing to all the piers being submerged!

The loch widens considerably south of Ross Point, and it is this wide and shallow 'sea' that has been known to freeze over in winter on several occasions, usually between Balloch and Luss, thus making it possible to walk or skate over to the southernmost islands. In 1855, 1881 and 1895, special trains brought huge crowds of skaters to Balloch from near and far. In 1895 they came from as far afield as London and various skating, curling and other sporting contests were held. At such times the Duke of Montrose had to employ men to prevent his fallow deer from escaping over the ice from the deer park on the island of Inchmurrin and in 1895 he even had to send a horse and cart laden with turnips over the ice to feed the starving creatures!

The steamer *Prince of Wales* frozen in at Balloch Pier during the great freeze of 1895 (Dumbarton Public Library Collection)

The loch's crowning glory is its archipelago of emerald islands. Most of them, and certainly all the larger ones, are scattered over the surface of the broad southern basin, adding beauty and interest to the wide vistas. Wordsworth, visiting the loch in 1803, thought 'the proportion of diffused water was too great', but the redoubtable Christopher North would have none of this. He indignantly retorted, 'It is out of our power to look on Loch Lomond without a feeling of perfection. The "diffusion of water" is indeed great; but in what a world it floats! At first sight of it how our soul expands!' The number of islands is debatable, depending upon one's interpretation of an 'island'. Henry Lamond, who probably knew the loch as well as anyone, listed 38 in his book *Loch Lomond* (1931). The largest is Inchmurrin, the southernmost, which is 3.2km (2miles) long and one of only three islands which is inhabited for all or part of the year.

Most of the loch's tributaries run from west to east, although the main drainage pattern is to the south, by the River Leven, and then westwards by the Clyde. The principal tributaries are the River Falloch, entering from Glen Falloch at the northern end which, despite draining an area less than half that of the Endrick, is the largest in terms of volume; the Inveruglas, Douglas, Luss, Finlas and Fruin Waters, which tumble down from lonely glens on the western shore; and on the eastern shore the sluggish, meandering Endrick Water, which enters near Balmaha from the broad vale of Strath Endrick and its catchment in the Fintry Hills and Campsie Fells.

The loch's only outlet is the River Leven at its southern end, the second-fastest-flowing river in Scotland after the Spey, which flows through the urbanised Vale of Leven for 9km to join the Clyde at Dumbarton Rock. Until the 1960s, the river supplied textile-dyeing and printing works in the Vale, which utilised the pure, clear waters for various processes. Cargo-laden sailing barges once ascended the Leven, hauled by horses, to serve the works and settlements around Loch Lomond. However, a barrage erected just below Balloch in 1971, in connection with the Loch Lomond Water Supply Scheme to supply a wide area of central Scotland, now precludes through navigation.

Many an ancient legend lends an aura of mystery to lovely Loch Lomond, perhaps the most famous being its claim to three wonders, 'Waves without wind, fish without fins and a floating island'. The 'waves without wind' may be caused by squalls which sweep down the glens among the mountains and whip up waves on the waters in their path, while leaving nearby waters undisturbed. Another phenomenon known as 'the Blue Belt' – long strips of alternately smooth and ruffled water caused by the way the wind strikes the surface – warns of a coming storm. The composer Felix Mendelssohn could testify to the fickleness of Loch Lomond's winds, for he recalled how he was crossing the loch in a small rowboat with his friend Klingemann one day in August 1829, '. . . when there came a sudden tremendous gust of wind from the mountains; the boat began to rock so fearfully that I caught up my cloak and got ready to swim'.

The 'fish without fins' may well be lampreys which, unlike the equally numerous eels which inhabit the loch, do not have pectoral fins. The 'floating island' was probably one of the many crannogs, or lake-dwellings, which were built at various locations on the loch during and after the Iron Age (from about 400BC). A small islet near the entrance to 'The Straits' between Inchtavannach and Inchconnachan is identified by tradition as (and is actually named) 'The Floating Island'. Although this wonder is now disappointingly stationary, it is supposed to have consisted of a mass of floating moss in former times. One nineteenth-century boatman on the loch, when asked by gullible tourists where the floating island was, always replied, 'Let me see, it was near Balmaha yesterday, an' by the way the win' is, I think it maun be aboot Tarbet noo!'

Another interesting legend relates how that part of the loch above Rowardennan was the old loch and all below it to the mouth of the Leven was inhabited country, until the old loch overflowed and flooded the area to the south. It was often claimed that during summer droughts the ruins of houses, churches and other buildings could be seen below the surface by boatmen. At Auchenheglish ('field of the kirk'), near Duck Bay, a heap of stones said to be the ruins of a submerged church appeared at times of drought. However, the church was actually situated on land, near the entrance to Auchenheglish House and when the house was being built in 1858 several stone coffins and human remains were found. Perhaps not surprisingly, the house had a reputation for being haunted ever after!

The loch holds many mysterious secrets beneath her sparkling waters and another legend tells of an underground tunnel which allegedly connects the loch to the sea. Certainly, there are strong underwater currents, drifts and eddies, deep holes, crevices and freezing cold waters which plunge to great depths just a few metres from shore, thus rendering these lovely waters dangerous at all times. The loch has therefore acquired a dubious reputation over the years for being quick to claim lives and slow to give up the dead. Indeed, many of those tragically lost have never been found. Loch Lomond has been justly crowned 'the Queen of Scottish Lochs', but she is a queen who demands the eternal respect of all who venture upon her waters.

Concluding on a more positive note, the pioneer novelist Tobias Smollett once wrote of Loch Lomond, in *Humphrey Clinker*, that 'Everything here is romantic beyond imagination. This country is justly styled the Arcadia of Scotland; and I don't doubt but it may vie with Arcadia in everything but climate. I am sure it excels it in wood and water.' Here you will find just over a quarter of the 2,000 flowering plants and ferns found in the British Isles; 200 recorded species of birds; 31 native and established species of mammal (including Australian wallabies!); about 13 species of fish, including the unique powan, a species found only in Lochs Lomond and Eck; and deep forests ranging from ancient oak woods to modern conifer forests of Norway and Sitka spruce, larch and other species. In the words of Sir Walter Scott, whose works provided the best advertisement that Loch Lomond has ever had:

'This noble lake, boasting innumerable beautiful islands of every varying form and outline which fancy can form – its northern extremity narrowing until it is lost among dusky and retreating mountains – while, gradually widening as it extends to the southward, it spreads its base around the indentures and promontories of a fair and fertile land, affords one of the most surprising, beautiful, and sublime spectacles in nature.'

BALLOCH–LUSS

Leaving Balloch by Carrochan Road or Balloch Road, take the A811 to Balloch roundabout on the A82. Heading north, the first glorious prospect of Loch Lomond suddenly unfolds as the road descends to the bonnie banks.

The first exit on the right leads to Cameron House Hotel and Country Club and Duck Bay Hotel and Marina. This loop of the old road, which rejoins the A82 about 1.5km further on, affords a grand view of the southern end of Loch Lomond, the island of Inchmurrin, the largest on the loch, and Ben Lomond, the highest mountain around the loch's shores. Be warned, though, that the Duck Bay road can be very busy indeed in summer! There are toilets (L, about 100m down the loop road), a car park opposite Duck Bay Hotel and a picnic area beyond.

Cameron House and Estate (R), home of the Smollett family from 1763 until 1989, has been beautifully restored as the prestigious Cameron House Hotel and Country Club with a luxury hotel, restaurants, luxury lodges, a leisure club, a 9-hole golf course and a marina all contained within the 108-acre estate. The original house, which took its name from the promontory on which it was situated ('cam sron' – 'crooked nose') appears to have been built around 1480 by the Dennistouns of Colgrain.

Tobias Smollett recalls a visit to his relatives at Cameron in 1766 in his novel *Humphrey Clinker*. Boswell and Johnson also called on their return from the Hebrides in 1773. The old house was largely rebuilt after a fire in 1864 and much altered again when it was converted to a hotel in 1989–90. Many stars of stage, screen and sport have stayed there since it opened in 1990, including Luciano Pavarotti, Cher, Cliff Richard, Clint Eastwood, Michael Jackson and U2.

The Duck Bay Hotel and Marina at Duck Bay enjoys a prime location on the loch shore. Opened in 1968, facilities include a hotel, restaurant, lounge bar, pleasure boat moorings and windsurfing, waterskiing and para-kiting are catered for.

Access to Loch Lomond Youth Hostel (Auchendennan House) is gained off the A82 (L) some 200m beyond the Duck Bay road junction. This grand mansion, which occupies a commanding position enjoying glorious views of the loch and surrounding hills, may be glimpsed from the A82. Auchendennan estate is said to have formed part of the hunting estate of King Robert the Bruce in the fourteenth century and certainly part of it was named Auchendennan-Righ, or King's Auchendennan.

The present mansion was built in 1866, to a design by Glasgow architect John Burnet, for George Martin, a wealthy Glasgow businessman who had made his fortune in India and the Far East. Martin was succeeded by his son John, a noted agriculturalist. The next wealthy owner, from 1898, was William Chrystal, head of J. & J. White, chemical manufacturers at Rutherglen and a Director of the Caledonian Railway. Auchendennan was purchased by the Scottish Youth Hostels Association in 1946 and converted into what was at that time the largest Youth Hostel in the world. The house still retains many splendid internal features and often appears as the exterior of 'the big house' in STV's *High Road*.

The Duck Bay loop road rejoins the A82 at the north end of the bay. It also provides access (R) to the Loch Lomond Castle Lodges – 55 timber holiday lodges.

Only the stark ruins of Auchenheglish House, latterly the Lomond Castle Hotel, remain behind the lodges. The mansion was built in 1859 for James MacKenzie, a wealthy Glasgow produce merchant who married the daughter of William Campbell of Tullichewan Castle and Auchendennan. Later it was occupied by the Brocks, who were involved in the local textile-dyeing industry and in the Clydesdale Bank, before passing to the Hamilton family in 1908. Then, in 1938 Sir Cargill McCowan bought Auchenheglish from the Hamiltons and in 1958 his son David converted it into the Lomond Castle Hotel. Many famous stars of the day stayed there, including Shirley Bassey, Cilla Black, Charlie Chaplin, Liberace, Jimmy Logan and the Bluebell Girls. Following several changes of ownership, the hotel was destroyed by fire in 1990.

The road swings away from the loch shore beyond Duck Bay and, on the approach to Arden (population c100 including Inchmurrin), Arden House is glimpsed briefly (R). This grand mansion was built in 1868 to a design by John Burnet in the then fashionable Scottish Baronial style. Its wealthy owner was

Sir James Lumsden, head of a wholesale stationery firm in Glasgow and Chairman of both the Glasgow and South Western Railway and the Clydesdale Bank. In 1982 the Lumsdens sold the house to an Australian businessman, who converted it into flats. In 1991, however, the occupants were suddenly evicted as a result of a dispute over ownership. The dispute was subsequently resolved and the flats advertised for sale again.

At Arden, the Black Hill road (B831/B832) goes off to Helensburgh and via Glen Fruin to Faslane on the Gare Loch. (For notes on these routes, see Route 2A.)

There is a noticeable change in the scenery north of Arden, for the high tops of the Luss Hills around Glen Finlas mark the gateway to the Highlands. The low, flat-topped Lowland hills of underlying old red sandstone, with volcanic lavas behind Dumbarton, give way to the higher, more rugged Highland hills, formed of tougher rocks known as Dalradian (after the ancient Scots kingdom of Dalriada), which are more resistant to weathering. The actual boundary line is the Highland Boundary Fault, a great geological fault line which extends right across Scotland from Stonehaven in the east, passes through Arden, and continues on to the Firth of Clyde.

The Fruin Water is soon crossed, on the final stretch of its tortuous course from lonely Glen Fruin, where the Colquhoun clansmen were massacred by the MacGregors in a bloody running battle on a bleak winter's day in February 1603. North of the Fruin, the Colquhouns were once lords of all they surveyed, all the way up the western side of Loch Lomond as far as Glen Douglas. After 1821, when they acquired the former territory of their ancient rivals, the MacFarlanes, their fiefdom extended to Inverarnan in Glen Falloch.

Fruin's waters must have run with blood in many a battle for, just beyond the old Bridge of Fruin (to the right of the present bridge), the burial mound of a Viking warrior was discovered in 1851. It contained an iron sword, a spearhead and a shield boss. This invader's tomb probably dated from 1263, when the Norwegian Vikings hauled their longboats across the narrow isthmus from Arrochar on Loch Long to Tarbet on Loch Lomond, before burning and pillaging the fertile lands around southern Loch Lomond.

At Midross, a road (R) leads to a jetty, from where the ferry to Inchmurrin Hotel on Inchmurrin Island sails on request in the summer months, from April to September. The hotel has a licensed restaurant and bar, self-catering flats, and small boats are available for hire.

The Loch Lomond Mail Boat at Inchmurrin Island hotel
(© Robert D. Campbell)

About a kilometre on, note (R) the imposing South Gate for
Rossdhu House, the seat of the Colquhouns of Luss until recent
years. The twin entrance lodges and arched gateway were built
for Sir James Colquhoun, 27th of Luss (1805–1836), who
greatly improved the grounds. The coat-of-arms is that of the
Colquhouns of Luss, featuring the cross saltire of the Earls of
Lennox, two greyhounds, a red stag's head, and the motto 'Si Je
Puis' (If I Can). Legend relates that the King asked the
Colquhoun chief to recover Dumbarton Castle from his enemies
and that he replied in Norman-French (then used at Court) 'Si
je puis', and then gave chase to a stag past the castle gates. The
garrison opened them and joined the chase, whereupon the
Colquhouns poured into the castle and captured it for the king.

At Duchlage another branch of the Helensburgh road (B832)
goes off (L) and about 500m beyond, on the same side, is the old
gamekeeper's cottage of Gallowhill. The hillock beside it is
known as Tom-na-Croich, 'the gallows hill'. There once stood
on its modest summit an ancient Scots fir known as 'the dule
tree', where wrong-doers paid the supreme penalty in far-off
days when the chiefs of Clan Colquhoun exercised the power of
life and death over their clansmen and enemies alike.

The adjacent hillock was Tom-na-Mhoid, 'the court hill', where
justice was dispensed. Just to the north of Gallowhill was Cnoc
Elachan, 'the armoury hillock', the gathering place of Clan
Colquhoun where clansmen rallied to the signal of the Fiery
Cross. 'Cnoc Elachan' was also the clan's war-cry, a cry which
must have resounded through the glens in many an encounter
with their fierce northern neighbours, the MacFarlanes and the
MacGregors.

The Finlas Water, 'the white stream', is crossed as it rushes down from Glen Finlas, just before the junction with the former Ministry of Defence road to Garelochhead via Glen Fruin (L), which was opened for public use in 1995. The track to Glen Finlas and Loch Finlas, which begins (R) some 100 metres along the Glen Fruin road, is not really suitable for motor vehicles but makes a fine walk.

In the eighteenth and early nineteenth centuries, heavy taxes on spirits made illegal distilling and smuggling of whisky rife in the side glens and islands of Loch Lomond, and indeed throughout the Highlands. In 1812 Colonel Peter Hawker, travelling between Dumbarton and Inverbeg wrote: 'In several of the most solitary glens we saw caves where smugglers manufacture famous Highland whisky, which is so superior to the ordinary by being distilled from the pure malt and smoked with the peat. They usually do this work in the dead of night.' Smuggling was often a necessary supplement to the meagre incomes of small tenant farmers. In addition to land-based patrols, the Customs and Excise Department had a Revenue cutter on the Loch by 1817 and there was many a pitched battle between the smugglers and the cutlass-wielding Excisemen, who were sometimes reinforced by a company of dragoon soldiers. Smuggling activity appears to have declined and then ceased within a decade of the cutter's appearance on the Loch, no doubt assisted by the introduction of an Act of Parliament of 1823 which legalised distilling in small stills upon payment of a moderate licence fee.

The main entrance to Rossdhu House, former seat of the Colquhouns of Luss and now the clubhouse of the Loch Lomond Golf Club, is passed (R) at Port of Rossdhu. Although this grand mansion is only 500m away across a small bay, it is unfortunately obscured by trees and is best observed from a boat on the Loch. Rossdhu is said to come from the Gaelic 'ros dubh', 'the black headland', as the promontory on which it sits was once covered in heather. However, industrious local historian, Donald MacLeod, maintained that since certain early charters show Rossdoe, and deer were commonly found in the vicinity, it was more probably 'point of the does'.

The Colquhouns were originally a Lowland family, whose ancestor Humphrey de Kilpatrick obtained a grant of the lands and barony of Colquhoun, which lay between Kilpatrick and Dumbarton, from Maldouen, 3rd Earl of Lennox, around 1246. Around 1368, Sir Robert Colquhoun of that ilk married the lady of Luss and so the extensive Luss estates on Loch Lomondside, between the Fruin and Douglas Waters, were acquired by marriage. The Colquhouns also retained possession of extensive territories south of the Highland line for many centuries.

The old Castle of Rossdhu, the ruins of which still stand near the present mansion, was built in the mid-fifteenth century for Sir John Colquhoun, 11th of Luss (1439–1478). A notable visitor to the castle was Mary, Queen of Scots, who stayed at Rossdhu on 15-16 July 1563. The ruins of what may have been an even earlier stronghold are to be found on nearby Elan Rossdhu, or Rossdhu Isle. North of Rossdhu House, by the shore, is the ruined private Chapel of St Mary, built in 1469, which was the burial place of the Colquhoun family for several centuries. A magnificent fifteenth-century Book of Hours which once belonged to the chapel is to be found in, of all places, the Central Library at Auckland, New Zealand.

The Colquhoun chiefs zealously upheld the law of the land and often held positions of authority, which tended to make them unpopular with the wilder clans. The MacGregors were particularly troublesome and often descended on the Colquhoun country bent on 'lifting' livestock, plundering and burning property. It appears to have been a minor sheep-stealing incident perpetrated by two MacGregors and the subsequent execution of the miscreants by the Colquhoun chief that led to the disastrous battle of Glen Fruin in 1603. The conflict ended with the massacre of the Colquhouns and the burning and pillaging of their lands by the MacGregors. A number of Colquhoun widows duly paraded the bloody shirts of their dead husbands before a horrified King James VI at Stirling. The King's retribution was swift and merciless, for he ordered proscription of the MacGregor name and tartan, the burning of their houses and they were ruthlessly hunted down in the hills. Alasdair, the MacGregor chief, was treacherously captured by the Campbell Earl of Argyll and hanged at Edinburgh with several of his clansmen. Persecution of the MacGregors was to continue almost until the end of the eighteenth century.

The male line of the Colquhouns ended in 1718, upon the death of the 22nd chief, Sir Humphrey Colquhoun. The estate then passed to his daughter Anne and her husband James Grant, son of the laird of Grant. The Colquhouns have therefore been Grants in all but name ever since that time.

Sir James Colquhoun, 25th of Luss, built the present house of Rossdhu in 1772–3 and in 1776 founded the town of Helensburgh, which he named after his wife, Lady Helen Colquhoun, sister of the 17th Earl of Sutherland. In 1773, Dr Johnson and James Boswell were received at the new house of

Rossdhu, when returning from their famous tour of the Highlands.

Sir James, 27th of Luss, enlarged Rossdhu, adding the two wings and the portico, unfortunately with stone from the old castle. He also greatly improved the grounds and had the arched gateway at the south entrance built. Sir James, the 28th chief, was drowned in a tragic accident in December 1873, while returning to the mainland by boat from Inchlonaig with his gamekeepers and a load of venison for distribution to people on his estate. Queen Victoria visited Rossdhu in 1875.

The present laird, Sir Ivar Colquhoun, 32nd of Luss, sold Rossdhu and no longer lives there. Since 1989 the estate has been redeveloped as the prestigious Loch Lomond Golf Club with a magnificent course designed by Tom Weiskopf, the 1973 Open champion, and Jay Morrish. The house of Rossdhu is now the clubhouse for what has been voted the best new course in the world. It is certainly one of the most scenic golf courses to be found anywhere in the world. The annual Loch Lomond World Invitational, first held in 1996, now attracts the cream of the world's leading golfers.

The village of Luss is reached along a stretch of the old A82 road which was replaced by the Luss by-pass, opened in 1991. As a visit to this pretty village is an essential highlight for visitors, the route via Luss is described here. However, by continuing on the A82 you can see the famous Scottish bagpipe, and the kilt, being manufactured at the Thistle Bagpipe Works (L). (01436 860250. Open all year 0900–1730, later in summer. Craft and gift shop.) There is access to Luss village a kilometre beyond.

The road drops down to Bandry, an attractive row of cottages facing Bandry Bay and the wooded island of Inchtavannach. Bandry is notable as being the place where the good St Kessog, or MacKessog, who brought Christianity from Ireland to the southern shores of Loch Lomond in the early sixth century, is said to have been martyred around 520AD or 560AD. However, some sources relate that St Kessog was martyred abroad and his remains returned to Luss for burial. A large cairn, known as Cairn-ma-Kessog, which once stood about 500m south of Bandry, was said to mark the spot where St Kessog was martyred. Unfortunately, it was partially destroyed by soldiers building the Military Road from Dumbarton to Inveraray around 1745 and thereafter gradually disappeared. The effigy which it contained, long believed to be that of St Kessog, but more probably that of Robert Colquhoun, Bishop of Argyll and Lismore, was removed to St Mary's Chapel, Rossdhu, along with a sculptured head which was probably of St Kessog, and a stone font. They were probably buried at Bandry for safe-keeping at the time of the Reformation. These relics were presented to the Church of St MacKessog at Luss in 1932 and they are now on display there.

St Kessog had his cell on nearby Inchtavannach, 'the island of the monk's house', and monks later had a monastery there, hence the island's name. The island's highest point is Tom-na-Clag, 'the hill of the bell', at its north-western end, where a large bell once tolled on the Sabbath to summon the good folk of Luss, Inchcailloch and Kilmaronock parishes to their respective churches. A farmhouse at the southern end, on the site of the monastery, is now let to tenants. The island supports many roe deer.

The statue of a boy nicknamed 'Wee Peter' projects mysteriously from the depths of the loch at the north end of Bandry Bay. Several legends have gained currency over the years to account for this phenomenon, a favourite being that it was erected in memory of a drowned child. Known as 'Kerr's Folly', the statue was in fact erected by William Kerr, an orphan brought up in Luss, who made his fortune in London as a stonemason. The statue had been intended to form part of a building erected in Balham, London, but it was rejected by the owner. Kerr brought it home to Bandry Bay and had it erected here in 1890, together with a cairn at the end of Bandry Bank on the Loch, where two Vale of Leven men had been drowned by the upsetting of a yacht. Luss Estates asked him to remove both structures. Kerr removed the Cairn, but left the monument. 'Wee Peter' has been blown off his pedestal several times, most recently in the Great Storm of January 1968, but concerned friends have always returned him to his pedestal.

Another pretty little bay soon comes into view at Aldochlay, 'the sword burn', graced by the picturesque islet Swan Island, once known as Eilean Aldochlay. Swans are indeed much in evidence in the sheltered waters of this corner of the Loch, which made it a favourite location for houseboat-dwellers earlier this century.

The next bay, Camstraddan Bay, lies at some distance from the road. Mounds of slate scattered along the shore about here are the only reminder of the once-busy Camstraddan slate quarries which worked the hillside above the road from the late sixteenth until the late nineteenth centuries. The Colquhouns of Camstraddan owned two quarries and a third was owned by the Colquhouns of Luss. The Luss family eventually purchased the Camstraddan estate, including Camstraddan House and the quarries, in 1826.

In 1796 the three quarries were producing between 350,000 and 530,000 slates a year and up to 30 men were employed. The slates were sent by barge to Glasgow, Paisley, Greenock, the Vale of Leven, and across the loch to places in Stirlingshire. Camstraddan House (private), at the north end of the bay, was built in 1739 by the 12th laird of Camstraddan and is now the residence of Sir Ivar Colquhoun of Luss.

LUSS

Luss (pop. c400) is entered by the bridge over the Luss Water, passing (R) the field where the annual Luss Highland Games are held in July. These popular games have been held since 1875. Beyond the Colquhoun Arms Hotel and Glendarroch Tea Room (L), there is a large car and bus park (T) with a Loch Lomond Park Board Visitor Centre (T) (01436 860601, open April to October). There is access beyond (R) to The Lodge on Loch Lomond Hotel; the Camping and Caravanning Club Site, with pitches for touring and motor caravans and tents; and (L) to the main A82 road. There are some shops, a Post Office and a tea room in the village.

There has been a travellers' inn on the site of the Colquhoun Arms Hotel since at least 1760 when Bishop Richard Pococke, Bishop of Meath, stayed there on a tour through Scotland. Not all travellers were so fortunate, as the French Professor Faujas St Fond and his companions were later to testify. Arriving at Luss inn late one stormy night in 1784, the weary travellers were herded into a stable by the hostess of the inn, ordered to keep quiet as a circuit judge was asleep at the hostelry and then ordered out in the heavy rain to battle on through the darkness to Tarbet inn!

William Wordsworth, his sister Dorothy and Samuel Taylor Coleridge did manage to stay at the Luss inn during their tour in 1803. However, Dorothy considered the landlady (probably the same one encountered by poor Faujas St Fond), 'the most cruel and hateful-looking woman I ever saw', which was certainly consistent with her having refused to light a fire for them!

Dorothy noted that, 'William and Coleridge had bad beds, in a two-bedded room in the garrets, though there were empty rooms on the first floor, and they were disturbed by a drunken man, who had come to the inn when they were gone to sleep.' The inn where the Wordsworths stayed was replaced by the present well-appointed hotel during the nineteenth century.

Walk through to Pier Road, the village's 'main street', which runs from the hotel to the pier. It will be readily appreciated why Luss, with its beautiful, flower-bedecked cottages and glorious panorama of the loch, islands and Ben Lomond from its sandy, gently curving beach, ranks as one of the most beautiful villages in Scotland.

Luss, which once boasted a corn-mill, a saw-mill and even a cotton-mill for some years after 1790, did not always make the most of its prime location. Dorothy Wordsworth regretted its 'want of loveliness' and she observed, 'Here we first saw houses without windows, the smoke coming out of the open window-places; the chimneys were like stools with four legs, a hole being left in the roof for the smoke, and over that a slate placed upon four sticks.'

Sir James Colquhoun, the laird of Luss, had most of the old village swept away soon after the steamer pier opened in 1850 and replaced by today's pretty cottages, occupied by his foresters, farm labourers and quarrymen. In a nine-year, £1.2 million project completed in 1992, the cottages were fully modernised and refurbished by a housing association for rental. They often feature in the popular STV series *High Road*, filmed at Luss and other locations around the loch, which transforms the village into 'Glendarroch'.

The impressive view from the beach or the pier (T) ranges round from Ben Lomond in the north to the archipelago of emerald islands scattered across the shallower southern reaches of the loch. A splendid scenic backdrop is provided by the Luss Hills around Glen Luss. Cruises around the islands operate from Luss Pier in the summer months. (Cruise Loch Lomond Ltd, The Boatyard, Tarbet. 01301 702356.)

The large, densely wooded island directly opposite Luss is Inchlonaig, 'the yew tree island', which was once held by the Luss family who preceded the Colquhouns as lairds of Luss. As the name implies, Inchlonaig is covered in ancient yew trees, which are said to have been planted by Robert the Bruce to provide bows for his archers. The island, which has over the years been farmed and used by the Colquhouns as a deer-park, is now in private ownership.

The islet to the south is Fraoch Eilean, 'Heather Isle', once known as 'the prison of Luss' where, it is said, errant wives were once marooned until they saw the error of their ways. Beautiful Scots firs which once clothed the islet were destroyed by fire after the First World War. The north end of Inchconnachan, 'the Colquhoun's island', can be seen beyond Fraoch Eilean.

Proceed south along the shore to the Church of St MacKessog (Luss Parish Church, Church of Scotland). This interesting little church was built in 1875 as a memorial to Sir James Colquhoun, the 28th laird, who accidentally drowned in the loch in December 1873. A memorial stone in the churchyard commemorates all five who drowned on that fateful day.

A church has stood on or near this site for many centuries. Tradition relates that the remains of St Kessog were, at some time after his death in 520 or 560AD, embalmed in sweet herbs and interred at Clachandhu, 'the black hamlet', as Luss was then known. One of the herbs sprang from his grave and spread over the wall of the church, thus giving name to the village, 'Lus' being the Gaelic for a plant or herb. The original church, probably a small oratory built on the shore by St Kessog, duly became the destination for many devotees on pilgrimages. Yet another source relates that 'Lus' comes from fleur-de-lys strewn on the grave of Baroness MacAuslan (the MacAuslans were ancestors of the Buchanans), whose husband had given distinguished service at the siege of Tournay in France. The flowers grew on her grave and miraculously cured a pestilence which was then raging.

The earliest mention of the church of Luss occurs in the mid-thirteenth century, when Maldouen, 3rd Earl of Lennox, confirmed the patronage of the living to Maldouen, Dean of Lennox, and his son Gillemore. In 1315, King Robert the Bruce granted the little church the privilege of Gyrth or Sanctuary for fugitives, extending to 5km (3miles) around by land or water, partly for the honour in which he held St Kessog and probably also as a token of friendship for his loyal supporter Malcolm, 5th Earl of Lennox.

In 1430 Bishop John Cameron of Glasgow built a 'theekit' (thatched) church at Luss, which was dedicated to St Kessog. This church was, to the chagrin of the Colquhouns, also used by the wild MacFarlanes of Arrochar as their parish church, until 1733 when they built their own church at Arrochar. A stone built into the north gable of the present church, erected by laird John MacFarlane in 1612 and transferred there from earlier buildings, marks 'The place of burial appointed for the Laird of Arroquhar'. A new church was built in 1771, which was in turn replaced by the present one in 1875.

The church (usually open to the public in the summer months) is of Gothic design and has a roof which is magnificently raftered with oak beams. Beautiful stained glass windows commemorate members of the Colquhoun family, apart from one which is to the memory of Sir James Lumsden of Arden. The 'laird's loft', or raised family pew of the Colquhouns, bears the armorial funeral hatchments of several Colquhoun chiefs. An ancient effigy on display was long believed to be that of St Kessog, who brought Christianity to the district in the early sixth century, but it is more probably that of Robert Colquhoun, Bishop of Argyll and Lismore (1475–c1495), who was a former vicar of Luss. A sculptured head, also on display, may be that of St Kessog. These items, together with a stone font, were discovered in a large cairn known as Cairn-ma-Kessog, which once stood just south of Bandry.

The lych-gates around the churchyard are an unusual feature in Scotland. Notable headstones include two cross-slabs, probably dating from the seventh to ninth centuries, a 'hogback' stone of the eleventh century and later stones commemorating the Colquhouns of Luss and the Rev John Stuart (1743–1821), a former minister of the church who first translated the Bible into Gaelic. However, perhaps the most famous person associated with the church (and still very much alive) is Noel Edmonds, the popular television personality. In July 1986, with his bride, he whirled across the loch by helicopter from the Buchanan Arms Hotel at Drymen, to be married in St MacKessog's.

The drive or walk up beautiful Glen Luss behind the village provides a pleasant excursion. A footbridge over the A82, just north of the Colquhoun Arms Hotel, provides pedestrian access to the Glen Luss road.

Some 2.5km up the glen the foundations of the pre-Reformation St Michael's Chapel, stand on a hillock above the road (R). In 1852 Sir James Colquhoun of Luss erected a memorial stone on the site, with Gaelic and Latin inscriptions, which reads, 'St. Michael's Chapel. James, Laird of Colquhoun and Luss, caused this monument to be erected to the memory of a bye-gone piety, and of those psalms formerly sung to the honour of God (in this place), now, alas, completely dilapidated.'

The public motor road ends opposite Glenmollochan Farm (L), where care should be taken not to obstruct farm access. The farm is notable as having been the place where Blackface sheep were first introduced to the Highlands in 1749 and a sheep's head is fittingly sculpted on the nearby Ramshorn Bridge, with the inscription, 'Wm. Johns Built This Bridge 1777'. The introduction of large-scale farming of Blackface sheep brought wealth to a few farmers on the old clan lands, but resulted in widespread depopulation throughout the Highlands as the old communal farms, each supporting several families, were swept away.

It is possible to walk through to Glen Fruin from the head of Glen Luss by a 350m-high pass, although the going becomes progressively harder.

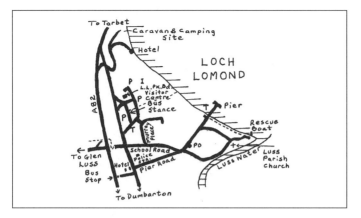

LUSS

Visitor Services
B CC Ch Cr G P PO PS PT SA SC T

Sport and Leisure
Cy Fi Go HB PB RC S VC W

Public Transport
Bus and Coach
Car park for Balloch, Alexandria and infrequent service from Clydebank or Helensburgh to Lochgoilhead and Carrick Castle. Stops on A82 behind Colquhoun Arms Hotel for Glasgow to Inveraray, Campbeltown, Oban, Fort William and Skye services.

Cruises
Luss Pier for cruises around the islands, usually from Easter to end of September. Cruise Loch Lomond, Tarbet, 01301 702356.

Accommodation
Hotels
Colquhoun Arms, Luss 01436 860282
The Lodge on Loch Lomond, Luss 01436 860201/202

Caravan and Camping Park
Camping and Caravan Club Site, Luss 01436 860658

Tourist Information
Loch Lomond Park Centre, car park 01436 860601 (April to October)

LUSS–TARBET

The A82 road, which is rejoined beyond the car park, has an adjoining foot and cycle path which provides easy walking as far north as Tarbet. The splendid vista to the north is dominated by the massive head and shoulders of Ben Lomond (974m), which has the distinction of being the southernmost 'Munro' (mountain over 914m/3,000ft) in Scotland.

The bonnie banks between Luss and Inverbeg were never busier than on 18 July 1932 when huge crowds lined the shore to witness the Irishman Kaye Don take the world's water speed record in Lord Wakefield's speed-boat *Miss England III*. Roaring to and fro, with spray flying high in the air, he achieved an average speed of 119.81 m.p.h. on his second return run of the measured mile from Luss. He actually attained 120.5 mph on one leg of the run, making Don the first person ever to travel at two miles a minute on water. Then, in June 1937 Sir Malcolm Campbell brought his famous speed-boat *Bluebird* to the loch for speed trials, based at Rossdhu. Unfortunately flotsam brought down by flooded rivers made conditions unsafe for the fragile craft and so *Bluebird* left Loch Lomond for safer waters.

While on the subject of records, there was a popular song in the 1950s which claimed that, 'I could swim Loch Lomond and be back in half an hour'! The loch was in fact first swum from end to end (Ardlui to Balloch Pier) on 1–2 August 1959 by Commander C.G. Forsberg of London in 15 hours 31 minutes 9.8 seconds. On 6–7 August 1960, Miss Susan Baddeley of Uxbridge became the first woman to swim the loch, in 26 hours 10 minutes.

North of Ross Point, which can be seen on the opposite shore opposite Culag (R), the loch becomes noticeably narrower and the mountains rise more steeply from its shores. About 2km beyond Culag, just beyond a lay-by (L), keep a lookout for one of the original Military Road bridges, built around 1747 by Redcoat soldiers.

INVERBEG

Inverbeg is soon reached. This tiny hamlet stands at the mouth of the Douglas Water where it issues from Glen Douglas, hence its Gaelic name which means 'the little river mouth'. The Inverbeg Inn (L) originated around 1814 as the ferryman's cottage for the Rowardennan ferry, which belonged to the Duke of Montrose. The inn was a favourite haunt of cattle drovers in its early days and had to be enlarged to meet the boom in tourism. It was rebuilt after a fire in 1978.

The old Inverberg Inn, now a fine hotel, was once frequented by cattle-drovers (R. D. Campbell Collection)

Just beyond the bridge over the Douglas Water, the Glen Douglas road goes off (L) to join the A814 at Craggan on Loch Long. The ancient chronicler Nennius relates that it was in Glen Douglas that Arthur (of Knights of the Round Table fame), fought certain of his battles against invading Picts and Scots. At a later period, the modest Douglas, or 'black water', marked the boundary between the clanlands of the law-abiding Colquhouns of Luss and the turbulent MacFarlanes of Arrochar. Glen Douglas, in common with other glens around the loch, suffered serious depopulation following the introduction of Blackface sheep-farming from the mid-eighteenth century. A map dated 1745 showed no fewer than 13 farms in the glen, each with several families, whereas there are only three today. The western end of the glen has been rather spoiled in recent years by a large nuclear defence installation.

The Glen Douglas road also provides access, by a bridge over the Douglas Water (L), to the Inverbeg Galleries (01436 860277), a large retail art gallery. It should be noted that the Inverbeg Youth Hostel is now closed, the nearest hostels now being Rowardennan (ferry from Inverbeg), Loch Lomond (at Duck Bay, Arden) and Ardgartan (near Arrochar).

The entrance to Inverbeg Holiday Park (R), a caravan and camping park, is just beyond the Glen Douglas turnoff. The land on which the park sits is actually an alluvial fan of material washed down by the Douglas Water over the centuries, a feature common to all the river mouths around the loch.

North of Inverbeg the loch occupies a deep, fiord-like trench carved by Ice Age glaciers, and the waters (which rarely exceed 60m in depth south of here) plunge steeply to over 150m, as far north as Inveruglas. Although the shallow southern basin has sometimes frozen over completely between Balloch and Luss during severe winters, the loch has never been known to freeze over north of Luss.

INVERBEG

Visitor Services
B CC F SA SC

Sport and Leisure
A Cy Fi PB RC W

Public Transport
Bus and Coach
Stops (see Luss for services) are on the main road near the Inverbeg Inn.

Ferries
An underpass leads from the inn to the ferry jetty. A ferry operates to Rowardennan in the summer months, usually April to September. Loch Lomond Ferry Service, Rowardennan Hotel, by Drymen, 01360 870273. Another ferry links with Rowardennan, Tarbet and Inversnaid, usually Easter to late September. Cruise Loch Lomond, Tarbet, 01301 702356.

Accommodation
Hotel
Inverbeg Inn, A82 01436 860678

Caravan and Camping Park
Inverbeg Holiday Park, A82 01436 860267

Leaving Inverbeg, the road curves to the right by a sheltered bay known as Camus-na-Glash, where a burn cascades down the hillside from Lochan Uaine, or the Fairy Loch. Legend has it that when local women had spun the yarn for cloth they brought it to this lochan, placed it in the water and left instructions as to the desired colour, together with a small gift for the fairy. Next morning, as the sun peeped over the shoulder of Ben Lomond, the yarn was found to be dyed in the desired colour! Then one day an evil shepherd tried to trick the fairy into dyeing a black fleece white. In anger she spilled all her colours in the water and disappeared forever. However, it is said that on a fine summer evening you may still see all the colours glittering in the water!

The new road cuts through the great headland of Rubha Mor, 'the big headland', an outcrop of rock known as schistose grit which occurs among the hard mica-schist rock about here and is also found on parts of Ben Lomond. When the Military Road was built, it simply climbed up and over this headland and the old route can still be traced to the present day. A later realignment, between Rubha Mor and Hollybank, near Tarbet, was abandoned when the present road opened in the late 1980s. It now provides a splendid walk down by the loch shore, either from Firkin car park and picnic area (R) (T), or from Luss or Inverbeg (Walk 3).

At Stuc-an-t-Iobairt, just beyond Firkin ('the grassy headland'), an ancient, gnarled yew tree, still bearing foliage, stands by the main road near a house (L). This is the historic Robert the Bruce's Tree, which recalls a desperate episode in his career. Fleeing from his enemies following defeat at Dail-righ (Dalry) near Tyndrum in 1306, the king is said to have rallied his men here after they had been ferried across the loch in a leaky boat, or had swum with their swords clenched in their teeth. They were fortunate enough to meet up with Bruce's loyal supporter the Earl of Lennox, who conveyed them to Rosneath. From there they carried onwards, to spend the winter at Rathlin Island before returning to renew the struggle for Scotland's independence.

Approaching Tarbet, Stuckgowan House, a large villa, stands on the hillside among some splendid trees. In 1799 the brothers John and Malcolm McMurrich, Glasgow merchants, purchased Stuckgowan from the heirs of John Syme, an Edinburgh burgess, and built the present Regency Gothic house. In 1836 John McMurrich entered into partnership with David Napier, the renowned marine engineer, and built the *Lochlomond*, the first iron-hulled steamer to sail on the loch. He also owned the Tarbet inn.

Francis Jeffrey (later Lord Jeffrey), the Lord Advocate and founder of the *Edinburgh Review*, often spent his annual holidays at Tarbet inn and then, after conducting a successful legal case for McMurrich, at Stuckgowan between 1822 and 1838. When the two brothers died, the property was inherited by their nephew James McMurrich, who eventually sold it to Sir James Colquhoun of Luss. As the Colquhouns had already acquired all the surrounding former territory of the MacFarlanes from Ferguson of Raith in 1821, this purchase completed their 'empire' on the west side of the loch. On the hillside above is the site of the Black Village, whose inhabitants were wiped out by the black plague in the seventeenth century.

TARBET

Entering Tarbet (pop. c300), the access road to Tarbet jetty for cruises on Loch Lomond (P) (T) is passed just before reaching Tarbet Hotel. (Cruise Loch Lomond Ltd., 01301 702356.) The A83 road, for Arrochar and Tarbet railway station, Arrochar, Inveraray and the Three Lochs Tour (Route 3), goes straight ahead at Tarbet Hotel, while the A82 goes right.

Take the A83 for the Argyll National Tourist Route (marked by white on brown signs) which goes by way of Inveraray, Lochgilphead, Oban and Ballachulish to Fort William, as an alternative to the more direct A82.

The Tourist Information Centre (01301 702260, April to October) is opposite the hotel and there is a Post Office/tea room, and a restaurant/coffee/craft shop a short distance along the A83. There are more restaurants, tea rooms and shops at Arrochar, 2.5km away.

The commodious Tarbet Hotel traces its origin back to a humble inn of the 1570s, which would seem to make it the longest-established hostelry on Loch Lomondside. The hotel was extensively rebuilt in 1880–2, to a Scottish baronial design by James Thomson. Famous visitors include James Boswell and Dr Johnson (1773); William and Dorothy Wordsworth with Samuel Taylor Coleridge (1803); Thomas Carlyle (1817); and Francis Jeffrey (later Lord Jeffrey), in the early years of the nineteenth century.

At Tarbet, the fresh waters of Loch Lomond are separated from the salt waters of Loch Long at Arrochar by an isthmus only 2.5km wide. In 1263 Hacco, King of Norway, despatched a hostile fleet of 60 ships from Norway, which sailed up Loch Long. At the head of the loch the Vikings dragged their smaller boats on rollers across to Loch Lomond, where they laid waste to the surrounding countryside by burning, pillaging and putting the unfortunate inhabitants to the sword. Retribution was not long in coming. Returning to Norway, the Vikings were driven ashore by a storm at Largs on the Firth of Clyde and decisively defeated by Alexander III.

Tarbet once lay at the heart of the territory of Clan MacFarlane, which extended from the Douglas Water to Inverarnan, beyond the head of the loch. The MacFarlanes earned a reputation for their feuding, cattle-lifting propensities and generally turbulent nature, but these were brutal times and their activities seem to have been directed mainly against their more lawless northern neighbours, rather than their law-abiding southern ones. The MacFarlane chiefs had one of their principal residences at Tarbet until 1697, when a new house was built at West Tarbet or Arrochar.

The old order finally passed away in 1785, when the MacFarlane lands were brought to a judicial sale and sold to William Ferguson of Raith. The MacFarlane clansmen soon began to drift away from their ancient homeland, and large farms running Blackface sheep replaced their small crofts which had grown subsistence crops and supported a few black cattle in summer, some goats and a few native (whiteface) sheep in winter. Their meagre incomes were sometimes supplemented by wood-cutting, herring-fishing and the illicit distillation of whisky, which was smuggled out to the Lowlands. In 1821 the old MacFarlane lands were purchased by Sir James Colquhoun of Luss, thus giving the Colquhouns control of nearly all the territory between the Fruin Water and Inverarnan.

Tarbet's strategic location made it a Mecca for travellers from very early times. In the sixteenth century the Knights Hospitallers of St John of Jerusalem had a hospital (a sanctuary for poor, sick and infirm travellers) here and from around 1570 there was an inn. The Military Roads brought the first tourists to the district in the mid-eighteenth century and Tarbet later benefited from the introduction of steamer and then rail services. In the 1850s the popular Three Lochs rail and steamer tour, embracing Lochs Lomond, Long and Goil, was introduced and for a century and more hordes of happy tourists were to be seen walking or coaching between Tarbet and Arrochar piers.

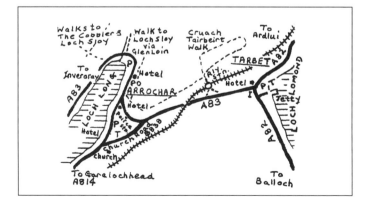

TARBET

Visitor Services
B Cr F G I MR P PO PT R SA SC T

Sport and Leisure
Cf Fi FP PB RC S W

Public Transport
Rail
Arrochar and Tarbet Station for West Highland Line Glasgow to Oban, Fort William and Mallaig services.

Bus and Coach
Tarbet Hotel (A83) for Glasgow to Inveraray, Campbeltown and Oban services, also for infrequent Clydebank or Helensburgh to Lochgoilhead and Carrick Castle via Arrochar service. Tarbet Hotel (A82) for Glasgow to Fort William and Skye via Crianlarich service.

Cruises and Ferries
Tarbet Jetty for local cruises and ferry to Rowardennan, Inverbeg and Inversnaid, usually daily Easter to end September. Cruise Loch Lomond, Tarbet, 01301 702356.

Caravan and Camping Park
Inverglas Holiday Park, A82, 5km N of Tarbet 01301 704224

Accommodation
Hotel
Tarbet, junction A82/A83 01301 702228

Tourist Information
Tarbet, Junction A82/A83 01301 702260 (April to October).

TARBET–ARDLUI

Leaving Tarbet, the old primary school (R) stands near the site of a house at Claddich which was once a seat of the Chiefs of Clan MacFarlane. Their principal stronghold was a castle on Inveruglas Isle, until it was burned down by Cromwell's men during the Civil War, whereupon the chief removed to a castle on the island of Eilean Vow. In 1697 a new seat, Inverioch House, was built at Arrochar. Tom-na-Croich, 'the gallows hill', stood opposite the house at Claddich and about a kilometre to the north, at Tom-na-Hianish, 'the hill of witness', the chiefs held Court and dispensed justice.

As the highway winds through Kenmore Wood at the eastern extremity of the Forestry Commission's 21,300-hectare Argyll Forest Park, picturesque, wooded Tarbet Isle comes into view. This lonely isle once supported a flourishing heronry among its pines, but alas these graceful birds have long since been replaced by colonies of gulls. About a kilometre on is the point where the loch reaches its greatest depth, at 105 fathoms (190m or 630ft), opposite the old shooting lodge of Blairannaich. This was ascertained by an Admiralty survey conducted from one of the loch steamers in 1861.

INVERUGLAS

Scarcely a hamlet, Inveruglas is entered by the bridge over the Inveruglas Water, where there is access (R) to Loch Lomond Holiday Park, a caravan park with chalets for hire. The private road to Loch Sloy goes off (L) immediately beyond the bridge. This bleak, mountain-encircled loch was the gathering place of the wild Clan MacFarlane and its name their war-cry. If walking to Loch Sloy (Walk 5), please do not park by the access road, but continue on to Inveruglas car park and walk back on the roadside verge.

On Wallace's Isle, hidden away at the mouth of the Inveruglas Water, Scotland's revered patriot William Wallace is said to have taken refuge during his guerrilla war against the English occupation of Scotland in the thirteenth century. It is always a pity to spoil a good story, but a more probable explanation is that the island was named in the early nineteenth century for a local farmer who rejoiced in the same name as the hero – and now lies buried in Arrochar churchyard.

Tiny Inveruglas has more definite connections with another famous historical figure. In June 1753, when the Military Road from Tarbet to Crianlarich was under construction, a young officer called James Wolfe camped with his regiment at Inveruglas. He was later to achieve fame as General Wolfe, the hero of Quebec.

The wooded islet in the bay is Inveruglas Isle, whose pine trees hide the ruins of the former principal stronghold of the chiefs of Clan MacFarlane. Walter, the 16th chief (1624–1664), a loyal adherent of Charles I and the Stewart cause, suffered for his loyalty during Cromwell's Commonwealth, when his castle on Inveruglas Isle was burned to the ground. This seems to have occurred in May 1654, when General Monck marched his forces over from Kilsyth to Buchanan House, near Drymen, whereupon he gave orders that all the boats on Loch Lomond were to be destroyed lest they be used by the Royalists. After the destruction of Inveruglas, the chief's main residence was either at Eilean Vow, near the head of the loch, or at Tarbet.

The Inveruglas Power Station of Scottish Hydro-Electric (L) is made conspicuous by the four giant pipelines (installed at a time when less consideration was given to environmental concerns) which bring the pure waters of Loch Sloy down from a three-kilometre-long tunnel through the shoulder of Ben Vorlich, to power four turbo-alternators of 130,450kw total capacity. The Loch Sloy Hydro-Electric project, the first major hydro-electric scheme to be completed in Scotland, involved the construction of a 353m-long dam at Loch Sloy; a tunnel through Ben Vorlich; the power station; access roads; diversion of the main road and railway at Inveruglas; and the diversion of many streams throughout the district.

Sleepy Inveruglas was transformed when construction commenced in May 1945. A railway station and a large workers' camp were built, together with another camp at nearby Ardvorlich. The labour force, which included German prisoners-of-war, Cornish miners and Polish tunnellers, numbered over 2,200 at peak construction. Many workers, including prisoners-of-war, travelled in daily by train from outlying camps at Faslane, Arrochar and in Glen Falloch. Sand was brought in by barge from Balloch while other materials were brought in by road and the West Highland Railway. The work was carried out under extremely arduous conditions. The area has a very high rainfall and records maintained during construction showed 230 wet days a year, with a maximum of 4,267mm during 1948! The mountains were often blanketed in mist and rain, and snow fell for days on end. When the project was finally opened by HM the Queen (now the Queen Mother), on 18 October 1950, all the local schoolchildren stood on the hillside above – in pouring rain.

At Inveruglas car park (R) (T), splendid views of the loch can be obtained from the viewing-point, which has a view indicator commemorating Tom Johnston, the first Chairman of the North of Scotland Hydro-Electric Board and former Secretary of State for Scotland. Rob Roy's Cave lies directly opposite, on the wooded eastern shore, and Inversnaid Hotel, Cruachan Hill (537m) and Ben Lomond (974m) are prominent towards the south east. A ferry operates from Inveruglas jetty to Inversnaid (usually from March to December, by arrangement with Inversnaid Hotel, 01877 386223). Fortunately it is no longer necessary (or indeed prudent) to light a fire, fire a gun or sound a coach-horn or bugle to attract the ferryman's attention, as was the case last century!

North of Inveruglas the road winds round a woody little bay, close by the grand masonry arches of Craigenarden Viaduct on the West Highland Railway. When the railway was under construction, around 1890, the engineers feared that the standard lattice-girder type of bridge employed throughout the line would be a blemish on the Loch Lomondside landscape. The handsome arches of Craigenarden Viaduct were therefore built of whinstone and, to enhance the scenic effect, were also provided with castellated parapets and balusters running up the piers.

On these remote sections of the line bordering the loch, tugs were used to tow in barge-loads of bridge sections and materials. Such was the skill of these bold Victorian engineers that in blasting the West Highlands through 160km of mountainous country, only one short tunnel was originally necessary, just to the north of Craigenarden. On a lighter note, it is recorded that a member of the workforce, a thirsty navvy camped near Inveruglas, whiled away a dull Sunday by lashing two planks together and paddling the 3km across to Inversnaid Hotel to down a glass of beer. Suitably refreshed, he paddled back again!

The loch narrows still further about here and it is now less than a kilometre across to the beautiful, oak-fringed shores on the eastern side, where only walkers on the West Highland Way, wild goats rooting among the undergrowth and the occasional birdcall disturb the silence. About 2km further on, the picturesque isle of Eilean Vow (which has been incorrectly recorded on Ordnance Survey maps as 'Island I. Vow' for many years now) makes a pretty picture in mid-loch. The ruins of one of the ancient strongholds of the MacFarlanes, described in the eighteenth century as 'a pretty good house, with gardens', lie mouldering among the vegetation.

The castle on Eilean Vow was built in 1577 by Andrew, the 14th chief of Clan MacFarlane (1547–1612), who succeeded at the tender age of three. The islet was then known as Eilean Ure, or Elenore, 'the new island', no doubt on account of the chief having built his new house upon it.

Andrew's clansmen had played a decisive part in the action against Mary, Queen of Scots' army at the battle of Langside in 1568 and, in recognition, the Regent Moray rewarded him with the MacFarlane crest and motto. This features the red cross saltire of the Earls of Lennox, flanked by two clansmen with bows and arrows at the ready, surmounted by a bare-chested man, or demi-savage, clutching a sheaf of arrows in his right hand and pointing to a crown with his left. The motto, 'This

I'll Defend' appears above and the war-cry, 'Loch Sloy', below.

Andrew was succeeded by his son John, who was apparently something of a firebrand in his younger days, for he was implicated, with some MacGregors, in the murder of Sir Humphrey Colquhoun at Bannachra Castle in 1592. He seems to have mellowed with age, however, for he was later described as, 'a man of piety and benevolence', and had an almshouse built for poor travellers at Bruitfort, or Croit a' phuirt (pronounced 'crutafoorst'), on the western shore opposite the island.

Eilean Vow became one of the principal residences of the chief following the destruction of the castle on Inveruglas Isle in the mid-seventeenth century. It was abandoned some time after the completion of a new house at Arrochar in 1697 and by the time William Wordsworth made his second visit to the loch, in 1814, the castle was falling to ruin. Wordsworth learned of an old MacFarlane kinsman who lived as a hermit on the island, and later wrote *The Brownie's Cell*, in which the castle ruins become those of an old religious establishment and the hermit a brownie, or fairy:

'Proud Remnant was he of a fearless Race,
Who stood and flourished face to face
With their perennial hills . . .

All, all were dispossessed . . . save him whose smile
Shot lightning through this lonely Isle!
No right had he but what he made
To this small spot, his leafy shade;
But the ground lay within that ring
To which he only dared to cling . . .'

It is recorded that the hermit was one Andrew MacFarlane, who stored goods in the kitchen of the old castle, which he sold to the local inhabitants as he sailed about the loch in his boat. He is said to have kept a calendar of passing events using strange hieroglyphics which only he could understand and seems to have passed away around 1830. When Wordsworth visited the loch again in autumn 1831, he composed *The Brownie*, on learning of the death of the old hermit, which begins:

'"How disappeared he?" Ask the newt and toad;
Ask of his fellow men and they will tell
How he was found, cold as an icicle,
Under an arch of that foreign abode . . .'

In the dark days of the Second World War yet another hermit lived on the island. Now, lonely Eilean Vow is left only with its mouldering ruins and a host of memories.

The road swings round the Rubha Ban, 'the white headland', where tradition relates that a chief of the MacFarlanes had the last of the uruisgs (goblins, or wild men of the hills credited with supernatural powers) hanged on a thorn tree. It appears that the chief had abducted the uruisg's wife and carried her off to Eilean Vow as a nurse for his infant son. In revenge, the furious uruisg attacked the chief's dairymaid while she was milking cows on the mainland. The chief then had the uruisg hanged at the Rubha Ban, in full view of his wife. The tragedy continued to unfold when the unfortunate wife attempted to poison the chief's infant son by applying a hemlock poultice to his feet! The fate of the uruisg's wife is not recorded. This episode is said to account for the 'savage' featured in the clan crest.

North of the Rubha Ban, the road winds round a small headland, where traffic lights controlling a short single-track section of road lend an incongruous, urban touch to such a magnificently scenic setting. About a hundred metres beyond the single-track section there is a tiny parking area on the left and just beyond, a path enters the woods through a wicket gate. A short walk takes you to the famous Pulpit Rock.

It is said that in the early nineteenth century, parishioners in the isolated northern part of Arrochar parish complained about the distance they had to travel to attend the parish church at Arrochar. The minister, the Rev. Peter Proudfoot, replied that if they built him a pulpit and vestry he would come and preach to them occasionally. In 1825 the congregation therefore arranged to have a vestry – or space large enough to hold the minister, an elder and the precentor – blasted out of this huge rock. Sad to relate, the man in charge of the explosives, Robert MacFarlane, was blinded in the process and known ever after as 'Blind Rabbie'.

The vestry, which was reached by a flight of steps, had a wooden door. A wooden pulpit was fixed to a platform bolted to the side of the great boulder and the iron bolts can be seen to this day.

Services were held in the summer months for about 70 years, with the congregation sitting on the ground around the rock. When Communion was held, which lasted for over a week, people gathered from near and far and a stall set up behind the rock sold bread, cheese and whisky. It is said that at such times there was usually a much larger crowd behind the rock than there was in front of it! Open-air services continued until 1895, when a mission church was built at Ardlui.

Before the rock assumed its religious function, it was known as the Clach nam Tarbh, or 'the stone of the bulls', resulting from an ancient legend. A red bull came from England to fight and put the bulls of Scotland to shame. He bellowed his challenge from the shoulder of Ben Vorlich, whereupon a black bull from Loch Lomondside accepted the challenge and found its way to the shoulder of the mountain. The black bull drove the red bull as far as a huge rock and killed it there. In the encounter, this great rock was pushed over and rolled down the mountainside to its present position on the level ground by the lochside.

Continuing on, the remains of four prehistoric burial cairns, probably dating from the Neolithic period of the Stone Age, about 4,000–5,000 years ago, were found by the loch shore near Stuckendroin Farm some years back.

ARDLUI

Entering Ardlui, meaning 'height of the calves' (pop. with Inveruglas c300), there is a camping site for walkers and cyclists (R), opposite Ardlui Railway Station on the West Highland Line (L). The Ardlui Hotel and Marina (R) has a small shop and petrol station, while the adjacent Marina provides berthing facilities, a slipway and boat sales. The Ardlui Caravan Park, a caravan and camping park, is behind the hotel.

Although the long and arduous ascent of Ben Vorlich (943m) can be made by experienced walkers from near the railway station, it is better approached from the Loch Sloy road (Walk 5). The West Highland Way can be reached by ferry or by a bridge over the River Falloch some 3km north of Ardlui (Walk 6). Great care is required when walking north on the main road to Inverarnan, or south to the Pulpit Rock, as there are no footpaths for much of the way.

There would have been a handy bridge over the Falloch at Ardlui today had it not been for a legal dispute between local landowners in the nineteenth century. The story begins early in the nineteenth century when the Falloch was busy with cargo boats, taking coal, sheep and general cargoes up to the farms in the glen and bringing down wool, cheese, heavy timbers, such as oak, and even lead from the Marquis of Breadalbane's lead mines near Tyndrum. Light timbers, such as birch, larch and ash were simply floated down to Ardlui and then rafted down the loch. Then, in 1844, passenger steamers also started sailing upriver to a point on the Marquis of Breadalbane's property near the Inverarnan Inn. From 1847 they actually reached the door of the inn – by canal!

In 1851, Sir James Colquhoun of Luss had the rival Ardlui Hotel built and served by a pier on the Falloch. However, it was soon found that floods, droughts and the windings of the river made navigation to Inverarnan difficult and so regular sailings ceased around 1858. Sir James built a new pier on the loch and the steamers terminated there.

Sir James had always objected to the steamers sailing up the river, which must certainly have deprived his new hotel of much business. In 1880, after his death, his trustees started building a bridge over the Falloch near the Ardlui Hotel to serve the Colquhoun estate's farms at Ardleish and Doune on the east side of the loch. However, the Marquis of Breadalbane and others, whom Sir James had annoyed by his objections to navigation of the river, quickly initiated legal action to have the work stopped on the grounds that the bridge would obstruct navigation! The objectors emerged victorious and the piers of the ill-fated bridge can be seen to this day, just north of the hotel.

Walkers on the West Highland Way must take the ferry or tramp the long way round by Inverarnan.

ARDLUI

Visitor Services
B CC Ch F G PO PT R SA SC

Sport and Leisure
Fi PB RC S SB W

Public Transport
Rail
Ardlui Station for West Highland Line Glasgow to Oban, Fort William and Mallaig services.

Bus and Coach:
Ardlui Hotel for Glasgow to Fort William and Skye service.

Ferries
Daily ferry from Marina Pier to Ardleish Jetty on the West Highland Way, April–October and out of season by special arrangement, 01301 704243. Ferry on request from camping site by railway station to Ardleish Jetty, April–October. Motor, rowing and sail boats also available for hire. Cuillins Yacht Charters, 01301 704244.

Accommodation
Hotels
Ardlui, A82 01301 704243
Inverarnan Inn, 3km N on A82 01301 704234

Caravan and Camping Park
Ardlui Caravan Park, A82 01301 704243

Camping Sites
Beinglas Farm, off A82, 3.5km N at Inverarnan 01301 704281
Cuillins Boat Hire, Ardlui 01301 704244

ARDLUI–CRIANLARICH

On a fine day, when the sun throws the bracken and heather-clad hills into sharp relief against the blue sky, it is a pleasant run up Glen Falloch, 'the hidden glen'. In the lower reaches of the glen, farms occupy the valley floor, deep forests clothe the hillsides and the River Falloch flows smoothly and ever wider. This lower part of the glen is actually a deeply incised glacial trench with tributary 'hanging valleys' and, on wet days, when mist hangs about the mountainsides, spectacular waterfalls plunge from the heights.

INVERARNAN
The old Garabal Toll House (L) (now Falls View Cottage) heralds the approach to the tiny hamlet of Inverarnan. In the nineteenth century, when the main roads operated under the turnpike, or toll, system, with toll houses and gates placed at strategic locations, the good folk of Glen Falloch found it cheaper to have their goods shipped up to Inverarnan by way of Loch Lomond and the River Falloch, rather than pay the road tolls. The horse-drawn passenger coaches, which connected with the steamers at Inverarnan for Fort William and Killin, likewise avoided the toll. Long, dry spells were not entirely welcome in these parts, for the river became too low for navigation, the toll-keeper had his day, and goods and passengers alike had to pay the tolls.

The quaint old Inverarnan Inn (R), which began as a cattle-drover's inn as far back as 1705, expanded as the tourist traffic flourished in the nineteenth century and, in the 1880s, became a popular venue for climbers. In recent years it has become a welcome stopping point for walkers on the West Highland Way. Opposite is the Stagger Inn restaurant/cafe.

Before the railways came to the Highlands, droves of black cattle passed through here en route from the Western Highlands and islands to the trysts, or markets, at Crieff or Falkirk.

Sometimes they were herded as far afield as the south of England. They reached Inverarnan by Glen Croe and the Arrochar gap or dropped down from the Lairig Arnan, west of Glen Falloch. In the early eighteenth century, when the Crieff market still flourished, droves made their way towards the head of Glen Falloch and then east by Glen Dochart. After 1770, when the Falkirk tryst replaced Crieff, they climbed to the watershed by the Ben Glas Burn, behind Inverarnan, and then dropped down into Glen Gyle. Yet another route was by a track down the western shore of Loch Lomond to Balloch, where the Leven was forded, before continuing by Dumbarton Muir and Killearn to Falkirk. Droves sometimes carried on down the Vale of Leven to the annual Dumbarton Fair, an important cattle fair held on Carman Muir above Renton.

The Inverarnan Inn, Glen Falloch, began as a cattle-drover's inn
(© Robert D. Campbell)

Sleepy Inverarnan first became a tourist rendezvous in 1844, when the Loch Lomond steamers started sailing up the Falloch to a point near the inn. Then, in 1847, a canal was built from the river to a pier and basin behind the inn, where the steamers connected with onward coaches. Several old claymores (heavy, two-handed swords) were found during the construction of the canal, which suggested that some fierce encounter between rival clans had taken place about here. This indeed seems likely, for in those days Inverarnan was something of a 'clan crossroads', with the MacFarlanes to the south, the Campbells of Glenorchy to the north, and the MacGregors just beyond the hills to the east.

Campbell country, part of the great Earldom of Breadalbane, once lay to the north of Inverarnan. The expansionist Campbells of Glenorchy purchased the Glenfalloch estate in 1599 and it was then held by a cadet branch of the family, the Campbells of Glenfalloch, until 1867 when, upon the demise of the main line of succession, John Campbell of Glenfalloch became the 6th Earl of Breadalbane. It was under his son, Gavin, 3rd Marquis of Breadalbane, that the Breadalbane estates reached their greatest extent, stretching all the way from Aberfeldy to the Western Isles. Following the death of the 3rd Marquis in 1922, the vast estates had to be sold off to meet heavy death duties and Glenfalloch passed into other hands.

Some 300m beyond Inverarnan Inn, there is pedestrian access to the West Highland Way by a bridge over the River Falloch (R) which serves Beinglas Farm. The Way is marked (R) at the end of the bridge (Walk 6).

At Glenfalloch Farm (R) the glen suddenly bends in a north-easterly direction, the road begins to ascend and the aspect changes. The forested slopes give way to a barer, but still splendid, landscape of mountain and open moorland. Nearby, the River Falloch cascades through a deep chasm, over the picturesque Falls of Falloch (R) (P).

The false impression that the glen is a cul-de-sac when it has more to unfold may well account for its name, which means 'the hidden glen'. In explanation of this sudden 'dog-leg', geologists have suggested that in pre-glacial times, when Loch Lomond did not exist, drainage was dominated by rivers draining eastwards to the Forth and Tay, so that the Falloch probably drained into Glen Dochart and eventually the Tay.

A great boulder, known as the Clach nam Breatann – 'the stone of the Britons' – can be seen from the West Highland Way (although not from the road) high on the hillside (L) above the Falls of Falloch. This strange monolith is said to have marked the northern boundary of the ancient British kingdom of Strathclyde, which extended all the way south from here to Lancashire. Its name was bestowed, not by the Brythonic-speaking Britons of Strathclyde, but by their Scottish Gaelic-speaking neighbours to the west, the Scots of Dalriada, just as they had also named Dumbarton Rock, capital of the kingdom of Strathclyde, Dun Breatann – 'the fortress of the Britons'. In the nineteenth century, when the Victorians had a penchant for imagining that every geographical feature looked like something else, this great boulder was known as 'the Mortar Stone', from a supposed resemblance to a cannon in firing position.

As the road climbs to the watershed near Crianlarich, a few stunted pines with gnarled and twisted trunks lie scattered along the rocky hillsides on the eastern bank of the Falloch. They are the last sad remnants of the ancient Caledonian Forest that once clothed the Highlands in the post-glacial period. Fire seems to have been the principal means of their demise, although many a storm has no doubt further thinned their ranks over the centuries.

A trio of 'Munros' can be glimpsed beyond the Falloch: Beinn Chabhair (931m); An Caisteal (995m) and Cruach Ardrain (1,045m). The last-named is notable for the fact that on each of its three faces water-courses rise which eventually serve three great rivers: the Clyde, the Tay and the Forth. Only in the last two kilometres before Crianlarich, where the road drops down from the watershed near Keilator Farm, does the drainage pattern switch its final destination from the Clyde in the west to the Tay in the east.

CRIANLARICH

Although scarcely a village, Crianlarich (pop. c300) boasts a reasonable range of accommodation and services – as befits an important road and rail junction – including a Post Office/shop, Youth Hostel, hotels, guest houses and a tea room at the railway station. The A82 goes left here, to run down Strath Fillan and on to Fort William and Oban (by A85 from Tyndrum). The A85 goes right down Glen Dochart, for Killin (A827 from Lix Toll), Lochearnhead, Crieff, and Callander by the A84 from Lochearnhead.

The village lies towards the western end of the fair district known as Breadalbane which embraces the upper River Tay catchment, extending from about Kenmore at the eastern end of Loch Tay through Glen Lochay, Glen Dochart and Strath Fillan to the water-shed beyond Tyndrum. The name is derived from 'Braghaid Alban', the uplands leading westwards to Druim Alban, the great dividing range of the country once known as Alba, the ancient name of Scotland. The Irish monk, St Fillan, brought Christianity to the district early in the eighth century and his name is preserved to the present day in Strath Fillan and the ruined St Fillan's Chapel at Kirkton Farm between Crianlarich and Tyndrum. St Fillan's mother, St Kentigerna, retired to the island of Inchcailloch, 'the island of the old woman, or nun', on Loch Lomond, where she died in 734AD.

Crianlarich, 'the little pass' (leading to Glen Falloch), or possibly 'the little farm', was the scene of one of the legendary incidents involving Rob Roy during the Jacobite Rising of 1715. In December that year, Graham of Killearn, the Duke of Montrose's lieutenant, backed by a large force of naval seamen and local militia from Dumbarton, tried to capture Rob, who was known to be sleeping in the Crianlarich change-house. Graham's men bolted the door from without and Rob's capture seemed assured, until the Highlanders were awakened and burst open the door by sheer force of numbers. Firing flintlocks in all directions and brandishing broadswords to awful effect, they charged out and presented such a fearsome spectacle that the potential usurpers turned tail and fled!

Crianlarich owes its development to the railways and not the roads, for the old Military Roads built in the mid-eighteenth century and the turnpike roads of the nineteenth century did little to stimulate development. The first railway to reach Crianlarich, in 1873, was the Callander and Oban, which was extended through to Oban in 1880. It came by way of Glen Dochart and carried on by the south side of Strath Fillan. The rival West Highland Railway arrived in 1894 by way of Glen Falloch, crossed the Oban line on a viaduct, and continued on to Fort William along the opposite side of Strath Fillan, so that tiny Crianlarich was served by *two* well-appointed railway stations for the next 70 years.

With the C. & O. controlled by the Caledonian Railway and the West Highland by their bitter rival the North British, such was the lack of co-operation between the two that, despite a connection having been completed between the two lines in 1894, it was not until 1897 that it was brought into use, and then only for goods traffic. It was only upon nationalisation of the railways in 1948 that the spur line was occasionally used by passenger trains. The C. & O. Line was closed between Dunblane and Crianlarich in 1965 and Oban trains diverted to run from Glasgow via the West Highland Line.

With several Munros in the vicinity, Crianlarich is an excellent centre for climbers and walkers. In addition to the peaks east of Glen Falloch already mentioned, Ben More (1,174m) and Stobinian (1,165m) to the east, and Beinn Dubhchraig (977m), Ben Oss (1,028m) and Ben Lui (1,130m) to the west, all lie within a day's walk. There are also splendid walks to north and south by the West Highland Way, in Glen Falloch and Strath Fillan. On day walks, the return can be made by train or bus if desired.

CRIANLARICH

Visitor Services
B Bk CC (10km E) Ch G MR P PO PS PT R SA SC T YH

Sport and Leisure
Fi PB RC S W

Public Transport
Rail
Crianlarich Station for West Highland Line Glasgow to Oban, Fort William and Mallaig services.

Bus and Coach
Crianlarich Hotel (junction A82/A85) for Glasgow–Loch Lomondside–Fort William and Skye service and Edinburgh–Callander–Fort William service. A82 layby for Tyndrum, Killin, Lochearnhead, Callander and Stirling. Post Office in Station Road for Royal Mail Post Buses to Tyndrum, Killin, Lochearnhead and Callander.

Accommodation
Hotels
Allt-Chaorain Country House, off A82 01838 300283
Ben More Lodge, A85 01838 300210
Crianlarich, junction A82/A85 01838 300272
Luib, 11km E of Crianlarich on A85 01567 820664
Suie Lodge, 11km E of Crianlarich on A85 01567 820417

Caravan and Camping Park
Glendochart Caravan Park, 10km E of Crianlarich on A85 01567 820637

Youth Hostel
Crianlarich Youth Hostel, Station Road 01838 300260

ROUTE 2A. THE BLACK HILL ROAD AND GLEN FRUIN

Arden (A82) to Helensburgh or Faslane (A814), via Glen Fruin, by the B831/B832

The Black Hill Road by Public Transport

Bus
The infrequent Clydebank or Helensburgh to Lochgoilhead and Carrick Castle via Luss and Arrochar service runs via the B832.

The Black Hill road (which has another branch starting from Duchlage further north on the A82) has an interesting history, for it was built in the 1760s for the 4th Duke of Argyll, in order to facilitate His Grace's travel by carriage between his castles at Inveraray and Rosneath. Thus did it come to be known locally as 'the Duke's Road'. On the final leg of his journey, the Duke boarded his private barge at Cairndhu Point, Rhu, and was rowed over the Gare Loch to Rosneath Castle. The 5th Duke later contributed towards the cost of a more direct route, by the east side of Loch Long to Garelochhead, and this was completed around 1788.

Around 1832 Sir James Colquhoun of Luss and others had 'the Duke's Road' realigned to terminate at Helensburgh instead of Drumfork (Craigendoran) and a toll was charged for its use. The toll house at the Helensburgh end still stands at the top of Sinclair Street, although passage is now free.

ARDEN–CROSS KEYS (B831/B832 JUNCTION)

Branching from the busy A82 at Arden by the B831, the Fruin Water is soon crossed at Dumfin, which once supported a thread-mill, a charcoal-mill for making gunpowder, a corn-mill and, more recently, a saw-mill. On the right bank of the meandering Fruin, some distance above Dumfin bridge, the crumbling ruin of ancient Bannachra Castle stands high above a bend in the river. Bannachra was once held by the Galbraiths, who had another stronghold nearby, on the small islet of Inchgalbraith on Loch Lomond. The castle later came into the possession of the Colquhouns of Luss and it was during their occupancy that a brutal murder was perpetrated within its walls.

It appears that Sir Humphrey Colquhoun of Luss had been in the habit of secretly dallying with the wife of John MacFarlane, who was later to become the 15th chief of Clan MacFarlane. MacFarlane, assisted by some MacGregors, duly raided the lands of Luss in July 1592, forcing Sir Humphrey to retreat to Bannachra Castle. The raiders followed him there and laid siege to the castle. When night fell, a servant who had been induced to betray Sir Humphrey was leading him up a winding stair to his room when he threw the glare of his lighted torch upon his master's person as he passed a loophole. A bowman's arrow swiftly found its mark and Sir Humphrey fell stone dead. The assailants continued their depredations by murdering three servants, violating Colquhoun's daughter Jean, inflicting certain indignities on Sir Humphrey's lifeless corpse and rounded off a good night's work by torching the castle. Other accounts relate that it was Sir Humphrey's brother John who betrayed him and that the castle was first set on fire to smoke Sir Humphrey out but, irrespective of the details, the outcome was the gory demise of the unfortunate Sir Humphrey.

Bannachra's name was made famous by Sir Walter Scott's *The Lady of the Lake* (1810), in which Scott uses poetic licence to place the Bannachra incident and the battle of Glen Fruin (mentioned later) some 60 to 70 years earlier, in the reign of King James V. As the boatmen of Clan MacGregor row on Loch Lomond they chant:

'Proudly our pibroch has thrilled in Glen Fruin,
And Bannochar's (*sic*) groans to our slogan replied;
Glen Luss and Rossdhu, they are smoking in ruin,
And the best of Loch Lomond lie dead on her side.'

The old stronghold also features in John Galt's novel *The Speywife*.

At the crossroads known as The Cross Keys, the single-track Glen Fruin road continues straight ahead to join the A814 at Faslane on the Gare Loch, while the B832 goes left for Helensburgh. The old cottage here was once the Cross Keys Inn. In the early years of the nineteenth century, when heavy excise duties and regulations made a drop of 'the hard stuff' hard to come by, a signal to the landlady of the Cross Keys from 'those in the know' would produce a drop of the purest 'sma still' (illicitly distilled) whisky!

CROSS KEYS–GLEN FRUIN–FASLANE

Glen Fruin (possibly 'the glen of sorrow' but more probably 'the sheltered glen') supported about 45 farming families and a number of cottars (small tenant-farmers) until the second half of the eighteenth century, when it was the most populous part of Rhu parish. Yet by 1839, only ten farming families and four cottars remained. The old farms grew subsistence crops, such as oats, peas and later potatoes on open land under the old 'runrig' system, while also raising black cattle, small hardy native (whiteface) sheep and some goats for southern markets. Depopulation came with the introduction of blackface sheep in the 1760s. As Glasgow's population soared during the Industrial Revolution, so did the demand for butcher meat and higher prices were obtained for it. The old farms that had supported three or four families and a cottar now gave way to larger farms with enclosed fields and were tenanted by only one family, often incomers, who were prepared to pay greatly increased rents.

At the head of the glen, as the road begins to climb, a cairn and plaque (R) mark the approximate site of the Battle of Glen Fruin (mentioned in Route 2) where, on 7 February 1603, the MacGregors slaughtered the Colquhouns.

On gaining the 197m-high summit of the road there is a wonderful vista of the Gare Loch and the Ardgoil Hills beyond Loch Long, the serrated tops of which have long been facetiously known as 'Argyll's Bowling Green'. From here, the road winds steeply down to join the A814 at Faslane (Route 3).

CROSS KEYS–HELENSBURGH

Returning to the Cross Keys and continuing towards Helensburgh, a hillock on the left, now sadly marred by quarrying, goes by the name of Dumfin, or Fingal's Hill. Ancient tradition relates that it was the site of one of the hunting seats of the legendary Celtic war-leader Fingal, whose exploits were related by his son Ossian, the famed Caledonian bard, hence Dumfin (properly Dunfin), 'the fort of Fingal'. Beyond the Fruin Water, the slopes of Ben Bowie (314m) mark the line of the great geological fault line known as the Highland Boundary Fault, which divides the Highlands from the Lowlands of central Scotland.

The road reaches its 106m-high summit at the Black Hill, near some reservoirs (R) which supply Helensburgh with water piped from burns in Glen Fruin. From here, the road begins its descent to Helensburgh by way of Sinclair Street, passing (R) the old Millig Toll House, where tolls for use of the road were once collected.

ROUTE 3. THE THREE LOCHS TOUR

Tarbet, Loch Lomond to Helensburgh and Dumbarton, via Loch Long and the Gare Loch, by the A83/A814

Helensburgh, The Gare Loch and Loch Long by Public Transport

Rail

West Highland Line trains from Glasgow (Queen Street High Level Station) to Oban, Fort William and Mallaig run via the Gare Loch and Loch Long, calling at Dalmuir, Dumbarton Central, Helensburgh Upper, Garelochhead and Arrochar and Tarbet. A frequent electric train service operates from Glasgow (Queen Street and Central Low Level Stations) to Helensburgh Central. When travelling from Glasgow Central, change at Partick.

Bus

A regular bus service operates from Helensburgh (Central Railway Station or Colquhoun Square) to Garelochhead and all places on the Rosneath peninsula to Coulport.

Cruises and Ferries

Cruises on the Firth of Clyde and nearby sea lochs operate from Helensburgh and Kilcreggan Piers in the summer months. A ferry for foot passengers also links Helensburgh with Kilcreggan and Gourock.

A magnificent round of the Three Lochs – Lomond, Long and Gare Loch – can easily be accomplished in half a day from Glasgow or Balloch by 'taking the high road' on the greatly improved A82 road along the bonnie banks of Loch Lomond to Tarbet, before striking west on the A83 for Arrochar. The return journey is by way of the A814, along the lovely shores of Loch Long and by the sheltered waters of the Gare Loch to enjoy salt-sea breezes at the attractive resort town of Helensburgh. For the final leg, the wide estuary of the River Clyde is followed past Dumbarton's historic castle and rock, to join the A82 again at Dumbuck for the return to Glasgow.

TARBET–ARROCHAR

Departure from Tarbet is by the A83. Tarbet is Gaelic for 'a portage for ships' and it was here that in 1263 hardy Norwegian Vikings hauled their long-boats on rollers over the isthmus from Loch Long to Loch Lomond, before plundering the fertile countryside around the loch's southern shores and returning to the River Clyde down the River Leven. As all the land between here and Dumbarton is almost surrounded by water on all sides (i.e. by Loch Long, the River and Firth of Clyde, the River Leven and Loch Lomond), the district rejoiced in the curious title of 'The Isle Above Leven' until the late nineteenth century. During the First World War there was in fact a proposal to link Lochs Lomond and Long here by canal as part of a Forth and Clyde Ship Canal which, had it proceeded, would indeed have surrounded the 'isle' with water!

The old Arrochar Free Church at Ballyhennan (R), now a licensed restaurant, coffee house and craft shop, was first erected in 1844 following the 'Disruption' of 1843 in the Church of Scotland. The present building, erected in 1867, is designed in the shape of a cross and has an unusual feature in that the church hall (now the craft shop) is built into the roof space above. The United Free Church rejoined the Church of Scotland in 1929. Neglected from the 1960s, when it was used as a builders' yard, garage and petrol station, the old church was beautifully renovated for its present use in 1989–90.

The historic Ballyhennan Burial Ground behind the old church is said to have originated in 1263, following a fierce battle between the progenitors of the MacFarlane and Viking invaders, when the dead were laid to rest here. Several eighteenth-century headstones bear the MacFarlane clan crest. In 1994, the centenary of the opening of the West Highland Railway, a memorial was erected to commemorate 37 workmen who died during construction of the line. Ballyhennan, 'the town of the old people', had some of the most fertile land in the MacFarlane country and was set aside by the clan for the old and helpless, so that they could be saved from poverty and want.

The approach road to Arrochar and Tarbet Railway Station on the West Highland Line goes off (R) just beyond the old church. This attractive station, built in 1894, is in Swiss chalet style with shingled boards and an island platform, a design which was typical of most stations on the line. A scenic circular walk on the hill Cruach Tairbeirt starts from the underpass at the station entrance (Walk 4).

Approaching the railway bridge over the A83, the modernised cottage (R) was once the Ballyhennan Toll House, back in the nineteenth century when main roads were financed under the turnpike or toll system with toll-houses and gates placed at strategic points. It is recorded that in much earlier times, the Earl of Lennox authorised his kinsman the chief of Clan MacFarlane to levy 'black mail' on all traffic that passed north and south and that MacFarlane always had a hundred armed men between Tarbet and Loch Sloy who were ready to muster for 'black mail' duty. Watchmen lived in a small hamlet called Tighvechtan, 'the house of the watch', which stood half way between Tarbet and Arrochar. They stood guard day and night on the shoulder of Cruach Tairbeirt and when any likely spoil appeared it was signalled from hill to hill to the chief's stronghold at Inveruglas.

From the Outdoor Centre and Mountain Rescue Post (R) the B838 (L) provides a shortcut to the A814 for southbound traffic. However, if stopping at Arrochar, continue along the A83 to the junction with A814 and go left to the car park (T). For Argyll Forest Park, the Forest Enterprise Caravan and Camping Site, the Caravan and Camping Club Site and Ardgartan Youth Hostel, all located at Ardgartan, some 4km beyond Arrochar, continue around the head of the loch. There is a car park beside the Loin Water, on A83.

ARROCHAR

Dramatically situated among the mountains at the head of Loch Long, Arrochar (pop. c600) is an excellent centre for the walker and climber. Wherever you go in the village, the vast bulk of The Cobbler (Ben Arthur) (881m) and his northern neighbour Beinn Narnain (926m) provide a stunning backdrop on the western side of Loch Long. The Cobbler appears to owe his nickname to a former Gaelic name, Ben Gobhlach (forked mountain), rather than to any supposed resemblance to a cobbler leaning over his last. Local tradition nevertheless avers that his wife is busy churning alongside him, hence the 'Soor-milk (or Buttermilk) Burn' that cascades down the mountain face to Loch Long! The peak's true name, Ben Arthur, may well be associated with Arthur, the famous war-leader of the Britons of Strathclyde, who is recorded as having fought certain battles in Glen Douglas, on the eastern side of the loch.

The name Arrochar possibly comes from the term 'arachor', a measure of land, since an early charter by the Earl of Lennox refers to the place as 'the upper arachor of Luss'. This word was in turn a corruption of the Latin 'aratrum', meaning as much land as could be wrought by a plough in a single year.

Arrochar and Cruach Tairbeirt from the old drove road
(© Robert D. Campbell)

The Loch Long Hotel is in Main Street, just north of the main
shopping area which includes a Post Office, general stores,
restaurants, tea rooms and St Peter and Paul R.C. Church.

The Arrochar Hotel stands at the junction of the A83 and
A814, near the remains of Arrochar Pier, which was built in
1850 to replace an earlier jetty. This was the busiest spot in
Arrochar in the days when crowds of happy day-trippers on the
popular Three Lochs Tour arrived and departed on sleek paddle-
steamers with tall, smoking funnels. Alas, the pier finally
succumbed to the all-pervading motor car in 1977.

The Cobbler Hotel, formerly Arrochar House, stands (L) at
some distance back from the road. It is a mainly nineteenth- and
twentieth-century building, built on to the front of the old
Inverioch House, seat of the chiefs of Clan MacFarlane from 1697
until 1785, when all the MacFarlane lands were sold by judicial
sale and acquired by William Ferguson of Raith. It was around
that time that the Duke of Argyll, chief of Clan Campbell, leased
Inverioch House from Ferguson, built the extension in front and
opened an inn for the use of his family and the general public
when travelling to and from Inveraray. The old MacFarlane lands
and the inn were purchased by Sir James Colquhoun of Luss in
1821. A further addition was made to the front of the house and
it then reverted to a private residence occupied by the laird's
relatives, before becoming a hotel again in 1932.

A stone from the original entrance to the house, dated 1697, is
installed above the present one. A free translation of the Gaelic
inscription reads, 'This stone was taken from the main entrance

of the house built by John, Chief of the MacFarlanes and Laird of Arrochar, in the year inscribed upon it.' Arrochar House hosted many famous visitors over the years, including the pioneer novelist Tobias Smollett (1766); General Ulysses Grant, later President of the United States (1874); and King George VI, during the Second World War.

 Church Road (L) leads up to Arrochar Parish Church (Church of Scotland), which was built by the Colquhouns of Luss in 1847. The MacFarlanes worshipped at Luss and their chiefs had their burial place there until 1733, when the first church was built at Arrochar. The ruins of this building, with a stone above the entrance showing the year of its construction, still stand in the churchyard. Built into a wall is the headstone of William Wallace, farmer of Inveruglas, who died in 1814 and after whom Wallace's Isle on Loch Lomond was probably named.

 Looking across the loch from Arrochar, a pier can be seen on the far shore, which was used by the Admiralty from 1911 until the 1960s as a base for testing torpedoes manufactured at Greenock and Alexandria. As soon as the torpedo range was established, Arrochar was invaded by heavily moustached Germans, all desirous of climbing The Cobbler, ostensibly to study the landscape but, it was suspected, more probably the torpedo range. Robert Burns spent a night in a hostelry which is believed to have stood behind this pier at Highlandman's Height, when returning from his tour of the Highlands via Loch Long and Loch Lomond. Burns was distinctly unimpressed by Arrochar, as a letter he sent to Robert Ainslie on 25 June 1787 reveals – 'I am writing this on my tour through a country where savage streams tumble over savage mountains, thinly overspread with savage flocks, which starvingly support its savage inhabitants.'

ARROCHAR

Visitor Services
B Bk CC Ch D G MR P PO PS PT R SA SC T YH

Sport and Leisure
Bw Cy Fi FP PB RC S SB W

Public Transport
Rail
Arrochar and Tarbet Station for West Highland Line Glasgow to Oban, Fort William and Mallaig services.

Bus and Coach
Braeside Stores (A83) for Glasgow to Inveraray, Campbeltown
and Oban services. Car park (A814) for infrequent Clydebank
or Helensburgh to Lochgoilhead and Carrick Castle service.

Accommodation
Hotels
Arrochar, junction A83/A814 01301 702484
Cobbler, A814 01301 702238
Loch Long, A83 01301 702434
The Village Inn, Arrochar 01301 702279

Caravan and Camping Parks
Caravan and Camping Club Site, Ardgartan
Forest Enterprise Caravan and Camping Site, Ardgartan 01301
 702293

Youth Hostel
Ardgartan Youth Hostel, Ardgartan 01301 702362

ARROCHAR–GARELOCHHEAD

The A814 road winds south from Arrochar along the eastern
shore of Loch Long, 'the lake of ships', a 26km-long deepwater
fiord occupying a deep glacier-carved trench. The name is at least
as old as the Viking invasion of 1263, for Icelandic chronicles of
that conquest refer to the loch as the Skipfiord ('Ship fiord').
  Loch Long provides some of the finest sea-angling in Britain,
species found including cod, herring, mackerel, plaice and
whiting. Birdlife which may be observed on or about the loch's
waters include oystercatchers, curlews, scoters, eider ducks and, if
you are really lucky, the white-tailed or sea eagle, one of the largest
birds of prey in Britain, which was reintroduced to the area. The
graceful heron nests beside some of the side streams. Buzzards,
sparrow hawks and golden eagles are among the more spectacular
residents of the surrounding hills. Wildlife includes red and roe
deer, squirrels, foxes and even mink – escapees from mink farms.
  On the loch's western shore, Ardgartan can be seen nestling at
the mouth of Glen Croe and further south the rugged peaks of
the Ardgoil Hills (facetiously known as 'Argyll's Bowling Green'
in reference to the Duke of Argyll!) rise steeply from the loch.
There was a time when this wilderness formed part of the great

City of Glasgow, for the Ardgoil Estate was gifted to Glasgow Corporation by Mr A. Cameron Corbett, MP (later Lord Rowallan) in 1906. This forest wilderness is now administered by the Forestry Commission as part of the 21,300ha Argyll Forest Park, which produces an average of 70,000 tonnes of timber a year, mainly destined for Scottish paper and sawmills.

This road south from Arrochar has an interesting history, for it was built around 1788 for John, 5th Duke of Argyll, to expedite his coach journeys between his castles at Inveraray and Rosneath, thus eliminating the lengthy detour by way of Loch Lomondside. Yet another interesting road threads the hillside high above: a steel road. In the early 1890s an army of engineers and Irish navvies, armed only with picks, shovels and steam excavators, swarmed over these steep hillsides as they drove the West Highland Railway through 160km of the wildest country in Britain. The opening of the line, from Craigendoran to Fort William in 1894 and on to Mallaig in 1901, first brought the Western Highlands and Islands within easy reach of all parts of the country.

At Craggan, a single-track road goes off (L) by way of lonely Glen Douglas to Inverbeg on Loch Lomond (Route 2). The old MacFarlane country is left behind here and the way now lies through Colquhoun country to Finnart. In the 1830s, two fine mansions were built here: Arddaroch, the country retreat of John White, chemical manufacturer at Rutherglen, and Finnart House, one of the residences of the Caird family, well-known Dundee jute manufacturers.

Finnart is now the site of the much less picturesque Finnart Deepwater Oil Terminal of British Petroleum (BP). In May 1951 a 92km-long pipeline was completed between Finnart and Grangemouth Oil Refinery, when tanker jetties capable of accommodating the largest oil tankers and a tank farm for fuel and diesel oils were built here. The whole installation was commissioned in November 1958. Finnart was chosen on account of its deep, sheltered waters and proximity to the oil refinery.

The road now climbs away from Loch Long to cross the moorland saddle which separates it from the Gare Loch. Above Portincaple (access R), the entrance to Loch Goil can be seen on the far shore, before reaching the 100m-high summit at Whistlefield.

In centuries past the main drove-road from Dumbarton to Argyll came by way of the Vale of Leven, Glen Fruin and high along the hillside above Loch Long to Arrochar. In those days Whistlefield was a small public house, much frequented by drovers, many of whom were taking cattle to or from the small fishing settlement of

Portincaple, where there was a ferry to Ardgoil. Whistlefield, with its well-appointed inn and (from 1896) railway station remained a popular refreshment stop for wayfarers well into the twentieth century. The old inn (R) is now a private residence.

A choice of route has to be made at the Whistlefield roundabout. The new by-pass (A814) (L) leads directly to Faslane and on to Helensburgh. For Garelochhead, keep straight ahead on the old road (B833), which descends steeply by the Whistlefield Brae past a viewpoint (T) (P), which offers a fine prospect over Garelochhead and the Gare Loch. At the foot of the brae go left and then right at Garelochhead Church to join up with the A814 again at Faslane roundabout. The round of the Rosneath Peninsula can be made by taking the B833 (R) at the foot of the brae. A third route from Whistlefield roundabout is by a new road (R), built by the Ministry of Defence, which offers splendid high-level views *en route* to Coulport for the circuit of the Rosneath Peninsula (Route 4).

GARELOCHHEAD

Garelochhead (pop. c600) lies in a sheltered nook at the head of the Gare Loch, or 'the short loch'. A mere 9.5km long and up to 22 fathoms (40m) deep, it occupies another glacier-carved trench. The village, which was little more than a cluster of thatched fishermen's cottages until the early part of the nineteenth century, developed with the introduction of regular steamboat services.

In 1812 Henry Bell, a Helensburgh hotel-keeper, placed the paddle-steamer *Comet* on the Clyde – the first successful sea-going steamship in Europe. By the 1820s the Gare Loch enjoyed a regular steamboat service and from the 1830s its beautiful sylvan shores were being 'feued out' to wealthy Glasgow merchants and professional men for the building of grand villas. During the Victorian era the lochside settlements were served by no less than eight piers for commuters to Glasgow, while the opening of the Helensburgh railway in 1858 helped promote further development and made commuting easier. There was even a commuter rail service on the West Highland Railway, operated by a quaint little train known as 'the Arrochar Bus', which shuttled between Craigendoran and Arrochar.

The steamer service finally ceased in 1942 during the Second World War, as the loch was being used extensively for military purposes. In any case, motor cars and buses were proving more convenient by then and Garelochhead Pier had already closed in 1939.

The most prominent building in the village is Garelochhead Church (Church of Scotland), which dates from 1838. This is now the oldest church on Garelochside, since Rhu and Rosneath churches were rebuilt at later periods.

Leaving Garelochhead, a plaque (R) at the south end of the village marks the site of Garelochhead Pier, which was built in 1845 and renewed in 1879. It was here that the 'battle of Garelochhead' was fought. This memorable mêlée occurred on Sunday, 22 August 1853, when the steamer *Emperor*, a 'Sunday-breaker', tried to land its passengers. The local laird, Sir James Colquhoun, a strict Sabbatarian, had his gamekeepers barricade the pier with boxes, barrels and gangways, and when the steamer tried to tie up, the ropes were thrown back into the water. The situation reached boiling point when some excursionists who had managed to land were apprehended by the gamekeepers. They were then bombarded with a volley of coals, bottles, potatoes and turnips, forcing them to retreat. A landing party duly followed and set about the vanquished defenders with walking sticks as they led the triumphant excursionists ashore! Legal action later succeeded where brute force had failed, and the sanctity of the Sabbath was preserved.

GARELOCHHEAD

Visitor Services
B Bk Ch D G PO PS PT R SA SC T

Sport and Leisure
Bw Fi L S SB W

Public Transport
Rail
Garelochhead Station (access by road which goes uphill opposite the church) for West Highland Line Glasgow to Oban, Fort William and Mallaig services.

Bus
Main Street, for Helensburgh to Rosneath and Coulport service (connecting at Kilcreggan with ferry to Gourock).

GARELOCHHEAD–HELENSBURGH

The road (unclassified) climbs away from the loch to by-pass the extensive Clyde Submarine Base of the Royal Navy at Faslane Bay, home to Britain's hunter-killer nuclear submarines armed with Trident nuclear missiles. An ugly razor-wire perimeter fence surrounding the base adds a chilling note and spoils the scenery for the next few kilometres. The massive 'shed' is a shiplift for the maintenance of nuclear submarines which, incredibly, won a Saltire Society Award in 1994.

This former beauty spot was sacrificed to warlike purposes during the Second World War on account of its sheltered, deep water, when it was developed as the secret Military Port No. 1. This vast complex had its own railway system, reached by a branch line from the West Highland line, with 36km of railway sidings. Extensive berthing facilities and a large floating dock for repairing ships were provided. Thousands of troops, tanks and guns poured through the port in 1942 en route to the successful North African landings, and preparations for the subsequent Normandy landings were also undertaken there. Many VIPs passed through the port, including the legendary Prime Minister Winston Churchill, who embarked on a trans-Atlantic voyage on 5 August 1943.

The northern half of the complex was used for shipbreaking by Metal Industries Ltd for some years after the war and many famous ocean liners, battleships and other vessels ended their last voyages there. *The Lucy Ashton*, the much-loved paddle-steamer which served the Gare Loch settlements for many years, came to a bizarre end at Faslane in 1950. Fitted with jet aero-engines for water-resistance experiments, she raced up and down the Clyde at unprecedented speeds for a couple of years before being broken up.

Faslane has a wealth of historical associations, for it was the site of one of the castles belonging to the powerful Earls of Lennox, with a mediaeval chapel near-by. The castle is long gone, but the remains of the Chapel of St Michael are still to be found in Faslane Cemetery, which is on the left just before the roundabout junction with the Garelochhead by-pass (A814). Near the cemetery entrance there are a number of carefully tended graves and a monument to the memory of ratings and shipbuilders' staff who perished in the tragic sinking of the new submarine *K13* in Faslane Bay on 29 January 1917 while on acceptance trials.

About 500m to the north, the new Garelochhead by-pass

crosses the West Highland Railway on a bridge. It was some 150m east of this bridge, on a grassy mound close by the railway at the junction of two streams, that Faslane Castle once stood. This was one of the principal seats of the Earls of Lennox from the fourteenth century, when Walter of Faslane married his cousin Margaret, Countess of Lennox. The chronicler Blind Harry relates how, in the late thirteenth century, William Wallace was welcomed at Faslane Castle by Malcolm, Earl of Lennox, after sacking the town of Dumbarton and burning Rosneath Castle, both held by the English.

At a later period, on a site now included within the naval base, the MacAulays of Ardencaple had a small house which was much enlarged over the years until it became Faslane House. The MacAulays once owned most of the territory south of here, as far as the present town of Helensburgh, but they fell on hard times due to extravagant living and most of their lands eventually passed to the Colquhouns of Luss. Faslane House stood on land 'feued' from the Colquhouns in 1693 and, when Ardencaple Castle became ruinous, Aulay MacAulay, the last of the MacAulay chiefs, took up residence there. But he had to give up Faslane too and died in abject poverty in a kinsman's house at Laggarie (Rhu) in 1767. The property then reverted to the Colquhouns.

The steep, single-track road to Loch Lomond by way of Glen Fruin (Route 2A) goes off (L) just beyond the Faslane roundabout. A dual-track former Ministry of Defence road, on much easier grades, now links the Garelochhead by-pass (A814) with the A82 near Arnburn, south of Luss.

The road soon returns to the loch shore at Shandon (meaning 'old fort'), at the southern end of the Submarine Base, where the Faslane Peace Camp stands opposite the base entrance. A constant vigil has been maintained in protest at the nuclear presence for many years now. Following the reorganisation of local government, the new local authority has been trying to have the protestors removed – so it is possible that they may not be there any longer.

It was about here that the renowned shipbuilder Robert Napier had his palatial mansion house, known as West Shandon, of which only an ornate gatehouse now survives (R). Born at Dumbarton in 1791, Napier began his career as a blacksmith apprenticed to his father and eventually built up one of the largest shipbuilding and marine engineering firms in Britain, through securing lucrative contracts to build ocean liners for the famous Cunard Line and warships for the Royal Navy at his Govan shipyard. A pioneer of marine steam propulsion and iron construction, he came to be known as 'the father of Clyde shipbuilding'. His first marine engine, for the paddle-steamer *Leven* (1824), outlived the three steamers to which it was fitted and can still be seen in front of the Denny Tank Museum in Dumbarton.

West Shandon, the palatial mansion of the shipbuilder Robert Napier, later became a hotel (R. D. Campbell Collection)

Napier built a small summer residence at Shandon in 1833 and later commenced the lengthy construction of West Shandon, which was completed in 1852. The massive house contained a wealth of treasures, including a large museum and picture gallery, whose contents fetched nearly £50,000 at auction after Napier's death in 1876. He lies buried in a grand tomb behind Riverside Church in Dumbarton.

After Napier's death, the house was bought by a company which extended it and ran it as a hydropathic establishment, a popular type of health spa in Victorian times. It was occupied by the Navy during the First World War and by the Army in the Second World War. This magnificent building was finally demolished in 1957.

Shandon, which did not exist as a community as late as 1830, emerged as a fashionable resort for Glasgow businessmen in the Victorian era, with numerous grand villas embowered in leafy grounds, a golf course, pier and railway station. The winds of change began to blow during the Second World War, when a large military camp was built on the hillside, near the station. After the war, German prisoners-of-war were billeted there and conveyed by train to work on the Loch Sloy hydro-electric scheme on Loch Lomondside. Much residential development has taken place since the 1960s in connection with the nearby submarine base.

The most prominent building locally is now Shandon Church (now converted into flats), which stands opposite the site of the old Shandon Pier. Built in 1844 by a Free Church congregation which had broken away from the Parish Church at Rhu during the 'Disruption' in the Church of Scotland of 1843, it was extended and had the spire added in 1884.

This sheltered reach of the Gare Loch, between Faslane Bay and Rhu, provides an excellent deep-water anchorage for ships and has acted as an indicator of the state of the nation all through the twentieth century. During the Great Depression of the 1930s, 33 rust-stained merchant ships – some 250,000 tons of shipping – swung idly at anchor here for nearly a decade. Then, after the last war, everything from mighty battleships and aircraft-carriers to minesweepers and landing craft lay at anchor here, until many made their last voyages to Faslane for breaking-up.

The day of the battleship has now gone and only dark, menacing nuclear submarines and their attendants disturb the loch's smooth waters now. There was also a time when the loch was used for testing ships' compasses, on account of its being free from magnetic interference.

RHU

Rhu (known as Row until 1927) enjoys a favoured location in a pleasant bay which sweeps round to Rhu Point at The Narrows, hence the village's name which – not surprisingly – comes from the Gaelic for 'a point of land'. From the point, Rosneath on the western shore seems little more than a stone's throw away. In past times the tide rushing through this gap was often dangerous, and a horse and coach with driver, waiting on the spit for a doctor to return from visiting a patient in Rosneath, once disappeared without trace. The Narrows have been deepened since then to allow large vessels to enter.

Although it remained but a tiny hamlet until as late as the mid-nineteenth century, when the introduction of steamboat services made it a desirable rural retreat for prosperous Glasgow businessmen, Rhu can boast of a particularly varied and fascinating history.

At the heart of the village is Rhu Parish Church (Church of Scotland), erected in 1851, whose distinctive spire is a prominent landmark all around the southern shores of the Gare Loch. Rhu was actually included in the parish of Rosneath until 1648 when the local laird, Aulay MacAulay of Ardencaple, undertook to erect a separate church and manse. A separate parish was then formed, extending along the eastern shore of the Gare Loch, up the eastern shore of Loch Long as far as Craggan, and including the whole of Glen Fruin. In those days the glen was the most populous part of the parish and for many years the faithful walked over the hill to Rhu on the Sabbath by an old drove-road, known as the Church or Highlandman's Road, which drops down the hillside behind the church (Walk 12). The first church, built around 1649, was replaced by a new one in 1763 and the remains of this building can still be seen in front of the present church.

The Rev. John MacLeod Campbell, the minister from 1825 until 1831, although very popular with his congregation, was dismissed from his charge following the famous 'Row Heresy Case', for preaching sermons which did not conform to the views of the Church of Scotland. However, Campbell had the last laugh on his accusers for he is remembered to the present day, while other ministers have faded into obscurity. In 1925 a memorial window in his memory was placed in the east side of the church and in 1981 a memorial plaque was affixed to the ruins of the old church, in which he had preached.

Poor Campbell had faced an uphill struggle. With 30 public houses scattered through his parish, drunkenness and immorality abounded, illicit whisky-distilling and smuggling was rife in the hills above the Gare Loch and in Glen Fruin, and many parishioners had turned their backs on the church. Despite this depressing situation, Communion time, which sometimes lasted for a week, was a great social gathering. Huge crowds converged on Rhu from all parts of the parish and a number of steamers would lie at anchor in the bay to take parishioners home at the end. A shed would be erected at the village inn to provide additional accommodation and stalls were set up to sell provisions.

In the years before 1833, when the first villa was erected and Robert Napier came to reside nearby at West Shandon, Rhu consisted of only a few thatched cottages, a church and the late eighteenth-century mansion house of Ardenconnel. Napier (who is commemorated by a memorial plaque within the church) considered the old church 'a scandal to religion' and offered £800 to build a new one. Sir James Colquhoun, as land superior, contributed a further £1,200 and the present church, in Victorian Revival Gothic style to a design by William Spence of Helensburgh, was completed in 1851. The building was enlarged in 1891 to accommodate a growing congregation and large numbers of affluent visitors who spent the summer months at Rhu.

The church's congregation was further swelled by contingents of boys in sailor-suits from the Industrial Training Ship *Cumberland*, an old man o' war, which lay off Rhu from 1869 until 1889, when she was spectacularly destroyed by fire. Indeed, many said it was the work of some of the boys. Her successor, HMS *Empress*, continued the work of training young offenders for the Royal Navy and mercantile marine from 1890 until 1923. The graves of some of the crew are to be found in the churchyard. A row of cottages in Cumberland Terrace, behind the church, was built by the Training Ship Association as officer accommodation and included a small hospital.

The Training Ship *Empress* was moored at Rhu on the Gare Loch from 1890–1923 (R. D. Campbell Collection)

A handsome monument stands in the churchyard, to the right of the church, near the last resting place of the steamboat pioneer Henry Bell (1767–1830) and his wife Margaret. Bell was tenant of the Baths Hotel in Helensburgh when he had the paddle-steamer *Comet*, the first successful sea-going steamer in Europe, built at Port Glasgow in 1812. When he died in 1830 all the shops in the district closed for the day and ships on the Clyde flew their colours at half-mast. Remarkably, Bell's grave remained unmarked and the monument was only erected some 20 years later by Robert Napier as a tribute to his memory. Nearby is the grave of the *Comet*'s skipper, Captain Robert Bain. Other famous people buried here include David MacBrayne, the renowned West Highland steamboat operator; William Teacher, of Teacher's Whisky fame; and Sir James Guthrie R.S.A. (1869–1930), the famous artist, who lived at Rhumore and had a studio there.

Stirling Castle was a favourite seat of the Stewart monarchs
(© Robert D. Campbell)

The ruined Old Kirk at Aberfoyle dates from 1774
(© Robert D. Campbell)

The historic Jean MacAlpine's Inn at Milton, Aberfoyle, has
been beautifully restored in recent times
(© Robert D. Campbell)

Lochan Balloch from Beinn Dearg in the Menteith Hills, with
Loch Venachar, Stuc a' Chroin and Ben Vorlich beyond
(© Robert D. Campbell)

The view of Ben Lomond from Loch Ard was admired by
Queen Victoria in 1869 (© Argyll, The Isles, Loch Lomond,
Stirling and Trossachs Tourist Board)

The busy tourist town of Callander, from The Meadows
beyond the River Teith (© Robert D. Campbell)

Loch Achray and Ben Venue lie at the heart of The Trossachs
(© Argyll, The Isles, Loch Lomond, Stirling and
Trossachs Tourist Board)

The steamer *Sir Walter Scott* sails on Loch Katrine in summer
(© Argyll, The Isles, Loch Lomond, Stirling and
Trossachs Tourist Board)

Ben Ledi from Loch Lubnaig
(© Stirling Council Countryside Rangers)

Loch Lubnaig and Strathyre from Ardnandave Hill
(© Stirling Council Countryside Rangers)

Balquhidder lies at the eastern end of Loch Voil. Rob Roy was buried in the kirkyard (© Stirling Council Countryside Rangers)

Cruach Ardrain from Inverlochlarig, where Rob Roy had his home and died in 1734 (© Stirling Council Countryside Rangers)

The Falls of Dochart at Killin, with the burial isle of the MacNabs in mid-stream and the Tarmachan Range beyond (© Robert D. Campbell)

The picturesque village of Killin lies near the western end of Loch Tay (© Robert D. Campbell)

Loch Tay and Ben Lawers from Sron a' Chlachain, Killin
(© Robert D. Campbell)

Ben Lawers, from the western end of Loch Tay
(© Robert D. Campbell)

Another famous, or rather infamous, person associated with Rhu was Miss Madeleine Smith, whose father James Smith, a wealthy Glasgow architect, owned a mansion there. In 1857 Madeleine was accused of poisoning her secret lover, Pierre L'Angelier, a penniless but opportunistic clerk, by passing him mugs of cocoa laced with arsenic from a window at the family home in Blythswood Square, Glasgow. The case, which created a sensation at the time, was found to be 'not proven' and Madeleine retired to her father's mansion at Rhu, then known as Rowaleyn but now as Invergare. (The house is at the end of Glenarn Road, off Pier Road, and is now converted to flats.) She married twice and later emigrated to America, where she died in 1928 at the ripe old age of 92. This fascinating murder mystery has been the subject of several books and a feature film.

Opposite the church, facing Rhu Bay, the Rosslea Hall Hotel is a former mansion built for Mr A.H. Dennistoun in 1849. Nearby is Ardenvohr, another large mansion, built in 1857 for Daniel Walkinshaw. The house was purchased by the Royal Northern Yacht Club (now the Royal Northern and Clyde Yacht Club) in 1937 for use as their clubhouse (01436 820332).

The grand old mansion house of Ardenconnel, built in the late eighteenth century by Andrew Buchanan, a Glasgow merchant, stands on the hillside above the church. The house was acquired by the Colquhouns of Luss in 1827 and remained in their possession for many years. By the 1930s it was a guest house for the Co-operative Holiday Association and was used as a headquarters for the Royal Air Force during the Second World War. It is now a private residence again. A tree-lined avenue (now Pier Road) once led all the way up to the house from Rhu pier (now gone), the opening of which in 1835 presaged a great influx of new residents and visitors.

Higher up the hill is romantic Aldonalt Glen (shown as Aldownick Glen on Ordnance Survey maps), made famous by Sir Walter Scott as 'The Whistler's Glen' in *The Heart of Midlothian*. This pretty glen was a hive of industry until the early part of the nineteenth century, for a slate quarry there worked the same band of slate that outcrops at Camstradden and Sallochy on Loch Lomond. A character who lived there, known as 'Duncan of the bourach', actually brought up his family in a sort of natural cavern, or 'bourach'.

In the early part of the nineteenth century, the glen became a favourite haunt of whisky-smugglers, who shipped out casks of the golden liquid in small boats at dead of night to Greenock and Dumbarton, where it was distributed to inns and public

houses. It is said that an inn-keeper on the lochside, on being
asked to settle a debt he owed, dug up a cask of smuggled whisky
from his garden and offered it as payment in kind.

  Before leaving Rhu, gardeners may wish to visit Glenarn
Gardens in Glenarn Road (off Pier Road), a woodland garden
featuring daffodils, primulas and bluebells in season, with
notable collections of rhodedendrons, magnolias and many
other trees and plants. The gardens are open daily from mid-
March to mid-June. A donation is requested.

RHU

Visitor Services
B Ch P PO PT SA T

Sport and Leisure
Fi HB L PB RC Ri S SB W

Public Transport
Bus
Main Road (A814), for Helensburgh to Rosneath and Coulport
service.

Accommodation
Hotels
Ardencaple, A814 01436 820200
Rhu Inn, 49 Gareloch Road 01436 821087/821048
Rosslea Hall, Ferry Road 01436 439955

Continuing towards Helensburgh, yachts can be seen riding at
anchor off Rhu Marina (01436 820238/820652). Yachting has
been popular in the district since Victorian times and many
splendid ocean-yachts, including large steam yachts, were to be
seen moored offshore here until the 1950s. The Royal Air Force
built an experimental station for seaplanes about here during the
Second World War, with numerous large hangars and landing
slips on the shore. Roads around the loch were closed to all but
essential civilian traffic for the duration of the war.

  The Ardencaple Hotel (L), a former coaching-inn, was built for
the Duke of Argyll in the late eighteenth century and was one of
the stages where horses were changed on the coach run from
Glasgow to Inveraray. The Duke, whose principal seat was at

Inveraray Castle, also owned Rosneath Castle on the far shore.

The mouth of the Gare Loch is reached at Cairndhu Point, now the site of Kidston Park (L), where the wide estuary of the Firth of Clyde opens up ahead.

A few cottages occupied by fisherfolk and cottars, and an inn, once stood on Cairndhu Point. From here a ferry – a six-oared barge with the Campbell crest (a boar's head) emblazoned on the bow – crossed to the opposite shore, near Rosneath Castle. In those days the headland was known locally as 'Neddy's Point', from a ferryman named Neddy who was a real character. Neddy was also the Duke's fisherman and his wife, a little English woman, helped him launch his boat every day and was on the beach waiting for his return, always with the same greeting, 'Welcome home Neddy, fish or no fish.' William Kidston of Ferniegair, a wealthy local resident, purchased Cairndhu from the Duke of Argyll in 1877 and presented it to the town as a public park. It was named Kidston Park in his memory.

The fifteenth-century castle of Rosneath, which stood close by the opposite shore, was destroyed by fire in 1802 and, in 1803, the Duke commenced building the new Rosneath Castle further inland, to a Romanesque or Modern Italian design by Joseph Bonomi. The Argyll family's links with Rosneath ended in 1939 and the castle was demolished in 1961. (See Route 4.)

Another fine residence, Ardencaple Castle, once stood on a commanding eminence behind Cairndhu Point. The site is now marked only by a surviving tower, used by the Royal Navy as a sea-mark for nuclear submarines, and a retaining wall in the midst of a modern naval housing development.

The MacAulays of Ardencaple (Ardencaple signifying 'the height of the mares') can be traced as far back as the thirteenth century, but the oldest part of the castle was thought to date from the time of Walter MacAulay, who succeeded as chief of the clan in 1566. Sir Aulay MacAulay succeeded him in 1583 and it was in his time that the family's fortunes reached their peak, with the ownership of extensive territories on the eastern side of the Gare Loch and in other parts of the Lennox. Decline and fall began under the seventeenth-century lairds Aulay and Archibald, due to gambling and extravagant living, and by the time Aulay the 19th chief succeeded, the family were virtually landless. As has been noted, Auley died in poverty at Rhu in 1767.

Ardencaple Castle was purchased by the 4th Duke of Argyll and in 1830, following a fire, Lord John Campbell (later the 7th Duke) made considerable additions. Sir James Colquhoun of

Luss bought the castle in 1862 and let it to various tenants. In 1923 it came into the possession of Mrs H. MacAulay Stromberg, an American who was connected with the old lairds of Ardencaple, and was subsequently acquired by Mr J.D. Hendry. The castle was occupied by the Admiralty during the Second World War and, having been allowed to become derelict, was demolished by 1959 leaving only the tower.

The grand mansion house of Cairndhu (L, at Cairndhu Avenue) took six years to build and was completed in 1871. Formerly a hotel and now a nursing home, it was designed by William Leiper for Lord Strathclyde, a High Court Judge and Lord Provost of Glasgow.

HELENSBURGH

The approach to Helensburgh (pop. with Rhu, c16,000) along West Clyde Street is a grand one, as the road hugs the seafront with its splendid promenade and wide vistas of the Firth of Clyde. The grassy lawns behind the promenade have provided a popular picnic spot for generations of visitors to this favourite resort. The wide reach of the Firth lying off Greenock and Gourock is known as 'The Tail o' the Bank', from the end (or tail) of a long sandbank which ends there. This was a departure point for many Scottish emigrants to Canada and the US who boarded ocean liners there by tender from Greenock. During the Second World War it became the assembly point for convoys of merchant ships before setting out to brave the German U-boat menace and the full fury of the North Atlantic in winter.

Just beyond the Commodore Hotel (L), a sculpture of John Logie Baird (1888–1945), pioneer of television, stands beside the esplanade (R). Baird, who was born and educated in Helensburgh, achieved universal fame by making the world's first successful television transmission. Yet another pioneer is commemorated on the esplanade by the Henry Bell Monument (R), a tall obelisk of polished pink granite, erected in 1872 by Sir James Colquhoun of Luss, Robert Napier and others, in memory of local resident Henry Bell, who placed the paddle-steamer *Comet* on the Clyde in 1812.

Passing Helensburgh Pier, the Tourist Information Centre (01436 672642, open April to October) is located just beyond the pier and car park (T), on the ground floor of the old Helensburgh Parish Church clock tower. The main part of the church, built in 1846 to a design by Charles Wilson, was demolished in recent times. Helensburgh Swimming Pool (01436 672224) is adjacent to the car park.

Helensburgh is a relatively modern town for, until the latter decades of the eighteenth century, only the few small cottages forming the crofting and fishing hamlet of Malig lay scattered along the shoreline about here, between the Millig and Glenan Burns. Earlier in the century, Sir John Shaw of Greenock had purchased the Malig or Milligs estate from Archibald MacAulay of Ardencaple, as the MacAulay family's fortunes declined. However, it was not until 1757 that Helensburgh's future was determined, when Sir James Colquhoun of Luss purchased the property from Shaw's daughter for £6,500.

Sir James promoted settlement of the land in the *Glasgow Journal* in January 1776, but the 'bonnetmakers, stocking, linen and woollen weavers' he was hoping to attract never came. Despite this setback, a feueing plan was commissioned from Charles Ross, surveyor to the Luss estates, while a second plan prepared by Peter Fleming of Glasgow in 1803, based on the New Town of Edinburgh, established the grid pattern of wide, tree-lined streets.

Helensburgh soon flourished into a fashionable holiday resort for the upper middle classes and as early as 1802 was created a Burgh of Barony. Wealthy Glasgow merchants and professional men built villas and arrived in the summer months with their families to enjoy the sea air and sea-bathing. Steamboat services from 1812 and the opening of the railway in 1858 made daily commuting to Glasgow possible, thus promoting a further increase in population. In summer, crowds of day-trippers also arrived by train and steamer from the metropolis.

The golden years of the 'big house' ended with the First World War and decline set in between the wars as costs increased and domestic help became increasingly hard to find. Many villas were converted for institutional uses such as nursing homes. Modern housing development, boosted by the expansion of the naval bases at Faslane and Coulport from the 1960s, has tended to spread over green-field sites to the east and west of the town. Today Helensburgh remains a popular spot for visitors, with a good selection of shops, restaurants, cafes, bars and hotels.

A remarkable number of famous people have lived in Helensburgh during its short history and mention has already been made of Henry Bell and John Logie Baird. Famous literary residents over the years include J.J. Bell (of *Wee MacGregor* fame); George Blake; Sir David Bone; James Bridie; A.J. Cronin and Neil Munro. The English poets C. Day Lewis and W.H. Auden were assistant masters at Larchfield Academy in the late

1920s and early '30s. Stars of stage and screen who spent their early years in Helensburgh include the actor Jack Buchanan; the Hollywood star Deborah Kerr; and (in his later years) actor and comedian Jimmy Logan. Jackie Stewart, the world champion racing driver, lived in the town for a time. Andrew Bonar Law, Prime Minister in 1922–3, stayed with relatives and received his education in the town as a young man. He is commemorated by a granite monument in Helensburgh Cemetery and a memorial window, unveiled by Stanley Baldwin, in the West Kirk in Colquhoun Square. This attractive red sandstone church, designed by J.W. and J. Hay, was built in 1853 and rebuilt after severe fire damage in 1924.

Many of Helensburgh's treasures are hidden away in the stately tree-lined drives which intersect with Sinclair Street, the start of the B832 Black Hill road to Loch Lomondside (see Route 2A), which runs uphill from opposite the Tourist Information Centre. Several key points of interest may be visited by taking a short excursion up Sinclair Street to the unique Hill House and return.

First, note the old Municipal Buildings at the junction with East Princes Street (R), erected in 1878 to a Scottish Baronial design by John Honeyman, featuring turrets and crow-stepped gables, in the days when Helensburgh administered its own affairs. A 1906 extension, to a design by A.N. Paterson, housed a Police Station and Fire Station. A plaque on the East Princes Street frontage commemorates John Logie Baird. Helensburgh Central Railway Station is also located in East Princes Street.

The ornate Victoria Halls, beside the entrance to Hermitage Park (R), were built by public subscription in 1887, Queen Victoria's Jubilee year. The Queen's likeness is carved above the entrance.

Beautiful Hermitage Park (R), which once formed the grounds of Hermitage House, home of the Cramb family, was purchased by the Town Council in 1911. The house was later demolished in 1963. The remains of the Milligs or Malig Mill, a cornmill, still stand beside the Millig Burn, near the entrance. Another historic feature preserved in the park is the fly-wheel of Henry Bell's *Comet*, together with an anvil once used by Bell.

The Helensburgh War Memorial, a distinctive design by local architect A.N. Paterson (1923), stands at the far (north) end of the park, in what was once the orchard of Hermitage House.

In Victoria Street, just above the park (R), A.J. Cronin, the best-selling novelist and creator of the popular television series *Doctor Finlay's Casebook*, lived at No. 7 Prince Albert Terrace (top flat) as a youth in the early 1900s. His novel *A Song of*

Sixpence (1964) was based upon the years when he lived here. Beyond is Helensburgh Upper Railway Station on the West Highland Line (L).

Some truly grand villas, dating from the late 1890s and early 1900s, are hidden away in the various 'Drives' on the left. A visit to the Hill House (signposted from Sinclair Street by Kennedy Drive and Upper Colquhoun Street) is recommended. This futuristic house, with its superb interior furnishings, was designed in 1902 by the famous Scottish architect Charles Rennie Mackintosh for the Glasgow publisher W.W. Blackie. The house is now owned by the National Trust for Scotland. (01436 673900. Usually open April to December. Parking; tea room; admission charge.)

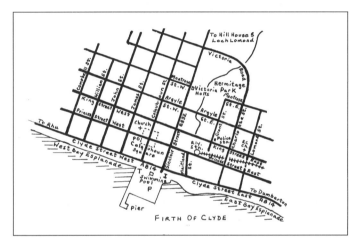

HELENSBURGH

Visitor Services
B Bk Ch Cr D F G I P PO PS PT R SA SC T

Sport and Leisure
A Bw Cf Fi Go HB L PB Pu RC S SP TC W

Public Transport
Rail
Helensburgh Central Station, in East Princes Street, for services to Dumbarton, Clydebank and Glasgow. Change at Dalreoch for Balloch. Helensburgh Upper, in upper Sinclair Street, for West Highland Line Glasgow to Oban, Fort William and Mallaig services.

Bus
East Princes Street, opposite Helensburgh Central Railway Station, or Colquhoun Square, for Garelochhead, Rosneath and Coulport service; the Dumbarton and (on Sundays) Balloch service, and the infrequent Clydebank or Helensburgh to Lochgoilhead and Carrick Castle via Luss and Arrochar service.

Cruises and Ferries
Helensburgh Pier for excursions on the Firth of Clyde in the summer months including the paddle-steamer *Waverley*, the last sea-going paddle-steamer in the world. Ferry to Kilcreggan and Gourock. (Sailing times from Tourist Information Centre.)

Accommodation
Hotels
Commodore, 112-117 West Clyde Street 01436 676924
County Lodge, Old Luss Road 01436 672034

Tourist Information
Clock Tower, car park near pier 01436 672642 (April to October)

HELENSBURGH–DUMBARTON

Leaving Helensburgh by East Clyde Street (A814), Queen's Court (R), just beyond Henry Bell Street, is a modern housing development incorporating the former Queen's Hotel. Originally known as the Baths Hotel, it was tenanted by Henry Bell and managed by his wife Margaret at the time he placed *Comet* on the Clyde in 1812. The little steamer actually plied between Glasgow and Greenock, with the crossing to Helensburgh being made in a sailing boat.

  Station Road (R) leads to the sad remains of Craigendoran Pier. When the Helensburgh railway opened in 1858 it was intended to extend the line to Helensburgh Pier. However, some influential residents objected on the grounds that it would detract from the amenity of the town and a legal battle raged for some years. Finally, in 1882, the railway company grew tired of the wrangling and opened a new pier and station at Craigendoran. Helensburgh residents then complained that they had been by-passed and petitioned to have the terminus at Helensburgh Pier, but it was too late! Craigendoran Pier closed in 1972 and, by a twist of fate, cruise vessels and the ferry to

Gourock now call at Helensburgh Pier in the summer months.

Leaving Craigendoran, Camis Eskan mansion house can be seen on the lower slopes of Ben Bowie (314m). This little Ben marks the gateway to the Highlands, for the great geological fault line known as the Highland Boundary Fault which divides the Highlands from the Lowlands passes through Ben Bowie and continues south by the Firth of Clyde. The Colgrain estate, on which Camis Eskan stands, belonged to the Dennistouns of Colgrain for almost 500 years until 1836, when it was sold to Colin Campbell, a merchant from Lanarkshire, who greatly altered and extended the existing house. Since the last war Camis Eskan had been used as a tuberculosis sanatorium, a geriatric hospital, and in 1979 was subdivided into luxury apartments.

The name Camis Eskan means 'fish bay', from a fish yair which once stood on the shore about here. There were several yairs between here and Dumbarton. They consisted of a dyke of stones arranged in the shape of a crescent or three sides of a square, extending from a point of land to enclose a bay. At spring tides the water receded quickly, leaving great quantities of fish, particularly herring, trapped inside. Small quantities of salmon were taken in spring and summer. Yet another method of salmon fishing was to drive several rows of stakes into the sand, supporting what were known as 'stell' nets, to catch the salmon as they swam along the shore. The fishing rights held by the Dennistouns of Colgrain and their neighbours, the Nobles of Ardardan, had been granted by Crown charter as far back as the thirteenth century. Curiously, these rights extended as far as a man could ride beyond low water – and then as far as he could throw a 12ft spear!

Beyond Colgrain, where an old farmhouse and smithy has been imaginatively refurbished as a restaurant (L), the road climbs past Lyleston mansion house (L). The splendid vista ranges over the Firth of Clyde towards Greenock and Port Glasgow and back towards Helensburgh and the Rosneath Peninsula. The Lyle family held Lyleston from 1466; the Nobles from 1537; and the Donalds, who were engaged in the shipping and tobacco industries in Glasgow, from 1708 down to the late nineteenth century. After reverting to the Nobles again and several more changes of ownership, the house is now divided into flats.

At Lyleston Farm (R) a road drops down to the Ardmore Peninsula, which was once owned by the Noble family. The property was purchased by General Thomas Geils in 1798 and in the early nineteenth century his son built the present mansion of Ardmore there. The property reverted to the Nobles again around 1890. It has been surmised that the Romans had an outlying fort on the Hill of Ardmore, with a landing place nearby. A ferry which once plied between Greenock and Ardmore brought travellers bound for the central Highlands, who tramped over the scenic Stoneymollan road to Balloch ferry (Walk 1). A nature trail, which gives magnificent views of the Firth of Clyde, now encircles the peninsula. Ardardan, a modern house (built in 1977), now stands (R) on the site of the Nobles' ancient seat of that name, just beyond Ardmore.

CARDROSS

Cardross (pop. c2,500), a relatively modern village which owes its origin to the church and its expansion to the railway, is soon reached. The village traces its origins to 1644, when the church serving Cardross Parish was built here to replace an ancient and rather inconvenient one which stood on the west bank of the River Leven at Dumbarton. The opening of the railway in 1858 prompted Glasgow businessmen to build villas, and further expansion, mainly public rental housing, occurred after the last war. The village now has a hotel, inn, general stores and a Post Office.

Entering Cardross, Geilston House (L) was owned by the Donalds of Lyleston in the eighteenth century, when it was rented by Dr John Moore of Glasgow. His son was Sir John Moore, of Battle of Corunna fame, and it is said that two mortars displayed in front of the house were used in the battle. The next owner, John Lennox, sold the house in 1805 to General Thomas Geils of the Madras Artillery, who had also purchased the adjacent Ardardan and Ardmore estates. Geilston passed to the Hendry family in 1910.

Beyond the Muirholm Hotel (L), the large mansion house Cardross Park (L) was built for Thomas Yuille of Darleith around 1810. Towards the end of the nineteenth century David MacBrayne, co-founder of the famous West Highland shipping company which bore his name (now Caledonian–MacBrayne), lived there. MacBrayne was a cousin of Sir John and James Burns, co-founders with Samuel Cunard of the famous Cunard Line. In 1859 James Burns purchased the Kilmahew estate behind Cardross, and it was his son John who built the grand Kilmahew House there (now derelict) between 1865–8. Early this century Cardross Park was home to Sir Archibald Denny, of the famous Dumbarton shipbuilding firm William Denny & Bros. Since 1925, the house has been used as a convalescent home for carters, as a children's hospital and home and, from 1964, a remand home and assessment centre. The mansion, disused at present, is now partly hidden from view behind a housing development.

Station Road (R) leads to Cardross railway station, where a level crossing and footbridge provide access to a grassy picnic area by the shore. Cardross Parish Church in Station Road, designed in an attractive Early English style, was built in 1871–2 as Cardross Free Church. As the famous shipowners James Burns and his son John financed its construction, it is also known as 'the Burns Church'. When the old Cardross Parish Church (erected at the east end of Main Street in 1826–7) was destroyed by a bomb during an air raid in 1941, 'the Burns Church' became the Parish Church.

It was in the last of four semi-detached houses opposite the railway station that A.J. Cronin, the famous novelist, lived as a child. Archibald Joseph Cronin was born in 1896 at Rosebank Cottage on the Murray's Road, which leads to the shore just beyond the west end of Cardross. He died at Montreux, Switzerland, in 1981.

Rosebank Cottage at Cardross, birthplace of the best-selling novelist A.J. Cronin (© Robert D. Campbell)

Cardross shore, now a quiet spot, was once the site of the ancient Cardross Whelk (or 'Wulk') Fair, held in late April or May, which attracted great crowds from near and far until after the First World War. Workers in the Vale of Leven textile printworks would tramp with their families over the Carman Hill road on Fair Day to enjoy the music, games and sideshows, and paddle in the waters of the Clyde. In those days the shore was a hive of industry, for coal was brought down in barges from pits around Glasgow and unloaded into horse-drawn carts in the bay. Farmers also gathered seaweed from the shore and had horse-dung shipped over from the streets of Greenock and Port

Glasgow to manure their fields. Two passenger ferries did a brisk trade, linking the southern shores of the Clyde with the east and west ends of the bay. In the early part of the nineteenth century smugglers also did a brisk trade – in conveying whisky that had been illicitly distilled on Loch Lomondside and the Kilpatrick Hills to Greenock and Port Glasgow.

Just beyond Cardross Golf Course (L), off the main road, there is a glimpse of Auchenfroe House, built around 1820 for John McInnes, a West Indies merchant, and later acquired by James Burns of Kilmahew. Hidden away in Peel Street (R) is Ardenvohr, a grand Victorian villa dating from 1885, which was once the home of Sir Maurice Denny, partner in Wm Denny & Bros, the famous Dumbarton shipbuilders. The old Cardross Inn (R), on the main road, had its origin as a farmhouse called Sealandbank.

The Auchenfroe Burn is crossed on a bridge with stone plaques at each end, one depicting a coat of arms and '1688', while the other reads 'Not We But God – Jean Watson'. The story goes that a servant girl, Jean Watson, took a piece of salt beef from the laird of Keppoch's larder for her poor mother. The meat had been specially reserved for the laird and Jean, fearing retribution, fled. It was a wet and windy night and, upon reaching the Auchenfroe Burn, she found it was in spate and could not be crossed until the waters receded next morning. It is said that she vowed to have a bridge built there, if she were ever able to do so. Jean married a shipbroker named Moore in Leith and later they moved to London, where they became wealthy. Towards the end of the seventeenth century she had the bridge, known as 'Moore's Bridge', erected at Auchenfroe and bequeathed a sum of money, known as 'Moore's Mortification', to be used for the relief of the poor of the parish residing between Auchenfroe Burn and Keppoch.

The ruined tower of the old Cardross Parish Church stands sentinel (L) near the eastern end of the village. The church was erected in 1826–7 to a Gothic design by George Dempster, on the site of an earlier church dating from 1644 which had formed the nucleus of Cardross village. Unfortunately, the second church was destroyed by German incendiary bombs on the night of 5–6 May 1941, during an air-raid on Clydeside. There are some interesting stones in the churchyard, marking the last resting places of many prominent figures in the history of the district.

The scenic Carman Road, which goes over Carman Hill to Renton in the Vale of Leven, goes off (L) just beyond the old church. The house known as Bainfield, opposite the road end, was once a ferry house and inn, known as 'Fraser's Inn' when the proprietor was John Fraser, ancestor of Hugh Fraser, Lord Fraser of Allander, founder of the House of Fraser chain of retail stores.

CARDROSS

Visitor Services
B Bk Ch G PO PS PT R SA

Sport and Leisure
Bw Go HB L PB RC Ri S TC W

Public Transport
Rail
Cardross Station, in Station Road, for services to Helensburgh, Dumbarton, Clydebank and Glasgow. Change at Dalreoch for Balloch.

Bus
Main Road, for Helensburgh, Dumbarton (and Balloch on Sundays only) service.

Accommodation
Hotels
Cardross Inn, Main Road 01389 841358
Muirholm, Main Road 01389 841286

Leaving Cardross behind, the road runs along the '25 foot beach' which was formed as the great glaciers of the Ice Age finally melted and the land rose as the weight of the ice was removed. As Stone Age man had appeared by that time, it is sometimes known as the 'Neolithic beach'. The red sandstone cliffs which lie at some distance back from the present shoreline between here and Dumbarton mark the former sea level. The glaciers brought down giant boulders – hard, old rocks known as 'erratics' – from north of the Highland line and these are to be found strewn along the shoreline. Glaciation drastically modified the drainage pattern, causing the river which is now the Clyde to reverse its direction of flow from east to west.

At Ardoch, Ardoch House (R) (c1780) was the home of the distinguished traveller, author and politician Robert Bontine Cunninghame Graham (1852–1936), laird of Ardoch, Gartmore and Gallangad, and a descendant of the Bontines of Ardoch. Graham, who led a most adventurous life, went out to

Argentina aged 17. He spent several years there and in Paraguay, where he became an expert horseman among the native Gauchos. In South America he was known as 'Don Roberto'. On returning to Scotland, Cunninghame Graham lived at Gartmore House until 1900, when he was forced to sell it for financial reasons. He moved to London until 1904 and then repurchased Ardoch House, which had been sold in 1887, remaining there until his death. Cunninghame Graham was the first president of the Scottish Labour Party when it was formed and later, when the Scottish National Party was formed in 1928, he also became that party's first president.

The road now climbs away from the raised beach by the Lea Brae, before entering the outskirts of Dumbarton (population c24,000) at Castlehill. Westbound traffic descending the brae enjoys a splendid vista of the ever-widening estuary of the Clyde, with the towns of Port Glasgow and Greenock on the far shore and the Cowal hills beyond.

Havock Road (R) opposite Dumbarton Joint Hospital leads down to the Clyde shore at Havock, where there are fine walks along the shore; westward to Ardoch, or east to Levengrove Park there is an impressive view of historic Dumbarton Castle perched on its precipitous rock. A cleft in the cliff at Havock (left, near Havock Road) is known as Wallace's Cave, from a legendary connection with Sir William Wallace. The chronicler Blind Harry relates how Wallace, having burnt the houses of the English soldiers at Dumbarton, hid in the cave and then escaped by following a subterranean passage to emerge on Carman Hill: 'In at the flow of Havock, And out at the yetts of Carman.'

Memorial Park (L), owned by the National Trust for Scotland, lies just beyond Castlehill Road. The park was long regarded as being the site of the manor house of Cardross, where King Robert the Bruce spent the last years before his death in 1329, supposedly of leprosy. The adjacent suburbs were therefore named Brucehill and Castlehill. However, subsequent research suggests that the house was actually situated further north, where the farm of Mains of Cardross once stood, near the River Leven. A monument commemorating R.B. Cunninghame Graham was unveiled at Memorial Park in 1937, but it had to be removed to Gartmore in 1981 owing to vandalism. The ancient-looking, single-storey building opposite the park has long been known as 'Bruce's Stables', but it was actually designed by architect Charles Ross in the mid-eighteenth century as part of Easter Hole (later Braehead) Farm.

For the return to Balloch, go left at Dalreoch on the A812

(continuing as B857 from Renton), via the former textile-printing and dyeing towns of Renton and Alexandria to the Balloch roundabout. Look out for the Smollett Monument (R) at Renton (mentioned in Route 1). Dalreoch, 'the king's field', may be named for Bruce's nearby manor house or the hunting estate which surrounded it.

  For Glasgow, cross the River Leven by the Artizan Bridge and continue ahead by Glasgow Road (A814). For Dumbarton town centre and the Denny Ship Experimental Tank Museum, turn into High Street (R) on leaving the bridge. (P at Risk Street (L); at Riverside, behind High Street (R) (T); and in Castle Street near the museum.) Historic Dumbarton Castle can also be visited by leaving the A814 just before reaching the overbridge at Dumbarton East railway station and going down Victoria Street (R) and Castle Road. The A814 joins the A82 just beyond the Dumbuck Hotel (L), at Dumbuck, for the return to Glasgow. (See also Route 1 for places of interest in Dumbarton.)

ROUTE 4. THE ROSNEATH PENINSULA

The Circuit of the Peninsula from Garelochhead or Whistlefield by the B833

The Rosneath Peninsula by Public Transport

Bus
A regular bus service operates between Helensburgh (Central Railway Station or Colquhoun Square) and all points on the peninsula to Coulport.

Cruises and Ferries
A ferry service for foot passengers operates from Helensburgh Pier to Kilcreggan and Gourock. Cruise vessels, including the paddle-steamer *Waverley*, also call at Kilcreggan in the summer months.

Note: A Rural Daycard for Zone A, obtainable on the ferry and also valid on buses around the Gare Loch, Gourock and Greenock, represents particularly good value (leaflet available).

The Rosneath Peninsula should feature prominently in the itineraries of cinema-goers who thrilled to Mel Gibson's adventures in the Hollywood block-buster film *Braveheart* (1995), for this is real 'Braveheart' country. Tradition relates that some of Sir William Wallace's most daring adventures during the Wars of Scottish Independence of the late thirteenth century were directed against English soldiers who then occupied Rosneath Castle. Another ancient tradition, which avers that the peninsula is 'hostile to rats', should, however, be taken with a large pinch of salt! Back in the eighteenth century a West Indies planter had several casks of Rosneath earth sent out to Jamaica, with a view to killing rats that were destroying his sugar-cane. Alas, this enterprising move did not work – and any lingering doubts were finally dispelled during the Second World War, when thousands of rats were caught and killed in the naval base at Rosneath!

The circuit of the peninsula, which is bounded on the east by the Gare Loch, to the south by the Firth of Clyde and to the west by Loch Long, provides a pleasant half-day trip from Glasgow, or it may be included in the round of the Three Lochs. The circuit can either be made from Garelochhead, by leaving the A814 northbound at Faslane roundabout, going down Gare Lochside and returning by the west coast to Whistlefield roundabout on the A814, or vice versa. The former direction is described here.

The name Rosneath is not easily accounted for. Several derivations have been suggested over the years, including 'bare or unwooded promontory', from its former state; 'the Virgin's promontory', from an early church at Rosneath dedicated to the Virgin Mary; 'the cape of the sanctuary', from the existence of St Modan's cell there; and 'the point of Neuet', from another early church at Rosneath, in the district of Neueth, which was dedicated to St Modan. More certain is the fact that, in contrast to the country to the east of the Gare Loch, the peninsula has long been noted for its mild, moist climate. There is often little or no snowfall in the winter months and tropical palms and shrubs can be grown. Much of the land surface is either woodland or moorlands grazed by sheep, and only on the limited amount of lower ground can crops and pasture be grown.

In 1790, when the population of Rosneath parish numbered just 394, the local minister noted that 'There are 98 houses in the parish – there being no towns or villages.' At that time the population had been declining, owing to the modernisation of farming methods, and the 96 herring-fishermen who resided on the peninsula greatly outnumbered the 48 farmers.

The coming of the steamboat in the early decades of the nineteenth century brought about a great change, for Glasgow's business and professional men were thereby enabled to build villas along the Clyde coast as summer or permanent residences for their families. On the peninsula, the first land for villas was laid out at Barremman in 1825 and many more appeared around the coastline by the end of the century, boosting the population to 1,923 by 1901. The development of defence installations, both during and since the last war, has further swelled the population.

GARELOCHHEAD–ROSNEATH

Heading south from Garelochhead along the western shore of the Gare Loch, the settlements of Mambeg, Rahane, Barremman, Clynder and Rosneath all owed their initial development to the construction of villas and, with the exception of Rahane, all had their own piers to facilitate commuting to Glasgow by steamer and rail by the close of the nineteenth century. At Clynder, where the pier was erected in 1866, a farcical situation developed when Robert Thom, the proprietor of Barremman House and estate a few hundred yards to the north, built his own pier in 1878, with a view to encouraging development on his estate. Thus did tiny Clynder end up with two piers, literally within a stone's throw of each other and with steamers calling at both! This remained the position until 1892, when Clynder pier closed in favour of Barremman.

CLYNDER AND ROSNEATH

The villages of Clynder and Rosneath are now contiguous. Rosneath (population with Clynder, Kilcreggan and Cove c3,000) is a place with many historical associations. In the sixth century St Modan, the patron saint of the district, left the monastery at Iona to preach in Argyll, before coming to spend his final years here at Rosneath. Pilgrims once came from near and far to listen to his preaching and take the healing waters of his well. The relics of St Modan are said to lie near the old church to this day.

Built in 1780, St Modan's Church at Rosneath is now in ruins
(© Robert D. Campbell)

The present St Modan's Church dates from 1853. However, the earliest reference to a church at Rosneath occurs as far back as the close of the twelfth century, although a cross-slab burial stone recovered from the churchyard in 1880 and now preserved inside the present church suggests that the site was in use at an even earlier date. The ruined old parish church nearby was built in 1780.

Among the numerous interesting stones in the churchyard, look
for the one that tells the story of a freed slave who accompanied his
master back to Rosneath from the sunny Caribbean.

Rosneath has literary associations, for it features in Sir Walter
Scott's *The Heart of Midlothian* as the parish of 'Knocktarlitie', to
which the Rev. Reuben Butler was presented by the Duke of
Argyll. Therefore it would have been in the old manse, which
stands behind the churchyard, that Butler and his beloved Jeanie
Deans made their home – had they been real persons. A very real
literary figure who did stay at the old manse was the young
Thomas Carlyle, who stayed there for three days in August 1817
as the guest of the Rev. Robert Story, during the latter stages of a
walking tour through The Trossachs and Loch Lomond districts.
Famous 'sons of the manse' associated with Rosneath include
John Anderson (1726–1796), founder of the Andersonian
Institution, Glasgow, the forerunner of today's University of
Strathclyde, and Dugald Stewart (1753–1828), Professor of
Moral Philosophy at the University of Edinburgh, who is
commemorated by a monument on Edinburgh's Calton Hill.

Other points of interest in the village include the picturesque
group of old houses near the church, known as The Clachan, and,
off Ferry Road (L), a surviving wing of the former Ferry Inn, built
in 1896–7 to a design by Edwin Landseer Lutyens (1869–1944),
designer of London's Cenotaph and the Vice-Regal Residence in
New Delhi, India. The contract was awarded by HRH Princess
Louise of Rosneath Castle, a daughter of Queen Victoria. As
proprietor, she often stayed there in her latter days as a widow. A
ferry once plied across the Narrows to Rhu from the old Ferry Inn.
(The house and approach road are private. It is best seen from the
beach, reached by footpath from the end of Ferry Road.)

Herring fishing was the principal occupation along these shores
until the early decades of the nineteenth century, when the advent
of steamers on the loch appears to have caused their numbers to
decline. There was a time when around a hundred herring 'busses'
could be seen in the loch during the season. Salmon were also
caught to a lesser extent, using stake-nets. In the early part of the
nineteenth century, the younger fishermen on the peninsula also
supplemented their income by illicit whisky-distilling and
smuggling, for which they found a ready market in Dumbarton,
Port Glasgow, Greenock and other towns. Their main haunts were
beside the burns that reach the loch near Clynder. Slate-quarrying
was also carried on at quarries behind Clynder and Barremman
during the late eighteenth and nineteenth centuries.

With the rise in popularity of yachting in the late nineteenth and early twentieth centuries, Rosneath and Clynder became noted centres for boat-building. Many famous pleasure and racing yachts were built at McGruer's yard at Clynder (now at Rosneath) and at James Silver's yard at Rosneath. McGruer's yard built the barges for the Royal Yacht *Britannia*, around the time that the old Royal Yacht, *Victoria and Albert*, was being broken up at Faslane, on the opposite shore.

A great change came to Rosneath in 1941, during the Second World War, when a large naval base housing 4,000 personnel was built at the south end of the village. The base was occupied by the Americans until 1945 and then by the British until 1948. Huge sheds and extensive quays and slipways were built along the shoreline. The Gare Loch was closed to civilian navigation, steamers ceased calling, the Rhu ferry ceased to operate and entry by road was strictly controlled.

CLYNDER AND ROSNEATH

Visitor Services
B CC Ch G PO PT SC

Sport and Leisure
L S SB TC W Ws

Public Transport
Bus
Rosneath Road (B833) for Helensburgh to Coulport Service.

Accommodation
Caravan and Camping Park
Rosneath Castle Caravan Park, off B833 01436 831208.

ROSNEATH–KILCREGGAN AND COVE

Leaving Rosneath, sheltered Camsail Bay was formerly a favourite anchorage for yachts. Camsail Wood (R) once formed part of the grounds of Camsail House, long in the possession of the Campbells of Carrick. Many splendid exotic trees graced the property, the most notable of which were Adam and Eve, two enormous 40m-high silver firs whose trunks measured nearly 9m in circumference at ground level. They were world famous and many Americans in particular came to view them. Alas, the cutting-down of the surrounding wood during the last war exposed the giants to the elements and brought about their demise.

The entrance to Rosneath Castle Caravan Park (L), a caravan and camping park, is opposite the wood. The park occupies what were once the beautiful grounds of Rosneath Castle (now demolished), a seat of the Campbells of Argyll.

This is truly 'Braveheart' country, for the earliest Castle of Rosneath, which appears to have been a royal castle before the close of the twelfth century, suffered grievously at the hands of Wallace during the Wars of Scottish Independence. This early castle, like its stone-built successor, was strategically situated on the shoreline at the entrance to the Gare Loch, at what is still known today as Castle Bay and Castle Point.

The chronicler Blind Harry tells how Wallace and his men burned the houses of the invading English at Dumbarton, before making their way to Rosneath, where the castle was also held by the English. Wallace's merry band made easy work of slaying all its occupants and then rounded off a good day's work by burning the castle to the ground. The hero then marched to Faslane Castle, where he was warmly welcomed by the patriotic Malcolm, Earl of Lennox.

On yet another occasion, Wallace made a daring escape from English soldiers at Rosneath, by jumping on horseback from a large rock, which is known to this day as Wallace's Leap. Wallace escaped unhurt and swam across the Gare Loch to land safely at Cairndhu Point, although his trusty steed was killed by the fall.

The second castle, long in the possession of the Campbells of Argyll and enlarged by them around 1630, also met a fiery end around 1800. The Campbells had benefited from the misfortunes of the Lennox family, whose lands had been divided up after Duncan, Earl of Lennox, his son-in-law Murdoch, Duke of Albany and other members of his family had incurred the displeasure of King James I – to the extent that most of them lost their heads on the Heading Hill at Stirling in 1425. Later, in 1489, the Lennox properties in the southern half of the Rosneath Peninsula were awarded to Colin Campbell, 1st Earl of Argyll.

John, 5th Duke of Argyll, commissioned the Anglo–Italian architect Joseph Bonomi to design a new castle, a magnificent porticoed mansion in Romanesque or Modern Italian style, and work commenced in 1803. The Campbells' long association with the district ended in 1939, when the Rosneath Estate was finally broken up, following the death without issue of HRH the Princess Louise. The Princess was also Duchess of Argyll, having married the Marquis of Lorne (later 9th Duke of Argyll) in

1871. The castle was then used as an administrative base by the American Forces during the Second World War, but it deteriorated after the war and was demolished in 1961.

The road now heads inland and reaches its summit behind Gallow Hill before descending to Kilcreggan. At Portkil Bay ('harbour of the chapel'), beyond Gallow Hill, several Bronze Age burials were discovered in 1815.

KILCREGGAN AND COVE

Upon entering Kilcreggan, Argyll Road (second right) leads to the Kilcreggan Hotel. A fine panorama of the Firth of Clyde estuary now unfolds: upriver to Dumbarton Rock; over towards Greenock and Gourock on the southern shore; and south-west and west to Dunoon, the entrance to the Holy Loch and the Cowal hills beyond. 'The Tail o' the Bank', off Gourock, was the assembly point for large Atlantic convoys during the last war and, until fairly recent times, the departure point for many Scots emigrating to Canada, America and other places.

Kilcreggan ('the chapel of the rock') and the contiguous village of Cove were particularly well situated for commuter travel by steamer and rail, either via Greenock or Helensburgh. Kilcreggan was served by steamer from 1850 and Cove from 1852. Builders did brisk business erecting villas and by 1865 the twin villages had achieved the distinction of becoming Dunbartonshire's smallest burgh. An all-year-round ferry service still links Kilcreggan Pier (P) (T) with Gourock and Helensburgh. (See Public Transport information below.)

Beyond the pier, look for a large rock on the shore, garishly painted like a man's head. Continuing past Barons Point, the westward view is over the lower reaches of Loch Long to the Highland hills of Cowal and the Argyll Forest Park. Looking down the Firth, the island of Bute and the peaks of Arran can be seen on a clear day. The famous Glasgow architect Alexander 'Greek' Thomson designed a number of villas in Cove and Kilcreggan and two splendid examples of his work are to be found in South Ailey Road at Barons Point. Craigrownie Castle (1854) is a great Scots baronial pile, while Craig Ailey (1850) is one of Thomson's earliest-known designs.

KILCREGGAN AND COVE

Visitor Services
B Bk Ch Cr F G P PO PS PT SA T

Sport and Leisure
PB S SB W

Accommodation
Hotels
Kilcreggan, Argyll Road 01436 842243
Knockderry, Shore Road, Cove 01436 842283

Public Transport
Bus
Main road (B833) for Helensburgh to Coulport service.

Cruises and Ferries
Kilcreggan Pier for cruises on the Firth of Clyde in the summer
months and ferry to Helensburgh and Gourock. (Clyde Marine
Motoring Co. Ltd, Greenock, 01475 721281.)

KILCREGGAN AND COVE–COULPORT–WHISTLEFIELD

About a kilometre to the north, the grand Knockderry Castle,
another Victorian mansion (1855), was once owned by John S.
Templeton, the well-known Glasgow carpet manufacturer. The
house stands on the site of 'an old Danish or Norwegian fort',
which may date from the era of the Viking invasions. On their
final incursion in 1263 the Norsemen sailed up Loch Long to
Arrochar, from where they hauled their smaller longboats
overland to Loch Lomond, before plundering and laying waste
the fertile countryside around the southern end of the loch.
Knockderry Hotel is to the north of the castle. The name
Knockderry may have inspired Scott's 'Captain of
Knockdunder' in *The Heart of Midlothian*.
 At Peaton a steep, winding road leads back over the hill to
Rahane. However, a new defence road from Coulport, about
1.5km to the north, provides a more scenically spectacular high-
level route, which joins the A814 at Whistlefield roundabout.
From there, Arrochar or Tarbet on Loch Lomondside may be
reached, or return to Dumbarton and Glasgow can be made
direct by the A814. Alternatively, Loch Lomondside can be
reached by the new Glen Fruin road, leaving the A814 just south
of Whistlefield.
 Cove Conservation Park, on the hill road (signposted at Peaton),
features practical demonstrations of major aspects of conservation,

for which visitors are recommended to wear stout footwear or wellingtons. (01436 850123. Open all year, 10a.m.–5p.m. April to October and 10 a.m.–4 p.m. November to March (weekends and holiday periods only). Tea room. Gift shop. Admission charge.)

COULPORT

Coulport, 'the back ferry' (to Ardentinny), was once a rather attractive 'sleepy hollow' at the end of the peninsula road, but it has been largely obliterated in recent years and transformed into a huge defence complex. The extensive Royal Navy Armaments Depot here was built to handle nuclear warheads for Polaris (and now Trident) nuclear submarines based at Faslane.

One of the casualties of defence development was Coulport House, built around 1860 and demolished in 1964. It had once been the residence of John Kibble, a rather eccentric engineer and businessman, whose main claim to fame was the donation in 1872 of the huge greenhouse that stood beside his home to Glasgow's Botanic Gardens. Known as the Kibble Palace, it can still be visited to this day.

Victorian enterprise knew no bounds, and this was well illustrated on 2 July 1886 when huge crowds of excursionists streamed ashore from five paddle-steamers at Coulport pier to listen to an open-air performance of Handel's *Messiah* on the Braes of Coulport. A subsequent excursion in 1900 brought more crowds to hear Glasgow's Orpheus Choir. It is all a long way from today's sinister nuclear 'hunter-killer' submarines, with their deadly cargoes. Alas, such is progress, and today's motorised excursionist hurries on to Whistlefield by the new defence road, with its scenic views over Loch Long and the Gare Loch.

The secluded village of Ardentinny which lies directly opposite Coulport on the far shore, was forever immortalised by Tannahill the Paisley weaver-poet's song 'The Lass o' Arranteenie':

'The langsome way, the darksome day,
The mountain mist sae rainy,
Are naught to me when gaun to thee,
Sweet lass o' Arranteenie.'

Ardentinny must have had a reputation for bonnie lassies, for much later Sir Harry Lauder, Scotland's 'King of the Music Hall', also had a song about tramping:

'Ower the hills to Ardenteenie,
Just to see ma bonnie Jeannie.'!

ROUTE 5. THE BUCHANAN COUNTRY

Balloch to Drymen, Balmaha and Rowardennan by the
A811/B858/B837, with Approach Routes to Drymen from
Glasgow (A81/A809) and Stirling (A811)

The Buchanan Country by Public Transport

Bus
A bus service operates from Alexandria (car park, opposite
railway station) and Balloch (Balloch Road near railway station,
or bus stance) to Drymen and Balmaha (car park), or via Balfron
to Stirling Bus Station. From Glasgow Buchanan Bus Station, a
service operates to Drymen via Milngavie (railway station) and
the Stockiemuir Road. From Stirling Bus Station, services run via
Balfron to Drymen and Balloch and also via Kippen, Balfron,
Killearn and Strathblane to Glasgow Buchanan Bus Station.

Cruises and Ferries
Cruises on Loch Lomond leave from Balmaha (boat-yard) and
ferries link Rowardennan pier with Inverbeg, Tarbet and Inversnaid.

Clan Buchanan's scenically magnificent territory once reached
all the way along the eastern shore of Loch Lomond, from the
Endrick Water to the southern slopes of Ben Lomond, straddled
the Highland boundary and stretched eastwards to the edge of
the Menteith district. Branches of the clan, which continued to
flourish long after the principal line had been eclipsed, also held
lands to the south of the Highland line, among them the Ardoch
and Ross and Drumakill branches, whose territory lay between
Gartocharn and Balloch, and Auchmar, on the Highland edge
between Drymen and Balmaha.

Sadly, the principal line of this proud clan failed upon the death
of the 22nd chief in 1682 and most of their lands passed to the
3rd Marquis of Montrose, chief of Clan Graham, whose son was
later created the 1st Duke of Montrose. This magnificent
wilderness of mountain, moor and loch remained in the hands of
the Grahams for the next two and a half centuries, until the 1930s

when the Montrose estates were sold off to meet heavy death duties. Huge tracts of the Buchanan country were acquired by the Forestry Commission and now form part of the 50,000-acre Queen Elizabeth Forest Park, created in 1953 to mark the Queen's coronation. The park affords visitors a huge natural playground for walking, cycling, fishing and other outdoor pursuits.

While the route described here starts from Balloch, the village of Drymen, the heart of the Buchanan Country, also lies within easy reach of Glasgow and Stirling. Therefore some account of the approach routes from these places is given by way of introduction.

Beyond Drymen, the route lies west to Balmaha, from where a scenic single-track road climbs to the Pass of Balmaha, the gateway to the Highlands and the lovely wooded eastern shore of Loch Lomond. This road more or less parallels the West Highland Way, which provides some delightful woodland walks with quiet beaches and bays never far away. Journey's end is Rowardennan, the starting point for the ascent of Ben Lomond, whose lofty summit affords unexcelled views over central Scotland and the Highland hills on a clear day.

Keen walkers may approach the district by the West Highland Way, a 152km-long-distance footpath which runs from Milngavie, on the northern outskirts of Glasgow, to Fort William. The route traverses Strath Blane and passes just to the east of Drymen, before climbing to the highest point on the Way at Conic Hill (358m) above Balmaha. Loch Lomond's lovely eastern shore is followed between Balmaha and the head of the loch, passing through Rowardennan and Inversnaid, before continuing through Glen Falloch to Crianlarich. As several guide books to the Way are available, the route will not be described in detail here.

Glasgow to Drymen by the Stockie Muir (A81/A809)

Leaving Glasgow by Garscube Road (A81), the suburb of Maryhill is entered beyond Queen's Cross, where Maryhill Road is joined. Queen's Cross Church (R) was completed in 1897–9 to an Art Nouveau Gothic design by the famous Glasgow architect Charles Rennie Mackintosh.

Maryhill, on the banks of the pretty River Kelvin, originated as a cotton textile-manufacturing and finishing village in the late eighteenth century. The opening of the Forth and Clyde Canal in 1790 promoted new industries, including iron-founding, saw-milling and shipbuilding, as well as serving coal and ironstone pits in the vicinity. The canal, which is now closed but due to reopen in time for the Millennium, crosses Maryhill Road by an aqueduct.

At the Kessington Toll junction take Drymen Road (L) (A809). This goes by way of Bearsden, a rural dormitory suburb developed from the 1870s, following the opening of the railway, for Glasgow's business and professional classes seeking to escape from the city smoke. The railway station was named after a solitary house nearby called Bearsden. The line of the Roman Antonine Wall, built around 142AD, is crossed at Roman Road (first right beyond Bearsden Station), which follows the line of the Military Way. The foundations of a bath-house attached to one of the Roman forts are preserved (L) beside Roman Road.

Beyond Bearsden the A809 continues (R, at junction with A810) as Stockiemuir Road, by-passing the town of Milngavie. The Stockiemuir Road winds along the foothills of the Kilpatrick Hills with pleasant views over Strath Blane to the Campsie Fells. The 193m-high summit is reached at the Queen's View (L), where a magnificent panorama of Loch Lomond and the hills along the Highland edge unfolds.

Descending over the bleak Stockie Muir, a favourite haunt of illicit whisky distillers and smugglers in the early years of the nineteenth century, the village of Croftamie is passed, before joining the A811 Balloch–Stirling road. Crossing the Endrick Water on Drymen Bridge, go left on B858 for Drymen and Balmaha (by B837).

Stirling to Drymen by the Valley of the Forth (A811/B858)

In the 1760s a Military Road was formed by Redcoat soldiers to link Stirling and Dumbarton Castles. It followed the Carse of Stirling and the valley of the River Forth between Stirling and Buchlyvie, which is roughly the route followed by the A811 road at the present day.

Departure from Stirling is by the A811 along Dumbarton Road, where the Tourist Information Centre is located (L) (01786 475019, open all year). Continuing along Albert Place, the Albert Hall (R) was erected in 1873 and the Smith Art Gallery and Museum in 1872 (01786 471917. Open all year; cafe and gift shop).

Stirling Golf Club (L) (01786 464098, clubhouse in Queen's Road) is pleasantly situated in the King's Park. This was the Royal Park until 1506, when the King exchanged it for Gallowhills (now Gowan Hill). King's Park then became the Burgh's common land. Opposite (R) is The King's Knot, once a royal decorative garden, which probably dates from 1628. In the early nineteenth century the use of the garden by farmers for grazing and raising crops brought public protests and so steps were taken to end the ploughing-up of the garden. Stirling Castle (see Route 7) towers above.

The way now lies between the River Forth (R), winding tortuously through the fertile Carse of Stirling, and the flat-topped Touch, Gargunnock and Fintry Hills, formed by the lavas of volcanoes which erupted some 345 million years ago. The ancient village of Gargunnock (population c700), perched on the hillside in the shadow of the Gargunnock Hills, was the site of the Peel of Gargunnock, a fortified tower sacked by Sir William Wallace in the late thirteenth century. About 1.5km west of the village is sixteenth-century Leckie House, where Prince Charles Edward Stewart was entertained in 1745 and where his baggage was later sent, after the Battle of Falkirk, in 1746.

The B822 road (R) crosses the Forth near the site of the Fords of Frew, an important crossing point in former times, where the outlaw Rob Roy MacGregor famously escaped from his captors while being taken on horseback to Stirling Castle by the Duke of Montrose in 1717. Some years later, in 1745, Prince Charles Edward's Highland army crossed the Forth there during their advance south into England, as Stirling Bridge had been breached to bar their progress. A year later they were back, this time retreating into the Highlands and final disaster at Culloden. Away to the north-west they would have been glad to see the hills of home – Ben Ledi, Ben Vorlich and Stuc a' Chroin – towering above the surrounding countryside.

The picturesque village of Kippen (population c1,400), famed for the saying, 'Oot o' the world and intae Kippen', can be seen on rising ground to the south. In 1692 the young Rob Roy skirmished with the men of Kippen during a raid on a valuable herd of cattle being driven from Menteith to Stirling. At a later stage in his career he was to levy 'black mail', for the protection of their property, on farmers in the surrounding countryside. The unfortunate Jean Key, abducted by Rob's son Robin Oig from the farm of Edinbellie, near Balfron in 1750, and forcibly married to him at Rowardennan, lies buried in the kirkyard of the old Parish Church of 1691. (A full-colour Kippen leaflet with walk maps is published.)

At Arnprior, where the dandy Henry Cunningham of Boquhan once routed Rob Roy in a duel (and thus became one of the few men ever to do so), the B8034 goes off (R) to Port of Menteith (7km, see Route 7), for the Lake of Menteith and Inchmahome Priory. The A811 soon traverses the hillside village of Buchlyvie (population c400), which was once a busy railway junction for visitors to The Trossachs, in the days when the old Forth &

Clyde Junction Railway (opened in 1856) linked Stirling with Balloch. Two other branches, opened in 1882, linked Buchlyvie with the gateway to The Trossachs at Aberfoyle and also with an existing line from Killearn to Glasgow.

At the Ballat junction with the A81 (Glasgow–Callander), the A811 goes right for Drymen. (See Route 6 for points of interest.)

Balloch to Drymen, Balmaha and Rowardennan (A811/B858/B837)

BALLOCH–DRYMEN

Leaving Balloch by Drymen Road, the A811 (Stirling Road) is soon joined at Mill of Haldane. A kilometre or so beyond lies the tiny hamlet of Ballagan, a busy place in the nineteenth century when a large saw-mill occupied the site where the bus garage now stands (R). This mill also cut red sandstone flagstones from the quarries at Kilmaronock (now Gartocharn) for paving the streets of Glasgow and Paisley. They were dispatched from a wharf at Townhead of Aber or sawn at Ballagan, then carted to Balloch and sent down the River Leven by boat.

Old Kirk and Shanacles Farms (from the Gaelic 'sean eaglais', 'old church'), on the hillside beyond Ballagan (R), owe their names to the mediaeval Chapel of St Ronan which once stood near Shanacles. The chapel appears to have been built in 1451 by the Friars Preachers of Glasgow on land granted them by Isabella, Countess of Lennox (widow of the beheaded Earl Duncan), who was then living at Lennox Castle on Inchmurrin. Several Bronze Age burials were discovered at Shanacles over the centuries, the most recent being in 1969. When the Military Road linking Dumbarton and Stirling Castles was built around 1765, it went over the hill and past the old chapel, but it was later realigned.

GARTOCHARN
The road soon drops down to the pretty village of Gartocharn (population c400), which nestles under the slopes of beautifully rounded Duncryne, or Duncruin, 'the round hill', better known to locals as 'The Dumpling'. In more superstitious times the hill was believed to be the haunt of the Lennox fairies or witches. An easy path to the summit from Duncryne Road (R) affords magnificent views of Loch Lomond, the Highland peaks and Lowland hills.

Approaching the village, Ardoch Farm, on the hillside (L), stands near the site of the old family home of the Buchanans of Ardoch, who acquired these lands in 1693. In the late eighteenth century Thomas Buchanan owned the biggest hat factory in Glasgow, and it was his son John who purchased much land around the south-eastern corner of Loch Lomondside, where he built Balloch Castle (1808) and Boturich Castle (1834). John Buchanan (1791–1868), 15th President of the US, was a descendant of the Buchanans of Ardoch.

A loop road that goes off (L) provides spectacular views of Loch Lomond and the surrounding countryside as it descends towards the loch. This road also leads to Ross Priory (private).

The Ross estate was held by the Ross and Drumakill branch of the Buchanans from 1624 and the family seat of Ross Priory erected in 1695. The male line of the family failed in the late eighteenth century, allegedly in consequence of a curse invoked by the Marquis of Tullibardine, whom a former laird had betrayed to the authorities while offering him sanctuary at the Ross during the 1745 Jacobite Rising. Hector MacDonald, an advocate, then married Jean Buchanan, adopted the name Buchanan and had Ross Priory rebuilt in 1810. He was a friend of Sir Walter Scott, a fellow advocate in Edinburgh, and it was on holidays spent at the Ross that Scott obtained much information for *The Lady of the Lake* and *Rob Roy*. Much of the latter work was actually written at Ross Priory, in an upstairs room facing Ben Lomond. Alas, the curse appears to have persisted and the male line failed again in 1830. A daughter of the last laird married Sir Alexander Leith in 1830 and thus the Leith-Buchanans became the lairds of Ross until fairly recent times. Major George Christie then occupied the house for some years, until it was acquired by Strathclyde University in 1971 for use as a staff club.

The loop road continues past Townhead of Aber, for the walk to Aber shore and Loch Lomond National Nature Reserve (Walk 7) and also for Lagganbeg Caravan Park, a caravan and camping park located beyond Townhead of Aber. The A811 is joined again beyond Gartocharn.

Gartocharn's peaceful, 'old world' atmosphere is deceptive, for the village is relatively modern. As late as 1839 the minister of Kilmaronock parish observed that there was '. . . no village in the parish: there are not even four dwellings in it closely contiguous'. Yet, just a decade later, the 1851 census recorded a flourishing new settlement at Gartocharn ('field of the cairn'), inhabited by farm and quarry workers.

The district had featured briefly on the stage of Scottish national history long before the village existed. In June 1685 Archibald Campbell, 9th Earl of Argyll, a Presbyterian, resolved to overthrow the Roman Catholic rule of King James II and duly marched on the Scottish Lowlands, while the Duke of Monmouth landed in the south of England to march on London. Fording the Leven at Balloch, Argyll marched his Highlanders towards Stirling but the way was blocked by a force of Government soldiers in the Kilmaronock district. The Earl's men could probably have prevailed if they had attacked, but a council-of-war was held instead and it was decided to march towards Glasgow and gather reinforcements. In the course of a strenuous night march over the Kilpatrick Hills Argyll's supporters gradually melted away. The disguised Earl crossed the Clyde at Old Kilpatrick, only to be captured near Inchinnan and executed at Edinburgh soon after.

Gartocharn has many literary associations. George Eyre-Todd (1862–1937), magazine editor and author of numerous Scottish historical works, came to Gartocharn in 1887 and spent seven happy years in a cottage here, before removing to the mansion Auchenlarich, which he had built at nearby Caldarvan. Many noted literary figures of the day and artists of the famous 'Glasgow School' visited Eyre-Todd at Gartocharn and Auchenlarich. Maurice Lindsay (1918–), author, poet, broadcaster, critic and latterly television executive, came to Gartocharn in 1949 and stayed until 1961. Tom Weir (1914–), the noted climber, hillwalker, journalist and author, well-known to readers of the *Scots Magazine*, arrived in 1959 and is happily still resident.

GARTOCHARN

Visitor Services
B CC Ch G PO PS PT SA T

Sport and Leisure
Cy PB RC Ri S W

Public Transport
Bus
Main Road, for the Alexandria or Balloch to Balmaha or Stirling via Balfron service.

Accommodation
Hotel
The Hungry Monk, Drymen Road (A811) 01389 830448

Caravan and Camping Park
Lagganbeg Caravan Park, off A811 01389 830281

Beyond Gartocharn, a grand view of Loch Lomond, Ben Lomond and the Highland hills opens up to the north. The farmlands here fall away to the marshlands at the mouth of the Endrick Water, which form part of the Loch Lomond National Nature Reserve, a favourite haunt for a wide variety of aquatic birdlife and a paradise for ornithologists.

The beautiful old Kilmaronock Parish Church (L), with its rounded windows, lies some 2.5km beyond Gartocharn village. Built in 1813, it stands on the site of a much earlier church dedicated to St Ronan, hence the name of the parish, meaning 'the church or cell of little Ronan'. 'Maronnan's Cell' receives mention in Scott's *The Lady of the Lake*. There was once a spring near the church known as St Ronan's Well, not to be confused, however, with Scott's *St Ronan's Well* which is at Innerleithen in the Borders. St Ronan, who died in 737AD, was active in the area some two centuries after St Kessog, the pioneer missionary on Loch Lomondside.

An ancient grey sandstone slab with unusual markings preserved at the church, known as 'The Crusader's Stone', may be connected with the Knights Hospitallers of St John of Jerusalem, who maintained several 'hospitals', or refuges for travellers, around the loch in the fourteenth to sixteenth centuries. Buried in the kirkyard are the Findlays of Boturich Castle; the author George Eyre-Todd; Hugh Fraser, Lord Fraser of Allander and his son and successor Sir Hugh Fraser Bt., who once owned Badshalloch Farm opposite the church.

Picturesque Kilmaronock Church, near Gartocharn
(© Robert D. Campbell)

From 1774 until 1929 Kilmaronock had a large breakaway, or 'dissenting', congregation who maintained their own church. This came about after Lord Stonefield, the then patron of the parish church, had tried to impose a minister on the congregation, whom they rejected. The present church in Gartocharn, built in 1854, was the Free or 'dissenting' church until reunion with the Church of Scotland in 1929.

Just beyond the church, the ivy-covered ruins of Kilmaronock, or Mains, Castle (L) are now all but indistinguishable from the encroaching vegetation. The story of this ancient tower goes right back to 1329, when the Earl of Lennox assigned the lands of Kilmaronock to Sir Malcolm Fleming for faithful service as the keeper of Dumbarton Castle. Later, in the mid-fourteenth century, Kilmaronock and the island of Inchcailloch were conveyed to Sir John Dennistoun of Dennistoun, or Danielston, in Renfrewshire, son-in-law of Malcolm Fleming, Earl of Wigton. As his sister Joanna was King Robert II's mother-in-law, the Dennistouns proudly maintained that, 'Kings have come of us, not we of kings'. Sir John would appear to have built the castle, as his arms appear on a shield above one of the windows.

Early in the fifteenth century Kilmaronock passed to Sir William Cunningham of Kilmaurs, who had married the heiress Margaret Dennistoun, and it remained with the Cunninghams (who later became Earls of Glencairn) until 1670. The next owner was William Cochrane, grandson of the 1st Earl of Dundonald, who built the splendid Levenside (later renamed Strathleven) House in the Vale of Leven around the beginning of the eighteenth century. Kilmaronock Castle was described as ruinous by 1724.

During Cochrane's time the Kilmaronock lands suffered greatly from the depredations of Clan MacGregor, who frequently swept down from their mountain fastnesses to lift cattle and plunder these fertile lands. The only way tenants could guard against this was to pay 'black meal', or 'black mail', as protection money to the freebooters. Cochrane was in an unfortunate position, since his lands had been made a barony held from the Crown on payment of 4d annually and, as laird, he was required to make good all losses sustained by tenants at the hands of reivers. In order to rid himself of this liability, Cochrane simply feued the lands out to his tenants at the rents they were paying. The tenants thereby acquired their own properties, but they had to bear losses from cattle-lifting themselves. 'Black mail' continued to be exacted until 1745, when the last, ill-fated Jacobite Rising sealed the fate of the old clan system. The several owners of these lands came to be known as 'the Aber lairds'.

Approaching the junction with the A809 Stockiemuir Road, the twin turrets of ruined Buchanan Castle can be seen peeping above the trees. 'The Watchman', a life-sized Highlander blowing a trumpet and wielding a pike once stood guard on the larger turret. This sad ruin, once a grand and stately mansion visited by royalty and the most notable people of the day, was completed in 1854 for the 4th Duke of Montrose to a Scottish Baronial design by William Burn. The castle replaced the old Buchanan House of 1724, which was destroyed by fire in 1852.

The Grahams, who were created Dukes of Montrose after acquiring their huge fiefdom on the bonnie banks, were comparative latecomers to the district, for their territory had hitherto been in Strathearn; the Montrose district; around Dundee; in the Menteith district; and in Strathblane. There was even a branch on the border with England. They first acquired a foothold here in 1682, when the principal line of the Buchanans ended and their lands and the family seat at Buchanan House passed to the 3rd Marquis of Montrose. When his ambitious son James succeeded as 4th Marquis, he also acquired the Duke of Lennox's remaining territory in the Lennox, in 1702. As a strong supporter of the Union with England, he was created 1st Duke of Montrose in 1707. However, he is probably best known for his long-running feud with Rob Roy, who often exacted his revenge on the Duke by raiding the Buchanan country.

The extensive Montrose estates were gradually sold off to pay heavy death duties after the death of the 5th Duke in 1925 and the family moved to Auchmar Farm nearby. The castle was used as a hotel through the 1930s and as a military hospital in the Second World War, when its best-known patient was Rudolf Hess, Hitler's deputy, who received treatment for injuries received when he parachuted into Scotland in 1941. The interior of the castle was stripped and the roof demolished in 1955. The once-beautiful grounds now form the Buchanan Castle Golf Course, whose clubhouse stands on the site of the old eighteenth-century house.

Catter House (R), an imposing Georgian mansion built in 1767 for James Buchanan of Catter, occupies a commanding situation facing Buchanan Castle and the Highland hills. Later it became the residence of the Duke of Montrose's factor and is now a private residence. Long before that, in feudal times, the Earls of Lennox had a castle at Catter – and a gallows where summary justice was dispensed.

At the junction with the Stockiemuir Road (A809), which comes in from Glasgow, the A811 turns left and crosses the

Endrick Water by Drymen Bridge. This fine, five-arched, red sandstone structure was built in 1765–8, when the Military Road was being formed, to replace a ferry and ford. It was completely rebuilt and widened in 1929.

The Endrick Water, variously interpreted as being 'the rising river', or 'the red river', rises in the Gargunnock Hills and is subject to damaging flash floods, so that the former name would appear to be the more likely one. The river has also been known to freeze over and the 6th Duke of Montrose recalled that, as a young man, during the great freeze of 1895, he skated all the way from Balmaha Bay to Drymen Bridge while roped to three companions. During that bitter winter, Loch Lomond remained frozen as far up as Luss for about eight weeks. Curling matches were held on the ice and a shuttle service of special trains brought people from Glasgow at weekends. On one Saturday alone around 20,000 people were estimated to be on the ice. There was a time when the Roman legions camped by Endrick's banks within sight of Loch Lomond, for the existence of a small advance fort at nearby Drumquhassle, 'the castle ridge', was confirmed by aerial photography as recently as 1977.

The Endrick Water marks the gateway to the Buchanan country, which extends along the eastern shore of Loch Lomond to Ben Lomond and eastwards as far as the River Forth in the Menteith district. The reputed founder of the Buchanans was Anselan, son of O'Kyan, King of Ulster in Ireland, who landed on the west coast of Scotland near the Buchanan country about 1016, hence the name McAuslan, 'son of Anselan', by which the clan was known for over two centuries. The family later assumed the name of their lands, Buchanan, from the Gaelic 'Both-chanain' – 'the canon's seat'. In 1225 a later Anselan, clerk to the Earl of Lennox, obtained a charter of the small island of Clairinch, in Gaelic 'Clar Innis', and the latter name was adopted as the clan's rallying cry. The island and some of the Buchanan lands were confirmed to his successor Gilbert (who appears to have borne the name of Buchanan) by Alexander II in 1231.

The family seat was Buchanan House until 1682, when the principal line of the family became extinct upon the death of John Buchanan, the 22nd chief. All the Buchanan lands, other than those held by branches of the family, were then sold to the 3rd Marquis of Montrose. Chiefship of the clan was resumed between 1826 and 1919, but it has been dormant since then. However, the name Buchanan attaches to the parish and district to this day. There were numerous branches of the Buchanans, including Auchmar, Ardoch, and Ross and Drumakill. Notable members of the clan include George Buchanan, poet, historian and teacher of the young King James VI and I, and James Buchanan (1791–1868), 15th President of the United States, who was descended from the Buchanans of Ardoch.

The Show Field (L), at the north end of Drymen Bridge, is the venue for the annual Drymen Agricultural Show, which has been held since 1816. Held on the last Saturday in May, the show features dairy and beef cattle, Clydesdale horses, sheep, goats, working and show dogs, poultry, ponies and horses, local produce, handcrafts and general entertainment. Beyond there is access to the Strathendrick Golf and Tennis Club (R) and the Buchanan Castle Golf Club (L). Go left at the road junction, on B858 (leading to B837), for Drymen, Balmaha and Rowardennan.

DRYMEN

The pretty village of Drymen (population c800), which takes its name from 'droman', 'the hill ridge', on which it is situated, grew up near the laird's seat at Buchanan House as an agricultural village which hosted regular cattle markets. The name was in turn adopted by the Drummond family, whose ancestor came from Hungary as a retainer of Margaret, the future queen of Malcolm Canmore, and was granted land here in reward for his services. The Drummonds, whose principal seat was at Drummond Castle near Crieff, owned much land throughout The Trossachs. They were created Earls and then Dukes of Perth.

In September 1715, during the Jacobite Rising, 300 armed MacGregors under their chief Gregor Glun Dubh, swept down Loch Lomond in their war galleys intent on raiding the southern shores of the loch. They ventured as far as Bonhill by sailing down the Leven, and looted the Buchanan country around Drymen and as far east as Menteith. Later that year, Drymen appears to have escaped lightly from the Jacobite-supporting Rob Roy's attentions. On 9 December, the Duke of Montrose was informed that Rob had arrived with a hundred men, before 'marching through Buchanan to Crigrostan without attempting anything upon the garrison of Drumakill, and having done little at Drunmon [Drymen] but proclaimed the Pretender and tore the gauger's [exciseman's] books'. Rob raided Luss instead, where a visitation upon the Colquhoun chief's property was every bit as agreeable to him.

The *Statistical Account* of 1792 relates that Drymen's inhabitants were then mostly tradesmen, day labourers and a few cottage-weavers who worked for manufacturers in Glasgow. As the village was situated on the Highland boundary, many inhabitants spoke Gaelic – and there were even some who did not understand a word of English. Drymen had become an important crossroads by then, with the completion of the Military Road from Dumbarton to Stirling in 1768, while other roads led to Glasgow via the Stockie Muir, to Balmaha and Rowardennan, to Aberfoyle and Killearn.

Illicit whisky-distilling and smuggling was rife in the hills around Drymen in the early nineteenth century, resulting from heavy taxes levied on spirits. The Stockie Muir was one of the smugglers' favourite haunts and on one occasion, in August 1818, excisemen reinforced by soldiers of the 40th Regiment destroyed an extensive private distillery which was operating less than a mile from the road. Crowds of people appeared from all directions and threatened them as they went about their work. The hated duties had thankfully been abated by 1841 when, to the intense chagrin of the local minister, Drymen boasted no less than *seven* inns to serve its 400 inhabitants.

Today, the village offers a good selection of attractive hotels, restaurants and pubs, a library, Tourist Information Centre, shops and other services. It is a popular stopping place for motorists, coach parties, cyclists and walkers on the West Highland Way (Walk 8).

Ascending through the village on the B858, note (R) the attractive, white-painted Drymen Parish Church, which was erected in 1771 on the site of a sixteenth-century church. Beyond (R) is the well-appointed Buchanan Arms Hotel, which was once owned by the Buchanans of Drumakill and run as part inn, part farm. It was later (1860–1931) owned by the Montrose Estates and rebuilt in 1935. The loch can just be seen from the little public garden opposite the hotel. The Salmon Leap (formerly The Plough) (R) dates from 1758 and is one of Drymen's long-established inns, although much modernised.

The Balmaha road (B837) goes off (L) just before reaching The Square. However, if you are stopping in Drymen, continue to The Square and go right on B858 to the car park (R) in Stirling Road.

The old United Free Church (formerly the United Secession Church), built in 1819, stands opposite the car park. A stone above the entrance bearing the date 1761 came from this breakaway group's original church, which stood behind Duncryne hill at Gartocharn. As the Free Church reunited with the Church of Scotland in 1935 it is now used as the church hall. However, you can still sit in the old pews – by visiting the public bar at the Clachan Inn. Eric Liddell, the famous athlete and missionary, made even more famous by the film *Chariots of Fire*, must have passed the old church often when, in 1907–8, he attended the old Drymen Primary School, situated further along Stirling Road. His grandfather's home and grocery shop was at No. 6 Stirling Road.

The village green in Drymen Square, an unusual feature in this part of Scotland, was once the venue for regular cattle markets and fairs. The Clachan Inn on the north side, dating from 1734 and once thatched, lays claim to being the oldest pub in Scotland. The Winnock Hotel, on the west side, began in the nineteenth century as the Drymen Inn (also part inn, part farm), when it was owned by the Montrose Estates. Drymen Public Library and Tourist Information Centre (01360 660068, open May–September) is located in the south west corner. (T, Balmaha Road, behind Library.)

DRYMEN

Visitor Services
B Bk Ch D G I P PO PS PT SA T

Sport and Leisure
A Bw Cf Cy Fi FP Go HB L PB RC Ri S TC W

Public Transport
Bus
The Square bus stop for the Glasgow –Drymen–Milngavie–Balfron service and the Balloch–Drymen–Balfron–Stirling service. Stops on Balmaha Road (B837), behind Library, for the Alexandria/ Balloch to Balmaha service.

Accommodation
Hotels
Buchanan Arms, Main Street 01360 660588
The Winnock, The Square 01360 660245

Tourist Information
Drymen Library, The Square 01360 660068. (May to September.)

DRYMEN–BALMAHA

The Balmaha and Rowardennan road (B837) starts just south of The Square. The way now lies through pleasant countryside, with the wooded grounds of the Buchanan Castle estate to the south and the conifer plantations of the Garadhban Forest clothing the Highland fringe to the north. This woodland, acquired by the Forestry Commission in 1931 when the Montrose Estates were being sold off, now forms part of the Queen Elizabeth Forest Park and is traversed by the West Highland Way on the approach to Conic Hill.

Buchanan Smithy is a row of early nineteenth-century houses built by the Montrose Estates to house their workers, with a smithy for the repair of agricultural implements, shoeing horses, etc. The smithy was returned to use in recent years by swordsmith David Smith, thus enabling visitors to watch demonstrations of metal-working over a traditional forge.

The next hamlet, Milton of Buchanan, was the location of the meal-mill for the district. The old mill, complete with waterwheel, is now an attractive residence (R). Milton also had a saw-mill for timber extracted from the Montrose Estates.

Negotiating a sharp left-hand bend (care required), the attractive old Buchanan Parish Church is on the left. Buchanan was originally included in Luss parish, while the district to the north and certain islands in the loch comprised Inchcailloch parish. The parish church for Inchcailloch was on the island of that name off Balmaha, but the church for Buchanan was at Luss, on the far side of the loch. These arrangements naturally proved extremely inconvenient for parishioners, as they had to row across the loch in winter storms.

Matters improved when Buchanan was transferred to Inchcailloch parish in 1621 and in 1643 the parish church was removed from the island to the old Buchanan family Chapel of St Mary, near Buchanan House. The parish then came to be known as Buchanan and the present church was erected in 1764, apparently with stones taken from the old Chapel of St Mary. The interior was destroyed by fire in 1938, but it was soon rebuilt. The graves of the 5th and 6th Dukes of Montrose and the Marquis of Graham are in the churchyard.

Approaching Balmaha, bonnie Loch Lomond comes into view again and there is a grand view towards the southern islands, the low-lying marshes around the Endrick mouth and the pleasant farmlands around Gartocharn. It is between Aber, near the Endrick mouth, and Rossdhu Estate on the opposite shore that the loch reaches its widest point, almost 7km across.

BALMAHA

The small clachan of Balmaha (population c400), overlooked by shapely Conic Hill, sits in a pretty, sheltered bay where a flotilla of pleasure boats ride at anchor. In the winter months Balmaha slumbers peacefully, but in the long summer days it is transformed into a Mecca for hordes of visitors. The access road is busy with cars and coaches, Balmaha Bay is thronged with small boats and hundreds of walkers stop for rest and refreshment as they tramp the West Highland Way.

Balmaha is a small but ancient settlement, whose name is said to come from the Gaelic 'baile Macha' – the village of St Maha. This saint, a disciple of St Patrick who was also known as Mahew or Mochta, founded an important monastery at Louth in Ireland in the sixth century. The name may have been bestowed personally by the saint or by missionary monks. On the moor above the Garadhban Forest there is St Maha's Well, credited with healing powers in former times and visited by pilgrims seeking a cure for various afflictions, while a pre-Reformation chapel at Cardross, on Clydeside (see Walk 1), was also dedicated to the saint.

Entering the village, the Loch Lomond Park Board Visitor Centre (01360 870470) is situated adjacent to the car and bus park (R). The new Oak Tree Inn tea room, restaurant, bar and accommodation and the entrance to MacFarlane's Boatyard for cruises on the loch to Inchcailloch, boat hire, boat maintenance and launching facilities, are directly opposite the car park (01360 870214). Just beyond the car park is the Highland Way Hotel, cafe, general store and filling station (R).

It is a short but pleasant stroll round the bay to Balmaha Pier, noting several points of interest on the way. The grand, red sandstone Montrose House (left, on leaving the car park, and now converted into flats) was built for the Duchess of Montrose in 1891 as the Montrose Holiday Home, to provide holidays for poor children from Glasgow who would otherwise not have the opportunity. The Montrose family were always active in providing facilities for tourists and the general public and in 1930 the then Duke had a large tea room built on the loch shore, almost opposite the car park. However, it was destroyed by fire in 1971.

Balmaha was a hive of industrial activity in the nineteenth century. In those days a small factory for manufacturing pyroligneous acid, used in the textile-dyeing and printing industry for the preparation of Turkey Red fabrics, stood on the site now occupied by the hotel and general store. Owned by Messrs Turnbull and Co., it was connected with a similar one established by the firm at Millburn in the Vale of Leven around 1791. Timber grown on the Montrose Estates, particularly oak, was harvested on a rotational basis, cut into small lengths and placed in retorts, where it was heated, liquefied and distilled to produce the acid. By-products included tar, creosote, pyrolixic spirit and Prussian

Blue. Scows, or barges, were used to bring timber to the factory and take the acid in wooden barrels to Millburn Works. At a later period, synthetic Turkey Red dyes were developed and, with no demand for the acid any more, the works closed around 1920.

Walking round the shore by the boardwalk, Passfoot Cottage, formerly a toll-house and then a tea room, stands at the foot of what is often termed the Pass of Balmaha, which is traversed by the Rowardennan road. However, you must climb higher up Conic Hill to find the actual pass through which Rob Roy and his men were accustomed to drive the cattle they had 'lifted' during forays into the rich Lowland districts.

If the loch is not too high, you may spot the remains of an old jetty opposite the cottage. It was used by the Duke and Duchess of Montrose when boarding their steam yacht *Lady Violet*, which usually lay at anchor in the bay. This graceful little steamer was named after the Duchess, Violet Jane Hermione Graham, the worthy founder of the Montrose holiday home. Several local landowners, such as the Marquis of Breadalbane and Sir James Lumsden of Arden, had private steam yachts on the loch in the nineteenth century.

Continuing towards the pier, the West Highland Way ascends steeply (R) through dense bracken to Craigie Fort. This rocky headland is topped by a cairn which commemorates the opening of the West Highland Way in 1980. The modest effort of the ascent is rewarded with grand views of the loch to north and south, and over to Inchcailloch and other islands.

The road ends at Balmaha Pier, now a mere jetty. The first pier was built by the Duke of Montrose around 1850 and it was always a stirring sight to see a crowded paddle-steamer suddenly slip round Inchcailloch, with coal smoke rolling from its tall funnel and a hoot on its siren, while the sound of a Scottish reel played by the band on board drifted across the water. Then, as the steamer manoeuvred alongside and gangways were raised, the delicious aroma of steam, hot oil and home-cooking in the galley would waft the summer air. A fair crowd would always be on hand in the summer months to watch passengers embark and disembark. Balmaha Pier closed in 1970 and it was a sad day indeed when the 170-year-old Loch Lomond steamer service ceased at the end of 1988.

An interesting rock formation is to be found near the pier, consisting of a peculiar type of old red sandstone called conglomerate, which contains large pebbles and boulders of quartzite belonging to the harder, more resistant Highland rocks. The Highland Boundary Fault passes just to the north of

Conic Hill about here and the underlying old red sandstone has
been sharply upturned against the fault, thus exposing the lower
levels of conglomerates washed down by rivers flowing from the
Highland region about 400 million years ago.

The dark, mysterious island of Inchcailloch, 'the island of the old
woman or nun', densely clad in oaks and a few Scots firs from shore
to summit, lies little more than a stone's throw from the pier. St
Kentigerna, the mother of St Fillan (the saint who brought
Christianity to the Breadalbane district), spent her final years on
the isle and died there in 734AD. Around the early part of the
thirteenth century, a church dedicated to her memory was built at
the north end of the island and for the next 500 years the good
parishioners of Inchcailloch rowed across the loch on Sundays to
attend worship. An ancient burial ground once used by Clan
MacGregor lies near the old church. The island, which was farmed
until 1770, is now administered by Scottish Natural Heritage as
part of the Loch Lomond Nature Reserve. An interesting circular
nature trail can be reached by ferry from Balmaha.

BALMAHA

Visitor Services
B CC Ch Cr F G P PO PT SA T

Sport and Leisure
Fi FP PB RC S SB VC W Wa

Public Transport
Bus
Car and bus park, for the Balloch/Alexandria service. There is no
public transport between Balmaha and Rowardennan at present.

Cruises and Ferries
MacFarlane's Boatyard (entrance opposite car park) for the all-
year-round mailboat service to the islands, cruises and ferry to
Inchcailloch. Rowing and motor boats are available for hire.
(01360 870214)

Accommodation
Hotel
Highland Way 01360 870270
Oak Tree Inn 01360 870357

Caravan and Camping Park
Camping and Caravanning Club Site, Milarrochy Bay, 2km N
of Balmaha 01360 870236

Tourist Information

Loch Lomond Park Centre, car park 01360 870470 (April to October)

BALMAHA–ROWARDENNAN

The Rowardennan road, a picturesque though narrow and winding route which is barred to all vehicles exceeding 3 tons laden weight, can be very busy on fine summer days, particularly at weekends. Yet for much of the year, these beautiful eastern shores provide a peaceful contrast to the constant procession of traffic on the loch's western side. As the public road ends at Rowardennan, it is necessary to return by the same route, although the scenery is such that this involves no great hardship.

The only steep climb is encountered at the start, as the road ascends through the wooded Pass of Balmaha. This is a true gateway to the Highlands, for the geological fault line known as the Highland Boundary Fault, which divides the Highlands from the Lowlands, runs just to the north of Conic Hill and through the islands of Inchcailloch, Torrinch, Creinch and Inchmurrin.

Descending from the pass, the Old Manse may be glimpsed (R). The manse was built in the days when the Parish Church was on the island of Inchcailloch and the oldest part dates from the seventeenth century. A new manse was built nearer the new Parish Church at Milton of Buchanan in the late eighteenth century. The Old Manse was home to John M. Bannerman, Lord Bannerman of Kildonan (1901–1969), who came to Balmaha in 1930 as farm manager and factor to the Duke of Montrose. Bannerman became well known throughout Scotland as a broadcaster, Chairman of the Scottish Liberal Party, President of the Scottish Rugby Union, President of An Comunn Gaidhealach and Chairman of National Forest Parks in Scotland, among other public offices.

At the foot of the brae the green and pleasant island of Inchfad 'the long island', comes into view beyond a field (L) at Manse Bay, much used by campers in the summer months. (A fee is payable.)

Early in the nineteenth century, Inchfad was the rather improbable site for a whisky distillery, the remains of which can be seen to this day. The distillery seems to have ceased production by mid-century, for by that time the island was a haven for female alcoholics or, as the author of *Robertson's Tourist Guide* (1858) delicately described it, '. . . for ladies whose peculiar relish for mountain dew precludes them from the unrestrained freedom of more populous districts'. The island was owned by the Dukes of Montrose until the 1930s and its beautiful green pastures tended by tenant-farmers. In July 1994, Inchfad, which has four cottages, was on the market for £550,000.

The road swings inland past Arrochymore Point, before the loch shore is regained again at Milarrochy Bay, where there is a large car park (L) (T). Milarrochy, the most easily accessible beach on the east side of the loch, is usually very busy and noisy in the summer months, owing to the activities of jet-skiers, power-boaters, and transistor radio-listeners. This pebbly, though potentially attractive beach is best avoided by those in search of peace and tranquility. The Caravan and Camping Club's Milarrochy Bay Site (L) is at the north end of the bay.

The road strikes inland again and passes Cashel Farm (R), before reaching the loch shore again at the Forestry Enterprise Cashel Caravan and Camping Site (L). In August 1992 the farm received a surprise visit from Queen Beatrix and Prince Claus of the Netherlands with the royal entourage, while touring Scotland. This is to be the headquarters for a 3,000-acre Millenium Forest, managed by the Scottish Forestry Society, the aims of which are to recreate natural woodland and promote public access.

The name 'Cashel' is said to come from the Gaelic for a castle, or a religious establishment of the Dark Ages. Hidden among the trees on Strathcashell Point, south-west of the camp site, lie the remains of an ancient stone-built building. An irregular, oval-shaped dry-stone retaining wall, 2m thick, has two entrances, one on the south-west side which has been blocked and another on the east side. A rectangular structure within the enclosure is apparently of a later date. An explanatory sign states that it was probably an Iron Age fort (400BC or later). However, the absence of outer defences has led some to suggest that it may have been a religious establishment in the Dark Ages.

Alexander Graham of Duchray, writing in 1724, relates that this structure was known as 'the Giant's Castle' and that its builder was one Keith MacIn Doill, or Keith the son of Doillus, who lived in the fifth century. Keith is also credited with having built an artificial island off Strathcashell Point, which was then known as Rownafean, 'the Giant's Point'. The island, based on 'large square joysts of oak firmly mortis'd in one another', is no doubt Strathcashell Islet, to the south of Strathcashell Point, which is an Iron Age crannog or lake-dwelling.

Crannogs were constructed by sinking boulders, logs and brushwood in the loch until the structure rose above the surface. Huts were then built on a timber platform placed on top of this foundation and there might even be sufficient room to accommodate some cattle. A number of crannogs are known to have existed around the loch.

Beyond the Cashell Burn, the road runs between the woodland of the Rowardennan Forest and the loch, with an open vista south towards Inchlonaig and the pretty village of Luss on the far shore. The Rowardennan Forest, which extends north from here, was acquired from the Montrose Estates by the Forestry Commission in 1951 and has been greatly extended since then by the planting of conifers. It now forms part of the giant Queen Elizabeth Forest Park, established in 1953 to mark the Queen's Coronation and extends as far east as Strathyre.

Inchlonaig, 'the island of yew trees', was owned by the Colquhouns of Luss for several centuries. It is said that the ancient yew trees which grow there were planted by Robert the Bruce in the fourteenth century to provide bows for his archers. The island was farmed until the beginning of the seventeenth century and was then converted to a deer park for the Colquhoun family with a resident keeper. There is a holiday home on the island.

At Sallochy the loch is again lost to view for some distance, as the road heads inland to avoid the prominent headland of Ross Point, where the loch narrows considerably. Sallochy, now little more than the name of a house and a wood, was a place of some importance in centuries past, in the days when these eastern shores supported a much greater population. The Kirk Session records for Buchanan Parish show that in 1759 there were 58 families and a total of 262 persons living between the Pass of Balmaha and Rowardennan. However, the population was already decreasing by the time the *Statistical Account* was compiled in 1790. Sallochy nevertheless boasted a charity school run by the Society for Propagating Christian Knowledge, which was run alternately at Sallochy for three years and then at Inversnaid for the next three years. Those able to pay had to contribute to the Master's salary, but the poor received free tuition.

In those days Sallochy was a hive of industry. Large quantities of slates were shipped out in sailing boats from its slate quarry, which worked the same band of slate as that found at the Camstraddan quarries on the loch's western shore. The extensive Sallochy and other woods along the eastern shore supplied coppiced oak timber on a 24-year rotational basis, known as 'coppice with standards'. Large timbers known as 'standards', which had been allowed to grow longer, were used for house and shipbuilding, while smaller timbers were used for manufacturing leather-tanning agents from oak bark, preparing charcoal for making gunpowder and making pyroligneous acid for use in textile-dyeing. Charcoal, peeled bark and oak timbers were loaded in sailing scows for transport to Glasgow and other places, while loads of birch wood were also sent to the thread-mills at Paisley for making bobbins. However, by the late nineteenth century, all the timber from the district was being consumed by the 'liquor factory' at Balmaha for making pyroligneous acid.

A car park (L), near the curiously named Camas an Losgain, or 'bay of the frogs', is the starting point for a circular forest or nature trail. The trail enters Sallochy Wood by a path on the opposite side of the road, heads south by a forestry road and returns to the starting point by following the loch shore on the West Highland Way (Walk 9).

The surface of the Dubh Lochan, 'the little black loch' (L), makes a pretty picture in the summer months when it is graced by yellow water-lilies. A road here (L) serves the Universities' Field Centre at Ross, established in 1967 by Glasgow and Stirling Universities for the study of flora and fauna. Beyond the lochan, the sheep farm of Blairvockie (R) and the slopes of Ben Lomond, which tower dramatically above the Forestry Commission's plantations, were purchased by the National Trust for Scotland in 1984. The road soon heads back towards the loch and there is access to the West Highland Way again on reaching the little inlet called Lochan Maoil Dhuinne, which means, literally, 'the little loch of the bald man'.

ROWARDENNAN

Rowardennan is a picturesque spot, with its sandy beach, beautiful oak woods and the massive Ptarmigan shoulder and head of lofty Ben Lomond towering above. Entering the tiny settlement (which can scarcely be called a village), some luxury lodges are passed (L) just before reaching Rowardennan Hotel (L). The public road ends at the car park (T), near the pier.

The start of the main path to the summit of Ben Lomond (974m) (Walk 10) is signposted behind the car park. On 11 November 1997 Donald Dewar, the Secretary of State for

Scotland, officially opened the Ben Lomond National Memorial Park, as a memorial to those who died in the two World Wars. He also unveiled the granite sculpture by Scottish artist Doug Cocker, which stands near the pier. The Park is managed by the Forestry Commission, the National Trust for Scotland and the Scottish Office.

The road behind the car park, part of the West Highland Way, leads to Rowardennan Youth Hostel, a former shooting lodge once owned by the Duke of Montrose and let out to wealthy tenants. The hostel is also an Activity Centre, offering tuition in windsurfing, canoeing, archery and orienteering by professional instructors.

It was at Rowardennan, 'the point of the height of St Adamnan', that the saint is supposed to have halted the plague by striking the soil with his crozier. Adamnan, who lived in the late seventh century and died c704AD, was Abbot of Iona and the biographer of St Columba.

As far back as the eighteenth century the Dukes of Montrose maintained a 'King's ferry' here, which had to operate on demand between Rowardennan and Lower Inveruglas (now Inverbeg). In 1790 the *Statistical Account* noted that the ferry had recently been made more convenient for travellers by the construction of a quay, 'for the safety of the boats, and for the covenience of horses getting out of and into the boats, as also a convenient public house'. At that time the road from Drymen had just been completed and so, with an improved ferry and a handy pub at the foot of Ben Lomond, there was little more that the intrepid traveller could desire.

In 1798 two English travellers, Dr Thomas Garnett and a Mr Watts, arrived at the inn from Inverbeg and enjoyed their stay so much that they were sorry to leave. When they enquired about supper, the inn-keeper's family went out on the loch to catch some trout, as their host was allowed by the Duke of Montrose to trawl for fish within 8km of the hotel. Next day they climbed Ben Lomond with the landlord's son, described as 'a civil and intelligent young man who serves as guide to those who visit the mountain. He took biscuits and a bottle of whisky.'

In later years visitors were taken up the Ben mounted on ponies and an 1847 guidebook advised, 'At this Inn, Highland shelties or ponies may be procured which may be used by the most timorous of gentlemen and the most nervous of ladies with the greatest of safety, till within a little of the top, they are such sure-footed animals.' Ponies and guides were still being hired out as late as the First World War. As they are no longer available, it

Tourists once ascended Ben Lomond mounted on hired horses or ponies
(R. D. Campbell Collection)

would seem that hill-walkers have become a more adventurous breed since then. An ancient tradition involved climbing the Ben to watch the sunrise on the longest day in mid-June and in 1932 it was estimated that between two and three hundred people had spent the night on the summit.

It was the opening of the Balloch railway and Rowardennan Pier in 1850 that brought the first hordes of day-trippers from the metropolis to conquer the Ben's lofty summit. As many as 800 'mountaineers' would arrive by steamer during the Glasgow Fair holidays. Angus MacLellan, an employee at the inn in the late nineteenth century, recalled that the day before their arrival the Irish proprietor made up a concoction in a hogshead, poured it into labelled bottles and sold it as whisky at prices ranging from 3/6d (17.5p) to 4/6d (22.5p) a bottle. People said it was good, too. Unfortunately, an Irishman working in the nearby woods nearly poisoned himself while drinking the stuff!

The shallow nature of the loch about here is betrayed by the small islet called Eilean Deargannan (possibly 'the purple island') lying just off the pier and by a sandbank in mid-loch, for the Douglas Water on the far shore brings down much silt into the loch. An ancient tradition maintains that in centuries past this was in fact the loch's southern shore, until the loch overflowed and flooded the inhabited country to the south.

North of Rowardennan, the precipitous eastern shore of the loch remains roadless and unspoiled all the way to the head of the loch, save for a forestry road (for walkers only) which continues for a few kilometres (Walk 11), the path followed by the West Highland Way and a road serving Inversnaid which drops down from the hills to touch the loch shore there.

ROWARDENNAN

Visitor Services
CC F P PT SA SC T YH

Sport and Leisure
Fi FP PB RC W Wa

Public Transport
Bus
There is no public transport service at present between Rowardennan and Balmaha. There are coach services to and from Glasgow, Helensburgh, Lochgoilhead, Campbeltown, Oban, Fort William and Uig (Skye) at Inverbeg, which is reached by ferry.

Ferries
Rowardennan Pier, for ferry to Inverbeg, April to September, weekends only until mid-May. Loch Lomond Ferry Service, Rowardennan Hotel, 01360 870273. Another ferry now operates to Inverbeg, Tarbet and Inversnaid, daily from Easter to end September. Cruise Loch Lomond, Tarbet, 01301 702356.

Accommodation
Hotel
Rowardennan 01360 870273

Caravan and Camping Park
Forest Enterprise Caravan and Camping Site, Cashel, 4.5km S of Rowardennan 01360 870234

Self-Catering
Rowardennan Lodge Rentals 0141 762 4828

Youth Hostel
Rowardennan Youth Hostel 01360 870259

ROUTE 6. THE MACGREGOR COUNTRY

Drymen to Aberfoyle, Stronachlachar (Loch Katrine) and Inversnaid (Loch Lomond) by the B858/A811/A81/A821/B829, with Approach Routes to Aberfoyle from Glasgow (A81/A821) and Stirling (A84/A873/A81/A821)

The MacGregor Country by Public Transport

Bus and Coach
Bus services operate from Glasgow Buchanan Bus Station to Aberfoyle, Port of Menteith and Stirling, via Strathblane and Balfron, and also to Balfron (change for Aberfoyle) via the Stockiemuir Road and Drymen. Another service operates from Balloch Railway Station (stop in Balloch Rd) to Stirling, via Drymen and Balfron. A Royal Mail Post Bus service runs between Aberfoyle Post Office, Stronachlachar Post Office and Inversnaid Hotel.

  The Trossachs Trundler coach operates a circular service in the summer months between Callander–Trossachs Pier–Aberfoyle–Port of Menteith–Callander.

Cruises
A steamer service operates on Loch Katrine between Trossachs Pier and Stronachlachar in the summer months.

The heart of the MacGregor or Rob Roy Country, a magnificent wilderness of bens, glens and lochs forever associated with the adventures of the famous outlaw Rob Roy MacGregor, lies around the head of Loch Katrine and over towards Inversnaid on Loch Lomondside. The MacGregors were dispossessed of their homelands in Glen Orchy, Glen Strae and Glen Lyon by Campbell guile in obtaining legal title to their lands and the clan gradually became scattered and landless. However, the Clan Dougal Ciar branch (named for an ancestor called 'mouse-coloured Dougal'!) fared better than most and by 1533 had laid claim to their territory on Loch Katrine and Loch Lomondside 'by right of the sword'.

  Life was hard in these remote Highland fastnesses and so the

MacGregors had perforce to resort to cattle-lifting, plundering and 'black mail' in order to survive, thus earning them much notoriety.

Thanks to the romantic works penned by Sir Walter Scott, the most famous member of Clan Dougal Ciar was destined to be the outlaw Rob Roy MacGregor. In 1694 Rob Roy ('Red Robert'), then a fairly respectable cattle-dealer, was granted the lands of Inversnaid by the chief. In 1706 he also acquired Craigrostan and in 1711 Ardess, both on the western flank of Ben Lomond. Rob's famous feud with the Duke of Montrose commenced in 1712, when one of his drovers absconded with a large sum of money Rob had raised from the Duke and others to buy cattle. In retribution, the Duke had Rob's family evicted from Craigrostan while he was absent and his house was destroyed. Sad to say, but the hugely successful block-buster movie *Rob Roy*, starring Liam Neeson and Jessica Lange (1995), was not shot on location here on Rob's home territory, but in Glen Nevis near Fort William, on the rugged west coast of Scotland, and at Drummond and Megginch Castles in Perthshire!

As the picturesque road that winds along the eastern shore of Loch Lomond from Drymen and Balmaha peters out at Rowardennan, in the very shadow of Ben Lomond, the scenic detour via Aberfoyle which will be described here is required to gain the heart of the MacGregor Country from Drymen. Some description of the approach routes to Aberfoyle from Glasgow (via Strath Blane) and Stirling (via the Lake of Menteith) is also given by way of introduction. The return trip may be combined with the round of The Trossachs (Route 7), thus making a pleasant day's excursion from Loch Lomondside, Glasgow or Stirling.

Glasgow to Aberfoyle by Strath Blane (A81/A821)

Departure from Glasgow is by the same route as for Drymen via the Stockie Muir, i.e. by Garscube Road (A81) and Maryhill to the Kessington Toll junction (Route 5). From Kessington Toll the A81 (R) is followed, which goes by way of Bearsden (population with Milngavie c41,000). The line of the Roman Antonine Wall, built around 142AD, is crossed at Roman Road, Bearsden (L), just before reaching Hillfoot Railway Station. Milngavie, which developed as a dormitory suburb along with Bearsden, had already become established as a milling and textile-manufacturing and finishing village from the late eighteenth century. The town is now the starting point for the West Highland Way long-distance walking track to Fort William, which begins opposite the railway station.

Leaving Milngavie by Strathblane Road (A81), a sharp right-hand bend avoids the Milngavie Waterworks, where the West of Scotland Water Authority's two large reservoirs, Mugdock dating from 1859, and Craigmaddie, completed in 1896, receive the pure waters of Loch Katrine by means of twin aqueducts. Together they hold 5.7 million cubic metres of water, which is equal to twelve days' supply to the city of Glasgow and surrounding districts. There are some pleasant walks in the grounds and also in Mugdock Country Park which lies beyond the north end of Mugdock Reservoir. Vehicular access to the park from Milngavie town centre is by way of Ellangowan Road (opposite the railway station) leading on to Mugdock Road.

Breasting the summit of the road, Ben Lomond's massive bulk suddenly appears before the descent is made to the contiguous villages of Strathblane and Blanefield (population c2,300), pleasantly situated in Strath Blane on the banks of the Blane Water. The flat-topped Campsie Fells, which provide a scenic backdrop to the villages, and the Kilpatrick Hills to the west are the result of lava flows from volcanoes which erupted some 345 million years ago.

Duntreath Castle (L), long the seat of the Edmonstones of Duntreath, dates from the fourteenth century with later additions. Approaching the tiny hamlet of Dumgoyne, the white-painted Glengoyne Malt Whisky Distillery (R) dates from 1833. (Open to visitors. 01360 550254.) Dumgoyne (427m), the prominent hill behind the distillery, is a basalt plug formed by one of the volcanic vents from which the Campsie lava flows emerged. George Buchanan, historian and tutor to Mary, Queen of Scots, and King James VI, was born at the farm of Moss (L), some 600m beyond Dumgoyne. The Buchanan Monument, a tall obelisk, was erected to his memory in the hillside village of Killearn (R on A875, population c2,200) some two centuries later, in 1788.

A minor road (L) leads to the village of Gartness in 600m. Gartness Castle, which once stood on the banks of the Endrick Water and is now no longer extant, belonged to the Napiers of Merchiston, near Edinburgh. John Napier of Merchiston, the famous mathematician and inventor of logarithms, was a frequent visitor to the castle in the late sixteenth century when, it is said, he had the nearby mill-wheel stopped to assist in his calculations. In autumn the bridge here provides a vantage point for watching salmon leaping up the rapids as they return to spawning grounds in the river's headwaters. The famous Pots of Gartness salmon leap is reached by a footpath (L) near the bridge. (The path is on private property and access is courtesy of the landowner. Restrictions may apply.)

One of the aqueducts conveying Loch Katrine water to Milngavie is crossed just before reaching the Ballat crossroads. The route from here to Aberfoyle is described in the Drymen–Aberfoyle section.

Stirling to Aberfoyle by the Lake of Menteith (A84/A873/A81/A821)

The A84 is followed from Stirling (see Route 7) to the junction a kilometre beyond the entrance to Blair Drummond Safari Park (R). Take the A873 (L) here for Aberfoyle. Traversing the rolling farmlands of the Carse of Stirling, there are distant views of the Gargunnock and Fintry Hills and the Campsie Fells to the south, while Ben Lomond's conical peak is prominent to the west and Ben Ledi's southern shoulder to the north. Entering the quiet agricultural village of Thornhill, the Mains Farm Caravan and Camping Site (01786 850605) is just off the A873 (L) on B822.

The way now lies along the northern edge of Flanders Moss, which was reclaimed from its former state as a vast peat bog over many years by the 'moss lairds', passing (R) the Farm Life Centre at Dunaverig Farm, Ruskie. (01786 850277. Open daily 10 a.m.–6 p.m. April–October and limited opening until Christmas. Tea room and gift shop. Admission charge.) The A81 is joined before reaching Port of Menteith (see Route 7) and the highway is soon skirting the pretty northern shore of the Lake of Menteith. At the Ballat junction go right on A821 for Aberfoyle.

DRYMEN–ABERFOYLE

Leaving Drymen by the B858, the main Stirling road (A811) is soon joined at the old Drymen School. The Stirling road follows the line of an old Military Road, built in the late 1760s to link Dumbarton and Stirling Castles. Note the farm names Templelea and Spittal Ballat (L), just before Ballat crossroads, which recall the existence in mediaeval times of a hospital, or refuge, for poor travellers, provided by the Knights Templar of the Order of St John of Jerusalem. In those days 'spittals' were to be found in many parts of Scotland. Spittal Ballat was the birthplace of the four Bilsland brothers, who founded the large bakery firm of Bilsland Brothers in Glasgow. One of the brothers, William, became Lord Provost of Glasgow.

The Aberfoyle road (A81) continues straight ahead at the crossroads to enter the fair district of Menteith, which was the province of the Earls of Menteith in feudal times. It is a name forever associated with treachery in the Scottish mind, through Sir John Menteith, son of one of the Earls, having betrayed William Wallace to the English in 1305. Menteiths, Comyns, Stewarts and Grahams all held the Earldom at various times, until the last Earl died in poverty in 1694.

The highway now hugs the edge of Flanders Moss, a vast flat expanse of reclaimed peat bog. Formed by the decayed remains of the ancient Caledonian Forest and said to owe its name to landowners of Flemish extraction who settled in the district around the fourteenth century, the moss has been gradually reclaimed for farming and forestry since the eighteenth century. The Peel of Gartfarran, an earthwork (R) about a kilometre beyond the junction with the B835, is a well-preserved homestead moat, which probably dates from around the thirteenth to fifteenth centuries. Trossachs Holiday Park, a caravan and camping site, is signposted (R) immediately beyond the bridge over the Kelty Water. A loop road here (L) leads to Gartmore.

GARTMORE

Gartmore (pop. c300), a pretty village on the old Drymen to Aberfoyle road, stands near the edge of the great Loch Ard Forest, which can be accessed at Cobleland, 1.5km to the north. Gartmore House, conspicuous on an eminence to the west of the A81, dates from the early eighteenth century with additions made in 1779–80. The house was long the seat of the Grahams of Gartmore, descendents of the Earls of Menteith. Robert Bontine Cunninghame Graham (1852–1936), author, traveller and politician, was the last of the family to reside there. A memorial to Cunninghame Graham stands on the village green. (See also Ardoch, near Cardross, in Route 3.)

In 1900 Gartmore House was purchased by Sir Charles Cayzer, the shipping magnate, who had extensive alterations made in 1902. It was later used as an approved school and then as a training centre for an American religious organisation. The ruin of sixteenth-century Gartartan Castle, which preceded the mansion, lies some 300m to the north.

There was a time when many of Gartmore's inhabitants were Glaswegians. Adults and children from Glasgow's poor and orphan institutions were boarded out in local farms and cottages until the early years of the twentieth century, when Sir Charles Cayzer ended the practice. South of the village, on the old Drymen Road, lies the farm of Chapelarroch, where a chapel attached to the Priory of Inchmahome once stood. There was also an inn, where Rob Roy famously kidnapped the Duke of Montrose's factor, Graham of Killearn, while he was collecting rents one day in 1716.

GARTMORE

Visitor Services
B CC Ch PO PT SA SC

Sport and Leisure
Cy Fi FP HB PB RC Ri W

Public Transport
Bus
The Stirling to Glasgow via Aberfoyle, Balfron and Strathblane service passes through the village. A Royal Mail Post Bus service links with Aberfoyle and Kinlochard.

Accommodation
Hotel
Black Bull, Gartmore 01877 382225

Caravan and Camping Parks
Forestry Enterprise Caravan and Camping Site, Cobleland, off A81, 2km N of Gartmore 01877 382392/382383
Trossachs Holiday Park, off A81 1.5km E of Gartmore 01877 382614

Forest Enterprise's Cobleland Caravan and Camping Site (01877 382392) is signposted (L) just before crossing the bridge over the infant River Forth, sometimes known locally as the Avon Dhu, or 'black water', at this point. At Braeval junction, take A821 (L) for Aberfoyle, or A81 (R) for the Lake of Menteith, Callander or Stirling. The Rob Roy Inn motel (L) stands by the junction and the Aberfoyle Golf Course is located just off the A81 (L).

ABERFOYLE

Aberfoyle (population c900), lies picturesquely situated in the shadow of Craigmore (387m) – a conspicuous, rocky eminence in the Menteith Hills. It stands at the gateway to the Highlands, for the great geological fault line known as the Highland Boundary Fault passes through the district about here, marking an abrupt transition from Lowland to Highland scenery.

Today's bustling tourist centre with its hotels, shops and restaurants consisted of nothing more than three primitive agricultural 'toons' prior to the first half of the nineteenth century. On the north bank of the Forth the tiny clachan of Aberfule ('the confluence of streams') comprised some thatched, stone-built cottages, described by Scott as 'miserable little bourocks', which straggled along the road between the ancient humped-back bridge over the Forth and the Milton to the west. Here, as the name implies, was the corn-mill for the district and an inn. South of the river, at the Kirkton, some thatched cottages huddled around the parish kirk and manse.

The Aberfoyle of old would have been well known to Rob Roy MacGregor on his frequent forays into the more prosperous Lowlands, and features prominently in Scott's *Rob Roy*. There was industry here too, for extensive slate quarries on Craigmore were worked from at least as far back as the mid-eighteenth century, continuing in production until 1958. Lime-quarrying at the Limecraigs, on the hillside to the east of the village, ceased much earlier around 1847.

Many inhabitants left the district in the century after the 1745 Jacobite Rising as the clan system was dismantled. In the Highland districts the small crofts and communal farms were made into large sheep-runs, while those in the Lowlands were absorbed into larger farms which engaged mainly in cultivation. As the Industrial Revolution gathered momentum, the clansfolk gradually deserted their native heath for the new towns and industries in the Lowlands and the native Gaelic language was heard no more in the district.

The early decades of the nineteenth century marked a watershed in the history of the district, for Sir Walter Scott's hugely successful romances *The Lady of the Lake* (1810) and *Rob Roy* (1817) brought the first huge influx of tourists. This was Graham country and successive Dukes of Montrose, as principal landowners in the district, actively promoted tourism and farming. The 5th Duke had a new inn built at Aberfoyle, succeeded by a fine hotel, and improved the local farm buildings. He was also a leading promoter of the Aberfoyle railway, opened in 1882, which not only encouraged tourism but allowed local farmers to get their produce to market much quicker.

The heart of the village now shifted to the north bank of the Forth and the population began to increase after having suffered decline for almost a century and a half. Grand villas for wealthy businessmen started to appear in Aberfoyle and along the Loch Ard road. Then, in 1885, the Duke had the 'Duke's Road' built over the Duke's Pass, so that tourists arriving by train (many of them Americans) could journey to The Trossachs by coach-and-four. Tourism, farming and forestry remain the main activities in the district to this day.

The splendid scenery and romantic associations of the Aberfoyle district have often attracted film-makers. Feature films shot on location here have included an earlier version of *Rob Roy* (1953), starring Richard Todd and Glynis Johns (which, alas, owed little to fact!) and *Geordie* (1954–5), a delightful tale about a Highland games champion, starring Bill Travers.

Entering Aberfoyle from the south, the car park (T) and Tourist Information Centre (01877 382352. Open April to October) are just off Main Street (L). Continuing on, Manse Road (L) leads over the River Forth to Kirkton, for the Covenanter's Inn, the old Parish Kirk and the walk to the fairy hillock Doon Hill (Walk 13). The Duke's Pass road (A821) for The Trossachs, Callander and the Queen Elizabeth Forest Park Visitor Centre, goes off (R) at the former Bailie Nicol Jarvie Hotel, now converted to flats. The B829 continues straight ahead, for Kinlochard, Stronachlachar and Inversnaid on Loch Lomond.

The Scottish Wool Centre, by the car park (01877 382850. Open all year. Tea room and restaurant. Admission charge to sheep display, Easter to October), tells the 2,000-year history of sheep in Scotland. There are daily presentations of spinning, weaving, sheepdog-handling (summer only) and a show demonstrating the evolution of sheep breeds in Scotland over the centuries.

At the junction of Main Street and the Kirkton Road, you may notice an old poker hanging from the lone tree here. This recalls an incident involving the fictitious Bailie Nicol Jarvie in Scott's *Rob Roy*. It came about when the Bailie was accosted one night by three trouble-making Highlanders as he entered the Aberfoyle Inn, which was then situated about a kilometre to the west. The Highlanders drew their swords and advanced menacingly towards him. The Bailie, who was a peaceable man, naturally reached for his sword, but it was stuck in its sheath. Thinking quickly, he grabbed a red-hot poker and struck out, setting the plaid of one of his attackers on fire. Honour was satisfied and this accounts for the poker which hangs in the tree to this day.

The former Bailie Nicol Jarvie Hotel, directly opposite the tree, was built for the Duke of Montrose around the time that the railway opened, in order to accommodate the hordes of visitors who were then converging on The Trossachs. Sixty fine horses were stabled there to haul four-in-hand coaches and brakes, driven by coachmen wearing red coats and grey top hats, over the Duke's Pass to Trossachs Hotel and Trossachs Pier. Alas, these colourful scenes were consigned to history when the new motor road opened in 1932 and even the Duke's fine hotel is now but a memory.

Baillie Nicol Jarvie's Tree, Aberfoyle, and the old hotel
(R. D. Campbell Collection)

Taking the Kirkton road (Manse Road), the infant River Forth is crossed on a picturesque old humpback bridge, beyond which a road (R) leads to the Covenanter's Inn and some fine walks in the Queen Elizabeth Forest Park. The post-war renaissance of Scottish Nationalism will forever be associated with Aberfoyle and the Covenanter's Inn, for it was here that the Scottish National Covenant was drawn up in April 1949. This document, pledging signatories to work by all constitutional means towards the achievement of self-government for Scotland within the UK framework, was subsequently signed by over two million people, a majority of the Scottish electorate.

The ruined walls of the Old Parish Kirk, dating from 1774, stand in the eighteenth-century graveyard, close by the site of the old clachan of Kirkton. Two cast-iron morte-safes by the kirk door recall the activities of the Resurrectionists in the early decades of the nineteenth century, when these grisly body-snatchers did a brisk trade in providing medical schools in the cities with fresh corpses. For a small payment to a morte-safe society, these cast-iron safes were fitted over coffins at the time of interment and remained until the corpse had lost its value for medical research. The remains of a prehistoric stone circle of ten upright stones once stood on a slight mound to the south of the old kirk, but the site is now occupied by a modern bungalow.

The road soon veers left past Auchinblae, the old Aberfoyle manse, which dates from around 1732. Between 1787 and 1828 this fine Georgian house was occupied by Dr Patrick Graham, the local minister, whose book *Sketches of Perthshire* proved a valuable source of information to Sir Walter Scott when writing *Rob Roy*. Scott often visited the house to talk about the history of the district with Dr Graham. A car park at the end of Manse Road caters for walkers in the Queen Elizabeth Forest Park (Walk 13).

An earlier minister of Aberfoyle, the Rev Robert Kirk (1644–1692), moved here from Balquhidder in 1685 and remained in charge until 1692, when he was allegedly spirited away to fairyland. Kirk, author of the book *The Secret Commonwealth of Elves, Fauns and Fairies*, was in the habit of visiting the fairy knoll at Doon Hill, a hillock in the nearby woods, and it was there that he died on 14 May 1692 while on one of his excursions, possibly as the result of a heart attack. Of course, his superstitious parishioners believed that he had been spirited away to fairyland for having revealed fairy secrets in his book. The existence of Kirk's grave in the old graveyard, at the south-east corner of the kirk, is explained by the fact that a stock, or changeling, was provided to replace him. Stretching credulity to its limits, it was long maintained that Kirk continued to be the minister of the parish and that all his successors were merely acting on his behalf.

Returning to Main Street, the Duke's Pass road (A821) leads in one kilometre to the Queen Elizabeth Forest Park Visitor Centre at David Marshall Lodge with its panoramic views of the surrounding countryside. There is a cafeteria, an audio-visual show about the wildlife of the park, way-marked trails, picnic places, cycleways, fishing, pony trails and a forest drive. (01877 382258. Visitor Centre open March to Christmas, subject to weather at certain times. Access to park all year.)

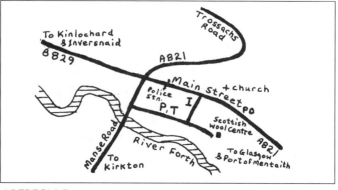

ABERFOYLE

Visitor Services
B Bk CC Ch D G I MR P PO PS PT SA SC T

Sport and Leisure
A Bw Cf Cy Fi FP Go HB PB RC Ri S SB* VC W Wa*

*Loch Ard

Public Transport
Bus
Car park, for Stirling, Balfron and Glasgow services and The Trossachs Trundler summer circular service (Callander–Trossachs Pier–Aberfoyle–Port of Menteith–Callander); Post Office, Main Street, for the Royal Mail Post Bus to Kinlochard, Stronachlachar and Inversnaid.

Accommodation
Hotels
Altskeith, Loch Ard Road, 5.5km W of Aberfoyle 01877 387266
Clachan, Main Street 01877 382216
Covenanters Inn, Kirkton 01877 382347
Forest Hills, Kinlochard, 6km W of Aberfoyle 01877 387277
Forth Inn, Main Street 01877 382372
Inverard, Loch Ard Road, 1.5km W of Aberfoyle 01877 382229
Rob Roy, A81/A821 junction, Braeval 01877 382245

Self-Catering
Barratt Forest Hills Trossachs Club, Kinlochard, 6km W of Aberfoyle 01877 387277

Caravan and Camping Parks
Forestry Enterprise Caravan and Camping Site, Cobleland, off A81, 3km SE of Aberfoyle 01877 382392

Dunglass Castle at Bowling, an ancient seat of
Clan Colquhoun (© Robert D. Campbell)

Dumbarton Castle was made a royal fortress
by Alexander II in 1222 (© Robert D. Campbell)

Balloch Castle lies at the heart of lovely
Balloch Castle Country Park (© Robert D. Campbell)

The village of Gartocharn nestles among pleasant farmlands
near Loch Lomond's eastern shore (© Robert D. Campbell)

Loch Lomond's islands, the Luss Hills and
Ben Lomond from Boturich (© Robert D. Campbell)

Around 60,000 people now climb
Ben Lomond each year (© Robert D. Campbell)

Wild goats inhabit Ben Lomond's western flank
(© Stirling Council Countryside Rangers)

The Loch Lomond steamer *Maid of the Loch* at Tarbet in 1964.
It is intended to resume sailings
(© Robert D. Campbell)

Inversnaid, which has a large hotel, was once home to the famous outlaw Rob Roy MacGregor (© Argyll, The Isles, Loch Lomond, Stirling and Trossachs Tourist Board)

Loch Arklet was a gathering-place of Clan MacGregor (© Argyll, The Isles, Loch Lomond, Stirling and Trossachs Tourist Board)

The Falls of Falloch in Glen Falloch,
frozen in winter (© Stirling Council Countryside Rangers)

The scenic West Highland Railway line runs through
Glen Falloch (© Robert D. Campbell)

Ben Arthur, by Loch Long, is nicknamed The Cobbler
(© Argyll, The Isles, Loch Lomond, Stirling and
Trossachs Tourist Board)

Garelochhead is pleasantly situated at the head of the
Gare Loch (© Robert D. Campbell)

The renowned Glasgow architect Charles Rennie Mackintosh
designed the futuristic Hill House at Helensburgh
(© Robert D. Campbell)

Kilcreggan, on the Rosneath Peninsula, enjoys fine views of the
Firth of Clyde (© Robert D. Campbell)

Trossachs Holiday Park, off A81, 5km SE of Aberfoyle 01877 382614

Tourist Information
Trossachs Discovery Centre, Main Street 01877 382352 (April to October and weekends only November to March)

ABERFOYLE–STRONACHLACHAR

Leaving Aberfoyle, the 'highway winding west' (B829) runs close by the infant River Forth. Near the church (R) a tramway once descended steeply from the extensive slate quarries high above, which produced over four million slates a year. The Inverard Hotel (R) is a former hunting lodge.

At the clachan of Milton, the great 4m iron wheel which once powered Milton Mill still survives. Built in 1667 as a lint-mill, it subsequently became a corn-mill, receiving grain from as far afield as Gartmore and Port of Menteith. Handloom and powerloom-weaving was also carried on in the district and in the mid-nineteenth century a factory manufactured pyroligneous acid for use in textile-dyeing, using abundant supplies of coppiced oak which grew in the vicinity. Behind a cottage (R) the old Aberfoyle inn, known as Jean MacAlpine's Inn, has been beautifully restored in recent years, complete with thatched roof. A road (L) gives access to forest trails for walkers and cyclists in the Loch Ard Forest, part of the Queen Elizabeth Forest Park.

The narrow Pass of Aberfoyle is entered close by Lower Loch Ard where an army could be held at bay by a handful of men in more troubled times. In fact, this actually happened in 1653, during the years of Cromwell's Commonwealth, when the Royalist Earl of Glencairn was joined by the local laird, Graham of Duchray, and some neighbouring clans numbering about 300 men in all, who camped about Duchray and Loch Ard. The Governor of Stirling Castle duly marched out to meet them with a squadron of horse and a regiment of foot. The English troops were hemmed in at the Pass of Aberfoyle and driven back with considerable loss. As R.B. Cunninghame Graham observed, 'Graham no doubt fought all the better because the Cromwellians had burnt his house (Duchray Castle) the night before.'

Fragments of the oakwoods that once existed throughout the district remain about here. They were worked on a 'coppice with standards' rotational system (as on Loch Lomondside) to supply bark for the tanning industry, until the development of aniline dyes around the time of the First World War caused prices to fall. Small wood was used for pit-props and peeled branches used by basket-makers, or sent to the 'liquor factory' at Milton or Balmaha. Birch wood was used to make charcoal for iron-smelting.

The road presently descends to beautiful Loch Ard, 'the high loch', at the 'Echo Rock' where, if there be little or no wind, one's voice can be heard echoing across the still waters. Queen Victoria, on a journey north in 1869, was entranced by the view here. She wrote, 'We came upon Loch Ard, and a lovelier picture could not be seen. Ben Lomond, blue and yellow, rose above the lower hills, which were pink and purple with heather, and an isthmus of trees in front dividing it from the rest of the loch . . . certainly one of the most lovely drives I can remember, along Loch Ard.'

Loch Ard, some 3.5km long, under a kilometre wide and about 33m deep at its deepest point, lies in a district which is associated with some of the most stirring passages in Scott's *Rob Roy*. Local features include the Bailie's Rock and Tree, where Bailie Nicol Jarvie swung from a bough suspended by his coat-tails, and on the far shore, Rob Roy's Cave. On Dundochil Islet, just off the far shore, are the ruins of the early fifteenth century Duke Murdoch's Castle, a stronghold of Murdoch, Duke of Albany, who was Regent of Scotland during James I's long captivity in England. Murdoch had incurred the king's displeasure during his enforced absence and, along with his uncle Duncan, Earl of Lennox, and his two eldest sons, was beheaded at Stirling in 1425, following James's return to Scotland. The extensive Loch Ard Forest now clothes the southern shore of the loch, the planting of conifers having been commenced by the Forestry Commission in 1929.

Approaching Kinlochard (PO), the Altskeith Hotel and, just beyond, the Forest Hills Hotel, which has a Watersports Centre on the loch-shore, overlook the loch. The Loch Ard Youth Hostel is now closed. The path to the summit of Ben Venue (727m) goes off (R) a short way beyond the Forest Hills Hotel (Walk 19). This path also leads to the Falls of Ledard where, in *Rob Roy*, Frank Osbaldistone said farewell to Rob's wife Helen MacGregor (whose real name was Mary). It was there also that Flora MacIvor had her sylvan retreat in Scott's *Waverley*.

Leaving Loch Ard, the road climbs to enter the Queen Elizabeth Forest Park, just before reaching the strangely named, and now ruined, house known as 'The Teapot' (R). The name comes not from its having been a tearoom, but from its use as a shebeen for slaking the thirst of workmen employed in the construction of the Loch Katrine to Glasgow water pipeline along the opposite hillside back in the 1850s. The excisemen were never able to prove the sale of whisky, for every time they raided the house the only liquor they found was a teapot on the hob infusing tea, hence the house's peculiar name.

A kilometre or so on, there are some pleasant forest walks around the lovely little Loch Dubh, 'the black loch'. Loch Chon (pronounced 'Con'), 'the loch of the dog', soon appears. This trout loch is more Highland in character than Loch Ard, although extensive planting in the surrounding Loch Ard Forest by the Forestry Commission has softened its former stern aspect. Lying some 88m above sea level, it is 2.5km long, just under a kilometre across at its widest point, and has a maximum depth of about 23m. A workmen's camp for 'navvies' employed on building the water pipeline to Glasgow was erected on the hillside beyond the loch's far shore in the 1850s and called Sebastopol, after the famous siege which was taking place at that time.

Climbing away from Loch Chon to the summit of the road, near the Forest Park's northern boundary, a path goes off (R) to Royal Cottage on Loch Katrine (Walk 21). This house, near the outlet which supplies the great city of Glasgow with 100 million gallons of water a day, was specially built to accommodate Queen Victoria when she came to inaugurate the great undertaking on 14 October 1859. A little way beyond the track and a cottage is the hillock (R) known as the Faery Knoll, a reminder of more superstitious times in the district. According to the good Dr Graham of Aberfoyle, it was believed that if on Hallow Eve any person went round one of these hillocks nine times, towards the left hand, a door would open into which that person would be admitted and enter into the fairies' subterranean abodes.

The eastern approach to Ben Lomond by the Bruach Caorainn Burn in
Loch Ard Forest (© Robert D. Campbell)

Leaving the Loch Ard Forest behind, the road drops down to Glen Arklet, close by the eastern end of wild Loch Arklet. At the road junction, go right for Stronachlachar on Loch Katrine or left for Inversnaid on the bonnie banks of Loch Lomond. The public road ends at both these places.

STRONACHLACHAR

Stronachlachar, 'the mason's point', a few scattered houses which provide a base for water authority workers, owes its existence to the establishment of the steamer service on Loch Katrine in 1843.

When Dorothy Wordsworth, accompanied by her brothers William and Samuel Taylor Coleridge, arrived here on foot from Inversaid in 1803, the loch seemed to Dorothy, 'but a dreary prospect – like a barren Ulswater – Ulswater dismantled of its grandeur and cropped of its lesser beauties'. There were no boats available for hire, no accommodation to be had and William had to ask for beds for the night at a house near the head of the loch. Following publication of *The Lady of the Lake* in 1810, there was an influx of tourists and a large rowing boat manned by eight strong Highlanders plied on the loch for some years before the first steamboat appeared in 1843. This craft landed its passengers at Coalbarns, near Stronachlachar, where Highland ponies were on hand to convey ladies, the elderly and infirm along the rough track to Inversnaid. Men often had to walk. On wet days that was bad enough, but the Highland ghillies who acted as guides often levied 'black mail' – just as their ancestors had once levied 'black mail' on Lowland farmers back in Rob Roy's time.

In 1859 the famous Tour No.1 began, a marathon day excursion by rail and steamboat, which involved travelling from Glasgow to Balloch by train; Balloch to Inversnaid by steamboat; on to Stronachlachar by horse-drawn coach; down Loch Katrine by steamboat to The Trossachs; on to Callander by horse-drawn coach; and returning to Glasgow by train. It also operated in reverse as Tour No.2. Sadly, this magnificent tour is no longer possible, owing to the withdrawal of the Loch Lomond steamer service. The present Loch Katrine steamer is the yacht-like *Sir Walter Scott*, a lovely little vessel which has sailed the loch since 1900 and is now owned by the Water Authority. (See Route 7 for details.)

The view from Stronachlachar Pier, now rather less barren than in Dorothy Wordsworth's time, is dominated by Factor's Island, or Eilean Dharag, little more than a stone's throw away. Some say it was there that Rob Roy imprisoned Graham of Killearn, the Duke of Montrose's factor, whom he had captured while collecting rents near Gartmore. Rob demanded a ransom of the Duke for his factor's release but, as none was forthcoming, he kept the rent money amounting to over £3,000 of Scots money (£1,000), to compensate for his losses at the hands of the Duke. Graham was then taken to the Lowlands and released unharmed. However, others maintain that Eilean Dubh, 'the black island', near the loch's western end, was the factor's prison. This indeed seems likely, since Rob often frequented the nearby farmhouse of Portnellan at that time.

A few hundred metres west of the pier, the old Stronachlachar Hotel can be seen, from where the horse-drawn tourist coaches for Inversnaid once departed. It is now a hostel for Water Authority workers. The first hotel, built near the loch shore in 1851–2, had to be replaced by this building in 1886–7 in order to allow the raising of the loch level.

At Portnellan, towards the head of the loch on the opposite shore, there is an ancient burial ground of the MacGregors. As with Factor's Island, it had to be protected against the raised water-level by stone walls. Also near the head of the loch is Glen Gyle House, once the seat of the MacGregor chief. Built around 1703, the house was soon burned and partly destroyed by a party of soldiers quartered at Finlarig, but it was quickly restored. It was in Glen Gyle that Rob Roy was born in 1671.

The North Loch Katrine Road, popular with cyclists and walkers, is not open to public motor traffic. However, farm and Water Authority motor vehicles, including heavy lorries, regularly use the road and so due care and attention is necessary.

STRONACHLACHAR–INVERSNAID

The Stronachlachar to Inversnaid road was built by the Duke of Montrose at the request of the Loch Lomond Steamboat Company, so that coaches could link with the Loch Lomond and Loch Katrine steamers. A toll was charged and the road remained in private hands until as recently as 1959. The four-in-hand coaches, complete with drivers magnificently attired in red coats and grey top-hats, were stationed at Inversnaid Hotel. A young lad hung precariously on the rear of every coach, in order to operate a special brake on the steep descents. It was a sad day indeed when they ceased running in 1937, to be replaced by more mundane motor buses.

Leaving Stronachlachar, the way now lies by the bare shores of Loch Arklet (possibly 'loch of the steep slope'), which was one of

These four-in-hand coaches once carried tourists between the steamers at
Rowardennan on Loch Lomond and Stronachlachar on Loch Katrine
(R. D. Campbell Collection)

the gathering places (the other was Lendrick by Loch Venachar)
of the Clan Dougal Ciar branch of the MacGregors. The loch,
which is about 4km long and a kilometre wide, was greatly
enlarged in 1909–14 by the damming of the Arklet Water at its
western end, so that Arklet's waters were diverted to flow towards
Loch Katrine instead of Loch Lomond, in order to augment the
Glasgow water-supply. The loch's surface lies some 145m above
sea level, which is somewhat higher than Lochs Katrine and
Lomond and makes the Arrochar Alps, an impressive sight
beyond its western end, appear much closer than they really are.
A trout-hatchery at the loch rears fish from spawn taken from
feeder streams, to provide fresh stock for the Water Authority's
reservoirs. Until fairly recent times the then owners, Glasgow
Corporation, kept the lochside road in a near impassable state, in
order to discourage visitors in the interests of water purity.

Corriearklet Farm (R) was the scene of Rob Roy's marriage to
Mary MacGregor of Comer in January 1693. Indeed, travellers
enquiring at a cottage here were once favoured with the sight of
an old duck-gun, which was said to have belonged to the famous
outlaw! Mary, or Marie (whom Scott calls Helen in *Rob Roy*) was
born at Comer Farm, which lies in the shadow of Ben Lomond,
behind Beinn Uamha (598m) on the far shore. Her uncles, John
and Alasdair, farmed the countryside around Corriearklet and
Corheichen, to the north of Ben Lomond.

The 320m-long, 10.6m-high red sandstone dam across the Arklet Water at the western end of Loch Arklet is now well screened by trees. A plaque (L) records details of its construction in 1909–14. Materials had to be brought to Balloch by rail, shipped up Loch Lomond in barges to a point just south of Inversnaid and then taken up the steep hillside to Loch Arklet on a specially-built aerial-ropeway.

The whitewashed farmhouse known as The Garrison (R) stands on the site of the Garrison of Inversnaid, a barracks built by the Hanoverian Government in 1718–19, at the instance of the Duke of Montrose following the Jacobite Rising of 1715. While it was under construction, Gregor Glun Dubh, the MacGregor chief, aided and abetted by Rob Roy, organised a raid which resulted in eight masons and quarriers being carried off to the Lowlands by the armed MacGregors, where they were released unharmed. The Garrison was later burned by the MacGregors during the 1745 Rising. Then, in the autumn of 1746, a young officer called James Wolfe arrived to effect repairs and remained briefly as its commander. He was soon to achieve universal fame as General Wolfe, the hero of Quebec.

The Garrison was out of use by the end of the eighteenth century and when Sir Walter Scott visited in 1792 he was told he would find the key under the door. It was becoming ruinous by 1823, when the only occupants were two women who kept 'a kind of inn'. Open-air church services were occasionally held at the Garrison, which brought worshippers from as far afield as Glen Falloch and the eastern end of Loch Katrine, until a mission station was established at Inversnaid in 1866. The tenants of the Inversnaid inn would bring along a keg of whisky to 'the preachings' and it was said that the congregation would sometimes partake a little too freely. The site of the Garrison is now occupied by farm buildings, many of which incorporate portions of the original structure, while parts of the barrack-block walls still stand.

The old military graveyard for the Garrison is situated behind Inversnaid Primary School (R) and contains a headstone erected by the 5th Duke of Montrose in 1895 to the memory of all those who died while serving at the Garrison. The original headstones are now virtually indecipherable. Children once attended the school from as far south as Rowchoish and Cailness on Loch Lomondside, which must have been an arduous journey in the winter months.

Descending towards Inversnaid, the attractive little white-painted St Kentigerna's Church (Church of Scotland) is on the left. At the time the church was built, in 1895, the area supported a much larger population and included Irish navvies working on the reservoirs and aqueducts. Some of the navvies who were killed in work accidents now lie in unmarked graves in the little kirkyard. The final church service was held in 1986 and in 1991 the building was converted into an Outdoor Centre by the Boy's Brigade.

Just before commencing the final steep descent to Inversnaid, a road (L) leads across the Arklet Water and uphill to a car park and viewpoint.

INVERSNAID

Descending to Inversnaid, Inversnaid Lodge (R), which cannot be seen from the road, was built in 1790 as a shooting-lodge for the 3rd Duke of Montrose, who was Lord Justice General for Scotland. Let to various wealthy tenants over the years and extended in 1906–7, the lodge now houses the Inversnaid Photography Centre, which offers photography holidays and accommodation (01877 386254).

World-famous Loch Lomond finally comes into view on the last steep descent to Inversnaid. A 1915 guidebook observed, 'The road descends rapidly to Inversnaid, and the coaches being supplied with specially constructed brakes are, after their wild rush, drawn up at the hotel door, to the great relief of the passengers, who momentarily expect to be dashed into the loch'. There is now a car park in front of the hotel – and little risk of motorists ending up in the loch.

The modest clachan of Inversnaid boasted a meal-mill from about 1753 and there was also a ferryman's cottage close by the picturesque Falls of Inversnaid where, in 1803, William Wordsworth was entranced by his 'sweet Highland girl'. This beauty, the ferryman's daughter, was immortalised in his poem 'To a Highland Girl':

'Sweet Highland Girl, a very shower
Of beauty is thy earthly dower! . . .

For I, methinks, till I grow old,
As fair before me shall behold
As I do now, the Cabin small,
The Lake, The Bay, The Waterfall,
And thee, the Spirit of them all.'

Wordsworth, who came with his sister Dorothy and Samuel

Taylor Coleridge, was but one of many famous people associated with Inversnaid. Back in 1306, King Robert the Bruce hurried through with a ragged band of men following his defeat at the battle of Dail-righ near Tyndrum, before crossing the loch south of Inversnaid. Some four centuries later, Rob Roy MacGregor made his home here.

Improvements in communications brought many famous authors to the area in the eighteenth and nineteenth centuries. James Hogg, 'the Ettrick Shepherd', passed through while herding a drove of sheep in 1791 and in 1803 passed over the hills behind Inversnaid while on a northbound walking tour. It was also around that time, in 1792, that Sir Walter Scott arrived. In 1819 the young Thomas Carlyle tramped over from Loch Katrine while on a walking tour. In 1857 American writer Nathaniel Hawthorne also passed through the area and in 1859 Jules Verne arrived by steamer, before crossing over to Loch Katrine and The Trossachs. The journey was later to feature in the adventures of his hero and heroine in the novel *Les Indes Noir* ('The Black Diamonds'), published in Britain as *The Child of the Cavern* (1877). The poet Gerard Manley Hopkins was a later visitor to Inversnaid. Arriving by steamer on a day trip in September 1881, Hopkins was so impressed that he later wrote the poem 'Inversnaid':

'What would the world be, once bereft
Of wet and wilderness? Let them be left,
O let them be left, wilderness and wet,
Long live the weeds and the wilderness yet.'

Inversnaid Hotel occupies a commanding situation by the loch, which affords splendid views of the mountains behind Inveruglas on the far shore: from right to left, Ben Vorlich (943m); Ben Vane (916m); Ben Ime (1,011m); and A' Chrois (849m).

The present large hotel began as a small inn around 1820, soon after the first steamboat started sailing on the loch in 1818. The inn/hotel was owned by the Duke of Montrose and let to tenants until 1931. It was an unlikely target for the German Luftwaffe on 5 May 1940, the night of the Clydebank blitz, when a bomber pilot apparently mistook a bracken fire on the hillside for Clydebank and dropped at least 28 bombs between The Garrison and Inversnaid, one of which struck the hotel.

The opening of the railway to Balloch in 1850 and improved steamboat services on Lochs Lomond and Katrine made Inversnaid an important staging-point for tours until fairly recent times. Steamboat tours are now only a memory but, with the opening of the West Highland Way in 1984, thousands of walkers now pass through Inversnaid every summer. The Way provides fine walks, north to Inversnaid Nature Reserve and Rob Roy's Cave and south to Cailness or Rowchoish.

INVERSNAID

Visitor Services
B F P SA T

Sport and Leisure
Fi FP PB RC SB W

Public Transport
Bus
Inversnaid Hotel, for Royal Mail Post Bus to Aberfoyle Post Office.

Ferries
Inversnaid Jetty, for ferry to Inveruglas car park where there are coach services to Glasgow, Fort William and Uig (Skye). March to end December. Sailing times from Inversnaid Hotel, 01877 386223. Another ferry operates to Tarbet, Inverbeg and Rowardennan, usually daily Easter to end September. Cruise Loch Lomond, Tarbet, 01301 702356.

Accommodation
Hotel
Inversnaid 01877 386223

ROUTE 7. THE TROSSACHS AND LOCH KATRINE

Stirling to Callander and Trossachs Pier by the A84/A821;
the steamer trip on Loch Katrine, and the return to
Callander and Stirling by the Duke's Pass, Aberfoyle and the
Lake of Menteith (A821/A81/A84 or A873/A84)

The Trossachs and Loch Katrine by Public Transport

Bus and Coach

Bus services operate from Stirling Bus Station to Callander via
Doune, and to Aberfoyle and Glasgow via Thornhill. The
Edinburgh–Fort William coach service also serves Doune and
Callander. The Trossachs Trundler circular service runs in the
summer months between Callander–Trossachs Pier–Aberfoyle
–Port of Menteith–Callander. Royal Mail Post Buses operate
between Callander and Invertrossachs (Loch Venachar),
Trossachs Pier and Aberfoyle.

Cruises and Ferries

A steamer service operates on Loch Katrine in the summer
months between Trossachs Pier and Stronachlachar and on
shorter cruises. A ferry operates on the Lake of Menteith in the
summer months between Port of Menteith and Inchmahome
Island, for Inchmahome Priory.

The scenic attractions of The Trossachs and Loch Katrine have
been justly famous ever since Sir Walter Scott penned his
historical romances *The Lady of the Lake* and *Rob Roy* in the early
decades of the nineteenth century. The true history of the
district, though poorly recorded, was no doubt every bit as
stirring as any of Sir Walter's fictional romances, for it was long
the haunt of lawless caterans, or robbers, who found refuge amid
its maze of hidden glens and silver lochs.

  The gateway to this wild region was the narrow, rugged defile
known as The Trossachs, where a handful of armed men could

hold a regiment at bay. From this hidden mountain fastness the caterans of old would launch their depredations deep into the fertile Lowlands, returning laden with stolen booty and driving before them the cattle they had 'lifted' through the Bealach-nam-Bo, or 'pass of the cattle', near the eastern end of Loch Katrine. Indeed, it is said that the Lowland spelling of the loch's very name is adapted from 'loch of the caterans'.

The proximity and ease of access to the Lowlands that made The Trossachs district attractive to the caterans of old now operates in reverse and thousands of motorists from the more populous districts of the Lowlands and beyond converge on the district every summer to enjoy its unexcelled beauty and recreational attractions. The Trossachs, variously said to mean 'the rough or bristly country' or 'the transverse country' is, strictly speaking, the name applied to the narrow, thickly wooded, rocky gorge that lies between Trossachs Pier on lovely Loch Katrine and pretty little Loch Achray. However, it has come to enjoy a much wider application and is now generally applied to the scenic triangle bounded by the head of Loch Katrine, Aberfoyle and Callander. In recent times it has often been extended northwards from Callander to embrace bonnie Strathyre and Rob Roy's burial-place at Balquhidder.

The route described here constitutes one of Scotland's most scenic circular tours. Starting from Stirling, the outward route lies by way of the bustling tourist town of Callander and Lochs Venachar and Achray to Trossachs Pier, for the sail on the sparkling, mountain-girt waters of Loch Katrine. The return is by the scenic Duke's Pass road, Aberfoyle and the pretty Lake of Menteith to Callander. Approach routes to Aberfoyle, from Drymen on Loch Lomondside (A811/A81/A821) and from Glasgow via Strathblane (A81/A821), have already been described in connection with the MacGregor Country. Trossachs Pier can be reached direct from Aberfoyle by the Duke's Pass road and the circuit completed in the reverse direction if desired.

STIRLING

The historic town of Stirling (population c29,200), guarded by its ancient castle on a crag, occupies a strategic site on the south bank of the River Forth, where routes converge from north, south, east and west. Stirling Castle was long the seat of the Scottish monarchy and regarded as being 'the key to the Highlands', on account of its geographical and political significance. Several key battles in Scotland's turbulent history were fought within sight of its walls. In 1297, during the Wars of Independence, Sir William

Wallace defeated an English army in the shadow of the castle at Stirling Bridge and in 1314 Robert the Bruce vanquished Edward II's superior army at Bannockburn. The unfortunate James III was not only defeated by dissident subjects at nearby Sauchieburn in 1488, but murdered as he lay wounded after the battle. Less decisive was the desultory struggle that took place in 1715, in the hills above Dunblane at Sheriffmuir, between the Jacobites under the Earl of Mar and Government forces under the Duke of Argyll.

Stirling's future prosperity was assured as far back as about 1124, when the town was created a Royal Burgh by David I, a status which afforded valuable trading privileges to its merchants. By the nineteenth century agricultural engineering, textiles and coal-mining had emerged as the principal industries in the district. Today, Stirling offers excellent shopping facilities, including the vast Thistle Shopping Centre complex, and is the industrial and commercial centre for the surrounding agricultural districts. The modern University of Stirling, founded in 1967, occupies a parkland setting near the town. For the visitor, Stirling not only offers an abundance of historic buildings, but provides a convenient base within easy reach of both Glasgow and Edinburgh by road and rail for exploring The Trossachs, Loch Lomond and the southern Highlands.

A detailed descriptive guide leaflet and map showing places of historic interest is available from Stirling Visitor Centre on the Castle Esplanade, or from the Tourist Information Centre, 41 Dumbarton Road. (Both open all year.) The main points of interest are outlined below.

Stirling Castle, whose recorded history dates back to the twelfth century and probably much earlier, stands on a crag at the highest point of the Old Town. Most of the present buildings date from the fifteenth to the seventeenth centuries. The castle played a crucial role in the struggle for Scotland's independence in the twelfth and thirteenth centuries. In 1297, it was captured by Sir William Wallace after the battle of Stirling Bridge and it was taken again by King Robert the Bruce in 1314 following his triumph over the English at Bannockburn.

As a favourite seat of the Stewart dynasty, the castle was the scene of many key events in Scotland's history. In 1451, King James III was born within its walls – and was also brutally murdered near-by, after the battle of Sauchieburn in 1488. James's father, James II, murdered the Earl of Douglas within the castle walls in 1452. The infant Mary, Queen of Scots, was crowned at Stirling in 1543 and her son James VI (James I of England) baptised there in 1566. Cromwell's forces, under General Monck, laid siege to the castle in 1651, forcing the surrender of the garrison, and it was again besieged unsuccessfully by Prince Charles Edward Stewart's men as they retreated north from Derby in 1746. However, Stirling Castle had long ceased to be a seat of royalty by that time and its history as a fortress also ended with the '45 Rising. (Open all year. Admission charge. Cafeteria. 01786 450000.)

Ladies' Rock, Star Pyramid and The Valley can be accessed from Castle Wynd or Castle Esplanade. The Ladies' Rock, now in the Castle Cemetery, was once a favourite vantage point for watching royal tournaments in the valley below. The Star Pyramid nearby remembers all those martyred while seeking religious freedom.

The Beheading Stone, Gowan Hill, was the scene of many gruesome executions, notably Murdoch, Duke of Albany and former Regent of Scotland, along with two of his sons and his father-in-law the Earl of Lennox, in 1425, when King James I took revenge for Albany's misuse of power during James's long captivity in England.

Argyll's Lodging, Castle Wynd, Old Town, is a beautifully restored seventeenth-century Renaissance mansion, built around 1630 by Sir William Alexander of Menstrie and the town house of Archibald, 9th Earl of Argyll, from 1666. (01786 450000, Historic Scotland.)

Church of the Holy Rude in St John Street, Old Town, has been Stirling's principal church since the mid-fifteenth century. James VI was crowned here in 1567. (Open May to September.)

The Guildhall, St John Street, Old Town, was built 1639–49 with funds bequeathed by John Cowane, a wealthy Stirling merchant. Originally its purpose was to offer charity to unsuccessful merchants, but it was later used as a school and epidemic hospital. It is now used for banquets, concerts, ceilidhs, etc.

Old Town Jail, St John Street, Old Town, is a former Victorian jail built in 1846 to replace the Tolbooth Prison. It features 'living history' tours by actors. (01786 450050. Open all year.)

The Tolbooth, in Broad Street, Old Town, was built in 1703–5 by Sir William Bruce as the town's old administrative centre. A courthouse and jail were added in 1809, the jail becoming one of Scotland's most notorious and inhumane.

The Town Wall and Back Walk can be accessed from various points around the Old Town, from the Corn Exchange to Castle Esplanade. Note the statue of the famous Rob Roy MacGregor near the Corn Exchange. The wall was built around 1547, when King Henry VIII of England sought to force the infant Mary, Queen of Scots, to marry his son Edward. The Back Walk, completed between 1723 and 1791 follows the line of the Town

Wall from Dumbarton Road to the Castle and then continues round the Castle Rock back to the Old Town, giving magnificent views of town and country.

The Smith Art Gallery and Museum, Dumbarton Road, was founded in 1874 with a legacy from Thomas Stuart Smith, painter and collector. (01786 471917. Open all year.)

King's Knot and King's Park, 1km west of town centre, is an octagonal stepped mound, now grassed over, but once part of magnificent formal gardens laid out beneath Stirling Castle about 1630. Opposite (now occupied by houses, a golf course and public park) lay the King's Park, hunting grounds for the Royal court at Stirling. Access from Dumbarton Road/King's Park Road.

Stirling Old Bridge, off Drip Road (A84), 1km north of the town centre, dates from the fifteenth century, and was once the only crossing over the Forth in the district. It stands near the site of an earlier bridge where Sir William Wallace inflicted a resounding defeat on the occupying English forces in 1297. The arch nearest Stirling was temporarily breached in 1745 to deny passage to Prince Charles Edward Stewart's (or more commonly Bonnie Prince Charlie's) Jacobite army. The Old Bridge features in an episode in Robert Louis Stevenson's *Kidnapped*.

Cambuskenneth Abbey, 1.5km east of town centre, is a ruined Augustinian Abbey founded by King David I in 1147. James III and his Queen are buried in the grounds. There is pedestrian access by footbridge from Riverside Drive and vehicular access from Alloa Road (A907). (01786 450000, Historic Scotland. Open April to September; grounds all year.)

The impressive National Wallace Monument, on the Abbey Craig, off Hillfoots Road (B998) one mile north-east of the town centre, was designed by J.T. Rochead and erected in 1861–9 to commemorate Scotland's national hero. His great sword is displayed within the 67m-high monument. Wallace assembled his men around the Abbey Craig before the battle of Stirling Bridge. (Monument open all year. Weekends only, November–February. Admission charge. 01786 472140.)

Bannockburn Heritage Centre, 3km south of town centre on Glasgow Road (A9), commemorates King Robert the Bruce's famous victory over a much larger English army at the Battle of Bannockburn in 1314. Close by is the Borestone, where Bruce planted his standard, and a magnificent statue of Bruce mounted on his war-horse. (01786 812664, National Trust for Scotland. Open March to December.)

At the Royal Burgh of Stirling Visitor Centre on the Castle Esplanade, the story is told of Royal Stirling from the Wars of

Independence through life in the mediaeval burgh to the present day. (01786 479901. Open all year, admission free.)

An open-top double-decker Heritage Bus Tour, with full guided commentary on historic places of interest, operates in the summer months. Details can be obtained from Tourist Information Centres.

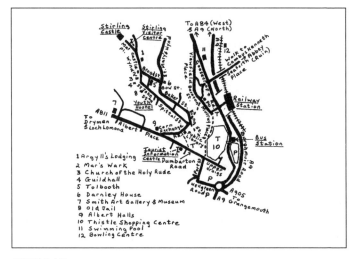

1 Argyll's Lodging
2 Mar's Wark
3 Church of the Holy Rude
4 Guildhall
5 Tolbooth
6 Darnley House
7 Smith Art Gallery & Museum
8 Old Jail
9 Albert Halls
10 Thistle Shopping Centre
11 Swimming Pool
12 Bowling Centre

STIRLING

Visitor Services
B Bk CC Ch D G H I P PO PS PT, R SA SC T YH

Sport and Leisure
A Bw Cf Cy Fi Go HB L M PB Pu RC Ri S SP TC VC W

Public Transport
A wide range of destinations in Scotland and England are served from the Railway and Bus Stations, which are both located in Goosecroft Road, close to the town's main shopping area. For particulars of some of the destinations served see the preceding section 'Getting There', about rail and coach approaches to the district, and also the introductory notes on public transport for routes 5, 6, 7 and 8.

Accommodation
Hotels
Allan Park, 20 Allan Park 01786 473598
Blairlogie House, Blairlogie 01259 761441
Golden Lion, Milton, 8 King Street 01786 475351
Holiday Inn Express, Springkerse Business Park 01786 449922

King Robert, Glasgow Road, Bannockburn 01786 811666
Park Lodge, 32 Park Terrace 01786 474862
The Portcullis, Castle Wynd 01786 472290
Stirling Highland, Spittal Street 01786 475444
Sword, Hillfoots Road, Causewayhead 01786 473338
Terraces, 4 Melville Terrace 01786 472268
University of Stirling, Conference and Vacation Campus 01786
 467140/467141
University of Stirling, Stirling Management Centre 01786 451666
Note: There are also several hotels close by at Bridge of Allan and Dunblane.

Caravan and Camping Parks
Auchenbowie Caravan Site, off A872, 2.5km S of Junction 9 on M80/M9 01324 823999
Witches Craig Caravan Park, Blairlogie, off A91 4km NE of Stirling 01786 474947
The Woods Caravan Club Site, Alva, off A91, first R beyond Alva (signposted Fishcross), 12km E of Stirling 01259 762802

Youth Hostel
Stirling Youth Hostel, St John Street 01786 473442

Tourist Information
41 Dumbarton Road 01786 475019 (Open all year)
M9/M80 Junction 9, Motorway service area 01786 814111 (April to October)
Royal Burgh of Stirling Visitor Centre, Castle Esplanade 01786 479901 (Open all year)

STIRLING–CALLANDER

Departure from Stirling is by Drip Road (A84) which begins at a roundabout at the north end of the town, near the picturesque Stirling Old Bridge over the River Forth. Approaching the M9 junction, there is a fine backward prospect, beyond the new Castle Business Park, to Stirling Castle. When approaching from the south or north by the M9, join the A84 here.

 Opposite the junction, the restored Craigforth House (L), built in 1675 for John Callander, now forms part of the Scottish Amicable Assurance Company's modern office complex. The River Forth is soon crossed near the quaint Old Drip Bridge (L) which dates from 1790, just south of the confluence of the Forth and the River Teith (R). Ben Ledi, Stuc a' Chroin and Ben Vorlich are prominent to the north-west.

Two splendid country houses can be glimpsed between here and Doune. The first, Ochtertyre (R), built in the 1760s, was the home of John Ramsay, celebrated diarist and correspondent of Scotland's national bard Robert Burns.

Some 2km on is Blair Drummond (R), designed in grand Scots Baronial style by J.C. Walker and erected in 1868–72. The house stands on the site of an earlier mansion, built in 1715, which was the home of Henry Home Drummond, Lord Kames (1696–1792), a law lord and prominent figure in the Scottish Enlightenment of the eighteenth century. In 1766 this truly enlightened landlord set about clearing the deep moss which covered the Moss of Kincardine as a first step towards developing today's rich farmlands. A huge water-wheel was used to wash the cut moss into the Forth, while tenants were introduced from the Balquhidder district and granted long leases to improve their holdings. The estate is now the Blair Drummond Safari and Leisure Park. (Usually open mid-March to early October. Restaurant, bar and gift shops. Admission charge. 01786 841456.)

At Kincardine-in-Menteith, the junction with A873 for Port of Menteith and Aberfoyle, the attractive Kincardine Parish Church (L) was built for Lord Kames's son in 1814–16 to replace a much earlier church, which stood in the ancient burial ground opposite (R). Blair Drummond School, of 1850 (L), is a new Tudor building with a fairytale central tower. Beyond the junction, on A84, there is access (R) to Cuthil Brae Caravan Site.

DOUNE

The A84 curves northwards, past the Creity Hall Hotel (L), before crossing the River Teith at Doune. Immediately before reaching the Bridge of Teith, a road leads (L) along the riverbank (where herons and roe-deer are often to be seen on the opposite bank) to the village of Deanston, a picturesque industrial village of former workers' houses, built in connection with Deanston Cotton Mill. The mill, first established in 1785, employed over 1,100 workers by the 1840s. Deanston, which once boasted its own school, library, savings bank, public hall and public baths, often featured in the popular 1960s television series *Doctor Finlay's Casebook*. The mill buildings now form part of a whisky distillery. Deanston House, behind the village and now a nursing home, was built in 1820 as the mill manager's residence.

The narrow, but picturesque, Bridge of Teith (care required), was erected as far back as 1535 and repaired and widened in 1866. Tradition avers that Robert Spittal, tailor to Queen Margaret, wife of James IV, built the bridge after the ferryman had refused to take him at this point because he had mislaid his purse and could not pay. However, the wealthy Spittal also built bridges elsewhere. An inscription and device featuring a pair of scissors appears on the left parapet.

Doune Castle, whose stout stone walls rise dramatically from the wooded banks of the River Teith, may be glimpsed from the bridge (R). This imposing fortress was built around 1370 as the principal seat of Robert Stewart, son of King Robert II, Earl of Menteith and Fife (by marriage) and later created 1st Duke of Albany. His son and successor Murdoch also resided there, until James I had him beheaded at Stirling in 1425. The castle then passed to the Crown and the Stewart kings often stayed there when hunting in the forests of Glen Finglas and Menteith.

Doune Castle and the Gallows Tree (R. D. Campbell Collection)

In 1581, Doune Castle passed to the Stewart Earls of Moray and in the 1745 Jacobite Rising, the castle was held for Prince Charles Edward Stewart when it was used as a prison. Several prisoners, including the Rev John Home, author of *The Douglas*, escaped by knotting several bedsheets together. The castle, which is mentioned in Scott's *Waverley*, later became ruinous until restored by the Earl of Moray in 1883. The building is now administered by Historic Scotland. Monty Python fans may wish to note that the film, *Monty Python and the Holy Grail* (1975), was shot on location there. (01786 841742. Open all year. Admission charge.)

The quaint old village of Doune (from 'dun', a fort; population c1,200) possibly owes its name to an ancient fort on the site of the castle, or it may come from a near-by Roman fort which was discovered in recent times by aerial photography. In the seventeenth century the village became famous for the manufacture of Highland pistols, when Thomas Cadell established a workshop there around 1646. Local demand declined in the late eighteenth century, as the pistol and dirk no longer formed part of Highland dress and southern and continental markets became more important. Skinning and the manufacture of Highland purses were also carried on in the village. Slaters from Doune were to be found working in the Lowlands in the summer months, returning to their native heath to work at shoe-making and weaving in winter. During the eighteenth century Doune was noted for its large cattle fairs, or trysts, which brought great droves of cattle from many parts of the Highlands, while the relocation of the Parish Church from nearby Kilmadock in 1746 brought further prosperity to the village. The ancient market cross dating from 1620 still stands in the main street, having been restored in 1953.

DOUNE

Visitor Services
B Bk C Ch D G PO PT SA T

Sport and Leisure
Bw Cf Fi HB L PB RC S W

Public Transport
Bus and Coach
The Stirling–Callander–Killin–Crianlarich–Tyndrum bus service passes through the village. The Edinburgh–Stirling–Callander –Fort William coach service stops at Doune Road end (A84) on request.

Accommodation
Hotels
Creity Hall, Stirling Road (A84) 01786 841215
Doune Arms, Stirling Road 01786 841237
Red Lion, Balkerach Street 01786 842066

Caravan Park
Blair Drummond Caravan Club Site, Cuthill Brae, Blair Drummond, off A84 3km S of Doune 01786 841208

Leaving Doune, the 'highway winding west' runs between the gently rising Braes of Doune and the banks of the River Teith. Doune Lodge (R) was once known as Cambus Wallace, from a tradition that Sir William Wallace had a camp about here. This attractive white-walled mansion, which dates from 1805, succeeded Doune Castle as the local seat of the Earls of Moray.

About 2km beyond the hamlet of Buchany, a backward glance reveals the ruins of the once-grand Lanrick Castle on the south bank of the Teith. This much-enlarged mansion was a seat of the Haldanes until the second half of the eighteenth century, when it was acquired by John Murray MacGregor, who was recognised as chief of the MacGregors in 1784 and created a Baronet in 1795. In 1840, Sir Evan John MacGregor sold the estate to William Jardine MP, who had made his fortune in the Far East as co-founder of the trading firm of Jardine Matheson & Co., initially engaged in the opium trade. The estate remained with the Jardines until 1905.

The extensive gravel quarries at Cambusmore (L) are comprised of debris left behind by the advance and retreat of Ice Age glaciers. The last advance, known as the Loch Lomond Re-advance, occurred when the climate deteriorated between 10,000 and 11,000 years ago and reached as far south as Callander, the Lake of Menteith, Drymen and Alexandria.

Approaching Callander, the mansion Cambusmore (L, obscured by woodlands) dates mainly from 1800, although it includes parts of an earlier building. In the early years of the nineteenth century Sir Walter Scott was often a guest of owner John Buchanan. He obtained much information about the Highlands on local excursions and it is said that he wrote part of *The Lady of the Lake* (1810) there. Callander is entered beyond the bridge over the Keltie Water.

CALLANDER

The bustling tourist town of Callander (population c2,800) enjoys a picturesque location on the Highland boundary, with the wooded heights of Callander Craig (273m) providing a dramatic scenic backdrop. The high slopes of shapely Ben Ledi are also usually clearly visible from the town's Main Street. Located on the old Military Road from Stirling to Fort William, Callander stands at an important crossroads where routes from Stirling, Aberfoyle and Glasgow meet. At Kilmahog, a short distance west of the town, scenic routes leading to The Trossachs by way of Lochs Venachar and Achray, and to the central Highlands by the Pass of Leny, also meet.

The oldest part of the town actually lies south of the bridge over the River Teith, at Bridgend. Plans had in fact been made to develop the north side of the river as far back as 1739, but there was a setback when the estates of the Duke of Perth, chief of Clan Drummond and the principal landowner in the district, were forfeited after the 1745 Jacobite Rising. The Duke's lands were administered for some years by the Commissioners for Forfeited Estates and it was they who in 1763 began laying out the present wide Main Street and Ancaster Square, specifically for the settlement of Army pensioners. This constituted a very early example of town planning in Scotland. The Baronetcy of Callander and a portion of its lands were restored to a branch of the Drummond family in 1784.

The village benefited from Scotland's Industrial Revolution, with the rise of linen, cotton and woollen-manufacturing in the latter decades of the eighteenth century. Linen and woollen yarns were spun and by 1798 about a hundred looms were engaged in weaving muslin on the cottage principle at Callander and in the adjoining village of Kilmahog. About a hundred girls also found employment in tambour (embroidery) work. The linen yarn and muslin were bought by Glasgow manufacturers and the woollen yarn by Stirling carpet-makers. While the women and girls worked in the textile industry, their menfolk were mainly employed in agricultural labouring.

Callander's rise to prominence as a tourist centre really commenced with the publication of *The Lady of the Lake* in 1810, which immediately brought a huge influx of visitors to view the beautiful scenery of the nearby Trossachs district which Scott had described. The coming of the railway in 1858 marked another important stage in the development of the village and in 1866 burgh status was achieved. By the 1880s a number of splendid villas had been erected to the east and west of the town, both for residents and well-to-do summer visitors who brought with them their entire households, including servants, for the summer 'season'. A large Hydropathic Hotel, a typical feature of Victorian 'health' resorts, was built south of the river and lasted until the Second World War.

Approaching Callander from Stirling by the A84, the town is entered beyond the crossing of the Keltie Water. The Keltie Bridge Caravan Park (R) (tent pitches) and Gart Caravan Park (L) are located near the road. Note (R) the attractive group of Veteran's Cottages, in Scots baronial style, built by subscription in 1927 by the Scottish Veterans' Garden City Association for soldiers, mainly from Perthshire, who had been disabled in the Great War. When built, they had several acres of ground attached to enable the occupants to engage in market-gardening, poultry-farming, etc. A war memorial to those who gave their lives in the two World Wars stands by the roadside.

The entrance to the Roman Camp Hotel is on the left. This unique country house, the oldest part of which dates from 1625, was built as a shooting-lodge for the Duke of Perth and is idyllically set in 20 acres of gardens beside the River Teith. The name is derived from an adjacent mound near the river, long considered to be a Roman camp, but in reality a glacial deposit left behind by an Ice Age glacier. Access to the Roman Camp can be obtained from Main Street, by a path just beyond the hotel entrance. A pleasant walk along the top of this long mound and then by the banks of the Teith affords views of Callander Craig and Ben Ledi.

Bracklinn Road, opposite the hotel entrance, leads to Callander Golf Course and some splendid walks (all signposted), including the circuit of the golf course; Bracklinn Falls; Callander Craig and Woods (Walk 15); walks in Cambusmore Estate; and the long-distance hill-walk to Comrie. Also in Bracklinn Road is Arden House (L), now a guest house, which achieved universal fame in the 1960s as the fictional home of Doctors Cameron and Finlay in the television series *Doctor Finlay's Casebook*. Callander featured as the town of 'Tannochbrae' in the series, which was originally based on A.J. Cronin's semi-autobiographical *Adventures in Two Worlds*. (See also the entry for Cardross in Route 3.)

Ancaster Square, named for the Earl of Ancaster, has been compared to the 'place' in a small French provincial town, with its large open space and the back alleyways leading off it. The date, 1773, and initials of the first residents appear above No.1 The Square. The impressive St Kessog's Parish Church, now the Rob Roy and Trossachs Visitor Centre, was designed by Robert Baldie and built in 1883 on the site of an earlier church of 1733. It became famous through appearing in the title shots of *Doctor Finlay's Casebook* and was used as a church until 1985. The Visitor Centre provides Tourist Information and has a souvenir shop, audio-visual presentation and toilet facilities. (01877 330342, March–December and weekends only January–February.)

Towards the western end of Main Street, the car and coach park in Station Road (R) (T) occupies the site of Callander railway station, which closed in 1965. It was from there that four-in-hand coaches, laden with happy tourists and with their drivers resplendent in scarlet coats with bright shining buttons and white beaver top-hats, once departed for The Trossachs.

The Dreadnought Hotel in Station Road was built by a chief of Clan MacNab in 1820, replacing the old Callander Inn of 1802

Arden House at Callander featured in the long-running TV series *Doctor Finlay's Casebook* (© Robert D. Campbell)

which stood opposite. The MacNab crest, the bearded head of a chief of Clan MacNeish (which recalls a bloody incident in the Loch Earn district), can be seen above the Leny Road entrance, together with the MacNab motto in Gaelic, which means 'Dread Nought'. Many famous people stayed at the old Callander Inn, including Keats, Ruskin, Southey and William and Dorothy Wordsworth. Today, the town offers a wide range of hotel, guest house, self-catering, caravan and camping accommodation, as well as restaurants, tea rooms and bars.

Tom-na-Kessaig, 'the hill of St Kessog', a grassy mound near the riverside car park, was the site of the original pre-Reformation church and overlooks the old graveyard. This is probably the most historic site in the town, for it is said that St Kessog, a sixth-century missionary who brought Christianity to the district (and who was also active on Loch Lomondside) preached there. A market or fair of St Kessog was held annually in March until as late as the early part of the twentieth century. The watchtower and most of the stones in the graveyard date from the eighteenth century onwards.

The 'Red bridge' carries the A81 (Aberfoyle) road over the Teith to Bridgend. Built in 1908 of red sandstone to replace a picturesque high-arched bridge dating from 1764, it became world-famous through appearing in the opening titles of the television series *Doctor Finlay's Casebook*. The view from the bridge, over the verdant meadows towards the long southern shoulder of Ben Ledi, is a memorable one.

Abundant supplies of mussels containing fine pearls were once found in the Teith and brought the villagers considerable profits, but they were exhausted long before Scott made the district famous in the early nineteenth century. In any event, the cultivation of tourists, rather than pearls, duly proved to be the more profitable activity. Salmon, sea trout and brown trout now provide good fishing in the river (by permit).

Only a few stones marking the site of Callander Castle lie mouldering among the undergrowth at the end of Manse Lane in Bridgend (1st L). This tower once belonged to the Livingstones, Earls of Linlithgow, whose principal seat was at Callendar, (not Callander) near Falkirk. In 1630 they sold their Callander (Perthshire) estate to the Drummonds, whose descendants, as Earls of Ancaster, still own much land around the town. The castle was mostly dismantled in 1737 and its stones used to build a mill and dam dike. A marriage stone bearing the initials 'AL:EH' and the date '1569' is now built into the entrance to the former, late eighteenth century, St Kessog's manse nearby. In 1645, during the Civil War, a skirmish known as the battle of Callander took place downstream from the castle, when 700 Royalists under the Laird of Inchbraikie defeated 1,200 Campbells under Campbell of Ardkinglas.

Just beyond Manse Lane, the Invertrossachs Road (R) leads to Callander Holiday Park, a caravan park which now occupies the site of the old Hydropathic Hotel. The road continues to the southern shore of Loch Venachar (no vehicular access beyond Invertrossachs Estate's East Lodge) and also gives access to the A821 (Trossachs) road (Walk 16).

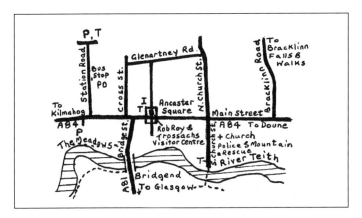

CALLANDER

Visitor Services

B Bk CC Ch D G I MR P PO PS PT SA SC T

Sport and Leisure
A Bw Cf Cy Fi Go L PB Pu RC Ri S SL TC VC W

Public Transport

Bus and Coach
Station Road, opposite Dreadnought Hotel, for buses to Stirling, Killin, Crianlarich and Tyndrum; the Edinburgh–Fort William via Crianlarich coach service and the Trossachs Trundler summer circular service (Callander–Trossachs Pier–Aberfoyle– Port of Menteith–Callander). Most services also call at Ancaster Square. The Edinburgh–Fort William service does not call at Ancaster Square. Post Office, Station Road, for Royal Mail Post Buses to Stronachlachar, Inversnaid, Trossachs Pier, Invertrossachs, Aberfoyle, Killin and Tyndrum.

Accommodation

Hotels
Abbotsford Lodge, Stirling Road 01877 330066
Bridgend House, Bridgend 01877 330130
Coppice, Leny Road 01877 330188
The Crags, 101 Main Street 01877 330257
Dreadnought, Station Road 01877 330184
Highland House, South Church Street 01877 330269
Lubnaig, Leny Feus 01877 330376
Roman Camp, off Main Street 01877 330003
Wolseley Park, Stirling Road 01877 330261

Caravan and Camping Parks
Callander Holiday Park, Invertrossachs Road 01877 330265
Gart Caravan Park, off A84, Callander 01877 330002
Keltie Bridge Caravan Park, off A84, Callander 01877 330811

Tourist Information
Rob Roy and Trossachs Visitor Centre, Ancaster Square 01877 330342 (March to December and weekends only January and February)

CALLANDER–TROSSACHS PIER

Leaving Callander by Leny Road (A84), the start of the Callander–Strathyre Cycling and Walking Path (Walk 17) is signposted and marked (L) by an old railway signal in the 'clear road ahead' position. It follows the track-bed of the old Callander and Oban Railway, which was opened in stages through to Oban in 1870–80 and closed between Dunblane and Crianlarich in 1965. The path also provides access to Little Leny, the ancient, walled burial-ground of the Nories and their successors, the Buchanans of Leny. It stands beside 'the meeting of the waters', at the junction of the rivers Garbh Uisge and Eas Gobhain.

Leny House, erected in 1846 to a Scots baronial design by David Bryce, stands on the hillside near the site of the old Castle of Leny, the ancient seat of the Buchanans of Leny, whose site is marked by a clump of trees near the road. It is said that the old castle was burned down in the sixteenth century, when the chief of the Buchanans of Leny was about to lead his clan to join the army of James IV at the disastrous Battle of Flodden in 1513. His wife had a premonition of disaster and in desperation locked her husband in his room. In trying to escape, he set fire to the door, but the flames spread and engulfed the building. A new castle was then built on the site of the present house.

The hamlet of Kilmahog is soon reached, where the Trossachs and Kilmahog Woollen Mills (R) both have a shop and a cafe. When James Hogg, 'the Ettrick shepherd', passed through Kilmahog on a walking tour in 1803 he wrote to Scott describing it as 'a paltry village. You may guess that I was glad at getting past this village, for its name signifies the burial place of Hogg.' Hogg was mistaken, however, for the name is said to mean, 'church of St Hog or Chug'.

According to tradition, the saint had a cell by the riverside here, which attracted pilgrims from near and far. At a later period, St Chug's Chapel (the foundations of which can still be seen) stood in the little burial ground (L) by the road junction. Kilmahog became a busy little community of corn, timber and woollen-millers and one of the mill-wheels is still preserved at the Kilmahog Woollen Mill. In those days the village was a typical Highland clachan, with houses built mainly of turf and the smoke from the hearth rising through a hole in the roof. Ferns pulled out by the roots were used for thatching roofs and lasted for many years. Today's modern hamlet is much less picturesque.

Taking the A821 (L) at Kilmahog for The Trossachs, the river Garbh-Uisge is crossed and Samson's Putting Stone soon appears on the slopes of Bochastle Hill (R). Tradition avers that Samson once tried to 'putt' the stone from the top of Ben Lawers to the top of Ben Ledi. On landing, it caused the depression which can still be seen near Ben Ledi's summit and then rolled down the mountain-side to rest here. It is more likely to be an 'erratic' boulder deposited by an Ice Age glacier.

The prominent hillock to the west, the Dun of Bochastle or Dunmore, is crowned by an early fortification which probably dates from the Iron Age. The fort's native occupants may well have looked down upon the nearby Roman fort of Bochastle, one of a series of forts built along the Highland edge by Agricola, the Roman Governor of Britain, around 83AD. These advance outposts were strategically placed to control egress by the mountain tribes, in this case by the Pass of Leny or by way of Loch Venachar. Some of the fort's earthworks can be discerned between the Strathyre cycle path and the river Garbh-Uisge. Scott's vivid imagination pictured:

'On Bochastle the mouldering lines,
Where Rome the Empress of the World,
of yore her eagle wings unfurled.'

Loch Venachar (possibly 'the pointed loch') soon appears. Venachar, which has a more open, Lowland aspect than its mountain-girt neighbours to the west, is about 6km long, up to a kilometre wide and has a maximum depth of about 34m. A road (L) leads to the loch's southern shore and the headquarters of the Loch Venachar Sailing Club's flotilla of sailing boats, which often add interest to the scene. The picturesque old Gartchonzie Bridge, over the Eas Gobhain on this road, which often featured in the television series *Doctor Finlay's Casebook*, was built by the Government out of the proceeds of estates forfeited after the 1745 Jacobite Rising. It bears an inscribed stone, which reads, 'This Building Erected AD1777. His Majesty Gave In Aid to It Out of The Annexed Estates.' There is no through road beyond Invertrossachs East Lodge (P), except for authorised traffic, pedestrians and cyclists (Walk 16).

When Loch Katrine was harnessed to supply water to the city of Glasgow in the late 1850s, a masonry dam was built across the eastern outflow of Loch Venachar in order to provide compensation water to the River Teith. Alas, the dam destroyed Coilantogle ford, the point where Roderick Dhu, chief of Clan Alpine, engaged James Fitz-James (the King of Scots in disguise) in mortal combat in Scott's *The Lady of the Lake*:

'They tug, they strain, down, down they go,
The Gael above, Fitz-James below.'

The loch's southern shore has been transformed since the last war by extensive conifer plantations on the Menteith Hills. An earlier landowner is said to have arranged his plantations there in accordance with the disposition of troops at the Battle of Waterloo.

Towards the western end of the loch, Invertrossachs House can be glimpsed nestling among the forests. It was in the old house, built around 1842 for a Mrs Eastmont and destroyed by fire in 1910, that Queen Victoria, Princesses Louise and Beatrice and other members of the royal family, stayed for ten happy days in September 1869. The royal party made several excursions from there, to The Trossachs, Loch Katrine, Loch Lomond, the Lake of Menteith and to Rob Roy's grave at Balquhidder. The present house was built in 1914–15.

Milton of Callander Farm (R) was the home of Mrs Burnett Smith for some years during the First World War. At that time she was better known by her pen name, as the popular 'kailyard' novelist and serial-writer Annie S. Swan (1859–1943). Approaching the wood here, there should really be a road sign warning motorists to beware of the water kelpie, an evil water spirit that was long believed to haunt the loch's waters. Scott relates how a funeral procession with all its attendants was once destroyed by this malignant demon about here, hence the name of the wood Coille-Bhroin, 'wood of lamentation'.

Ben Venue (727m), 'the little ben' (compared with Ben Ledi), now fills the western skyline ahead. Lanrick Mead (L), a flat meadowland surrounded by wooded knolls at the western end of Loch Venachar, was (with Loch Arklet) one of the muster places of the Clan Dougal Ciar branch of Clan Alpine or MacGregor. Much of the meadow was lost forever when the level of the loch was raised.

Lendrick Lodge (R) was once a shooting-lodge belonging to the Earl of Moray, which was later used as a Youth Hostel for some years. James Stewart, Earl of Moray, was appointed Hereditary Keeper of the Royal deer forest in nearby Glen Finglas back in the early seventeenth century. This was certainly no sinecure, for the records show that he had a particularly hard task in preventing poaching by the local populace. The Earls of Moray later acquired the forest for their own use.

BRIG O' TURK AND THE TROSSACHS

An exquisite view of Ben Venue and The Trossachs region, with lovely Loch Achray in the foreground, soon unfolds as the road reaches its summit, before entering the pretty village of Brig o' Turk (population with Trossachs, c100). This was the 'Duncraggan' of Scott's *The Lady of the Lake*, where 'Duncraggan's huts peeped like moss-grown rocks half-seen'. The Oriental-sounding name actually comes from the Gaelic 'torc', a wild boar, for tradition holds that one of the Buchanans of Leny hunted and killed a wild boar here that had been ravaging the countryside.

The village, which was once a favourite resort of artists, featured in a famous scandal. In July 1853 the famous artist John Everett Millais arrived with his friend, the critic John Ruskin, and Ruskin's wife Effie. The group stayed for four months, while Millais sketched and painted, his works including a famous portrait of Ruskin standing by a waterfall in Glen Finglas. They stayed initially at the Trossachs New Hotel (burnt down in 1864) and then moved into lodgings in a nearby cottage. The group appeared to be happy enough, but all was not as it seemed, for Millais and Effie had fallen in love. Her marriage to Ruskin was dissolved by decree in the following year and she wed Millais in 1855.

Not long after this episode, Horatio McCulloch, the renowned Scottish landscape artist, made his base in the village during 1859 and 1863 while he completed several large landscapes. Later in the century, this was one of the first haunts where the group of artists known as 'the Glasgow Boys' gathered for a summer's painting, their work concentrating more on the intimate details of the surroundings rather than portraying vast landscapes. James Guthrie's *A Highland Funeral* (now in Glasgow Art Gallery), based on a funeral they attended here in 1882, established the group's reputation.

The 200-year-old Brig o' Turk (1797), successor to an earlier structure which featured in the chase in *The Lady of the Lake*, is crossed just beyond the village:

'Few were the stragglers following far
That reached the lake of Vennachar;
And when the Brig o' Turk was won,
The headmost horseman rode alone.'

BRIG O' TURK AND THE TROSSACHS

Visitor Services
B Ch Cr P PO PT SA SC T

Sport and Leisure
Cy Fi FP PB RC SB VC W

Public Transport
Bus and Coach
The Trossachs Trundler summer circular service and the Callander–Trossachs Pier and Callander–Aberfoyle Royal Mail Post Buses pass through Brig o' Turk.

Accommodation
Hotels
Loch Achray, off A821 01877 376229

Self-catering
Tigh Mor Trossachs (time-share), A821, Loch Achray 01638
660066

Approaching Loch Achray (possibly 'loch of the level field'),
another beautiful prospect opens up, over the loch to Ben
Venue. This pretty little loch, about 2km long and under half a
kilometre wide, was vividly described thus by Scott:

'The copsewood grey
That waved and wept on Loch Achray
And mingled with the pine trees blue
On the bold cliffs of Ben Venue.'

The authors of an 1890 guide book enthused, 'We believe it is felt
and acknowledged by every visitor to Loch Achray, that to raise
one's voice above a whisper is a profanation.' Now, alas, the peace
of this pretty spot is often shattered by the inevitable power-boat.

Blair House (R) is a former mansion, later converted to an
Eventide Home, which featured in the original *Doctor Finlay's
Casebook* television series as Tannochbrae Cottage Hospital. Just
beyond, Trossachs Church, or St Kessog's Kirk (L), a Gothic
chapel designed by G.P. Kennedy in 1849, occupies a scenic site
near the loch shore. St Kessog brought Christianity to the
district as far back as the sixth century, even before St Columba
had set foot on Iona. Apart from featuring in countless tourist
photographs, the little church also featured in a wedding scene
in the 1953 Walt Disney film *Rob Roy* (which owed little to fact).
The film was mainly shot on location near-by, in the hills above
Loch Ard, with men of the Argyll and Sutherland Highlanders
staging the battle scenes between opposing forces.

The Tigh Mor Trossachs (R), a time-share holiday centre, was
formerly the Trossachs Hotel. This grand edifice, featuring
fairytale towers known as 'candlesnuffers', was designed by the
aforementioned G.P. Kennedy in 1852 for the grandly named
landowner Lord Willoughby d'Eresby, a member of the Ancaster
family. The hotel offered its upmarket guests a tennis court, post

and telegraph office, and a flotilla of boats for use on Loch Achray, where residents enjoyed free fishing. The four-in-hand tourist coaches bound for The Trossachs also stopped there for lunch and in the 1890s Robert Blair, the hotel proprietor, kept about a hundred fine horses at the hotel stables for hauling them. The American writer Nathaniel Hawthorne, who arrived in July 1857, was but one of the many famous people who stayed there while visiting The Trossachs.

The Wordsworths visited Loch Achray twice in 1803, but did not stay. In those early days, there was only a farm and some cottages here, which rejoiced in the name Ardcheanochrochan. When, in 1810, the first rush of visitors came, following publication of Scott's *The Lady of the Lake*, James Stewart, the astonished farmer, first converted his dwelling into a public house and then an inn.

Serious overcrowding, poor fare and Stewart's high-handed manner brought bitter complaints. Thomas Carlyle, who passed through in 1817, recalled The Trossachs as being grand and impressive, and Loch Katrine exquisitely so, but the farm-inn he described as a dirty, smoky farm-hut, with no provision in it but bad oatcakes and unacceptable whisky. Lord Cockburn, in his amusing *Circuit Journeys* (as a judge), recalled that the inn could accommodate two dozen people at the very most, but in 1837 he had witnessed a hundred apply for admittance and, 'after horrid altercations, entreaties and efforts, about 50 or 60 were compelled to huddle together all night'. Cockburn, noting that 'they were all of the upper rank', concluded that 'the pigs were as comfortably accommodated'.

Ben A'an (461m) may be ascended by a path which starts opposite the car park (L), some 180m west of the Tigh Mor. Despite its modest height, splendid views are to be had from the summit, ranging over Lochs Katrine and Achray and the entire Trossachs district (Walk 18).

The true heart of The Trossachs is entered beyond the junction with the Duke's Pass road (L). The name 'Trossachs' is, notwithstanding the district's universal fame, of indeterminate origin. The Rev. Patrick Graham, in his *Sketches of Perthshire* (1806), gives the meaning as 'the rough or bristled territory', although some maintain that it comes from the obsolete Gaelic word 'troiseachan', meaning a transverse glen joined by two others. The former derivation seems appropriate, for the road traverses a thickly wooded, rocky gorge, clad in birch trees, heather, bracken and moss and is described thus by Scott:

'Where twined the path, in shadow hid,
Round many a rocky pyramid.'

In *The Lady of the Lake*, it was about here that Fitz-James, having ridden his horse to the death in pursuit of a stag, found himself lost and alone, before finding his way to the island home of the outlawed chief Roderick Dhu, on Loch Katrine. It would have been no easy journey, for Scott recalled that 'Until the present road was made [in Scott's day north of the present one] there was no mode of issuing out of the defile excepting by a sort of ladder composed of the branches and roots of trees'. A picturesque walk to the sluices at the eastern end of Loch Katrine goes off by a water authority road (L), about half way through the gorge.

Emerging from the pass, the mountain-encircled waters of Loch Katrine come into view. The neat little rustic Trossachs Steamer Pier stands in a sheltered bay by the car and coach park. Facilities here include a spacious tea room in a Victorian stone-built building, a gift shop, toilets, cycle and boat hire and a Visitor Centre for interpreting local and natural history and technical aspects of Glasgow's water supply.

The public motor road ends here and unauthorised vehicles are not allowed on the scenic road that continues along the loch shore to Glen Gyle and Stronachlachar. Visitors may walk or cycle, but care must be taken, as the road is narrow, winding and steep, and operational vehicular traffic may be encountered.

Loch Katrine is some 14km long, up to 1.5km wide and has a maximum depth of 152m. Its surface level has been raised on three occasions, in 1859, 1895 and 1919, by a total of 4.26m, for the purpose of supplying water to the city of Glasgow. Twin aqueducts convey the water from intakes at Royal Cottage, on the loch's southern shore, to reservoirs at Milngavie, some 42km distant. In 1920 Glasgow Corporation purchased all the land in the catchment areas of Lochs Katrine and Arklet in order to protect the water supply, while affording reasonable public access for walking and cycling. The whole undertaking, including the loch steamer, is now managed by the West of Scotland Water Authority.

In the days before Scott's *The Lady of the Lake* was published, only a few hardy tourists, most notably William and Dorothy Wordsworth with their friend Coleridge, managed to reach Loch Katrine. A carriage road existed by the 1780s and the Drummond family, as landowners, had erected two booths on a high rock at the southern end of the loch 'for the accommodation of strangers'. Dorothy Wordsworth (accompanied by her brother William) recalled how 'Coleridge hailed us with a shout of triumph from the door of one of them, exulting in the glory of Scotland'.

The Trossachs became internationally famous upon publication of Scott's romance and tourists converged on the district, bent on viewing the fictional scenes Scott had described. Many artists of the day portrayed these scenes in romantic style, notably the Edinburgh artist John Thomson (1824), Scott's friend and protege; Turner (1831); and the Glasgow landscape painters John Knox (c.1834) and Horatio McCulloch (1866). On the other hand, the Rev. Patrick Graham observed that the native Highlanders perceived no beauty in such scenery and frequently expressed their surprise at the crowds of admiring strangers who arrived every summer.

Accommodation and transport in the district could scarcely cope with the demand for some years. Before the first steamer was placed on the loch in 1843, a large rowing boat called *Waterwitch*, manned by eight stalwart Highlanders, conveyed tourists up and down the loch. The pioneer steamer, the *Gypsy*, disappeared under mysterious circumstances one dark night, and it is said that she was scuttled by the crew of the rowing boat, who feared that she would deprive them of their livelihood. Their enterprising vandalism was to no avail, for the steamer was soon replaced by another, the aptly-named *Rob Roy*.

The development of railway and steamboat services in the 1840s and '50s heralded the era of tourism for the masses. In 1847 the pioneer travel agent Thomas Cook conducted his first tour through The Trossachs, Loch Katrine and Loch Lomond, and in 1859 the famous No.1 Circular Tour, by rail, road and steamer from Glasgow and Edinburgh commenced, which endured for almost a century and a quarter.

The Cruise on Loch Katrine

The Cruise on Loch Katrine is an essential highlight of a visit to the district and should not be missed. The yacht-like steamer, SS *Sir Walter Scott* (built 1900), operates daily from the beginning of April to late October. Only the morning cruise calls at Stronachlachar, except on Saturdays. (01877 376315/6 and ask for 'Steamer Enquiries', or timetable from Tourist Information Centres.) The Trossachs Trundler vintage bus provides a daily connecting service from Callander and Aberfoyle from Easter until the end of September. (Timetable from Tourist Information Centres.)

The main points of interest on the cruise are as follows:

Glen Finglas Intake (R). Water from Glen Finglas Reservoir,

completed in 1965, reaches the loch here by a 3.5km-long tunnel which pierces the mountains.

Am Prison, or The Prison (R) is a small peninsula where the MacGregors kept their stolen cattle under guard, until they could be distributed.

Coire nan Uiruisgean, or 'Hollow of the uruisgs or goblins' (L) was a legendary haunt of the uruisgs (wild men of the hills possessing supernatural powers), who were once feared in the Highlands. This was the setting for Scott's *Goblin's Cave*. On the slopes of Ben Venue above is the Bealach nam Bo, 'pass of the cattle', through which the MacGregor caterans drove herds they had 'lifted' from Lowland farms. At a later period, droves of Highland black cattle were herded in the reverse direction, to the cattle trysts at Doune, Crieff and Falkirk.

Ellen's Isle, formerly Eileen Molach, 'shaggy island', was the haunt of the MacGregor caterans who held 'lifted' cattle there. The island may well have been the 'Ilanvernack', referred to in the Register of the Scottish Privy Council, which a party of soldiers was sent to besiege in February 1611. The MacGregors had fortified the island, 'with men, victual, powder, bullets and other warlike furniture'. Accounts differ as to the outcome of the expedition, one stating that the MacGregors decamped before the soldiers arrived, another attributing the failure of the besieging expedition to a violent snowstorm.

The island was also a place of refuge for women and children when there was danger of attack. One of Cromwell's soldiers once swam to the island to bring back a boat, so that his party could raid the island in retribution for a comrade's death in an ambush. No sooner had he landed than a woman named Helen Stewart sprang forward, produced a dagger, and decapitated him with a single blow. The soldiers prudently decided to desist. It is said that the heroine Helen suggested to Scott a name for *The Lady of the Lake*, hence Ellen Douglas and the present name by which the island is known.

In Scott's romance the isle was the location for Roderick Dhu's 'rustic hall' and so, in the early part of the nineteenth century, the Earl of Ancaster, as landowner, erected a suitably rustic building containing trophies of the chase and old armour. Sad to relate, it was abused by early vandals and destroyed by fire in 1837. The mountain above the island is Ben A'an.

The Silver Strand (R), behind Ellen's Isle, was once a beach of fine sand, made famous by *The Lady of the Lake*. Unfortunately, it was covered by the last raising of the loch level.

Brenachoile Lodge (R) is a former hunting lodge. It has been said that Dr Archibald Cameron, brother of Cameron of Locheil, was captured at Brenachoile by Redcoat soldiers in 1753 while plotting another Jacobite rising, taken to the Tower of London and hanged at Tyburn. However, evidence points to Glen Buckie, near Balquhidder, as being the actual scene of his capture. Iron-slag from a 'bloomery', or small foundry, was found near Brenachoile in 1895, one of several such sites around the loch. Records show that an iron industry flourished in The Trossachs from the mid-fifteenth to sixteenth centuries.

The loch, which occupies a typical glacier-carved trench, reaches its maximum depth of over 152m off Brenachoile. The broad valley in which it lies is known as Strath Gartney.

Jonathan's Island, near the farm of Glasahoile (L), was submerged when the loch was raised in 1859. Passengers on the rowing boat *Waterwitch* landed here to enjoy a drink of Jonathan's 'goat's milk' which, unknown to the excisemen, was really illicitly distilled whisky. The Glasahoile Burn tumbles down from the Tinker's Loch, in which the legendary water-bull was said to dwell.

Lettre, Edra and Strone (R) are sheep farms on the north side of the loch. The Water Authority owns one of the biggest sheep farms in Scotland, covering 27,000 acres and running 8,500 breeding ewes. James Hogg, on a walking tour in 1803, recorded that decaying stumps on the north shore indicated the extensive cutting of timber and noted that sheep were being raised on the cleared areas. As on Loch Lomondside, the oak woods around the loch were cut on a rotational basis, on the 'coppice with standards' principle, and burnt to make charcoal for gunpowder, or stripped of their bark for making leather-tanning agents. 'Standards' were allowed to grow longer, in order to provide timber for building purposes. Reafforestation was undertaken after Glasgow Corporation acquired the land around the loch in 1920.

Ben Lomond's conical peak towers above the western hills (L) approaching Royal Cottage.

Royal Cottage (L) was built for Queen Victoria in 1859, but she only had lunch there! On 14 October 1859 the Queen arrived by steamer to inaugurate the Glasgow Water Supply project, by opening the sluices which controlled the flow of water to the reservoirs at Mugdock and Craigmaddie, near Milngavie. The tunnel air-vents can be seen on top of the hill behind Royal Cottage. The Glasgow bailies once enjoyed the privilege of a fortnight's holiday at Royal Cottage or, even better, Stronachlachar Hotel.

The Arrochar Alps (L) can be unexpectedly glimpsed through a gap in the hills, approaching Stronachlachar.

Loch Arklet Intake (L) receives water diverted from Loch Arklet by an aqueduct.

Factor's Island, or Eilean Dharag (R), is said to be the islet where, in 1716, Rob Roy imprisoned Graham of Killearn, factor to the Duke of Montrose. However, some sources maintain that Eilean Dubh, 'the Black Island', near the western end of the loch, was the factor's prison. This indeed seems likely, since Rob is recorded as having lived at nearby Portnellan at various times.

Stronachlachar and points west to the head of the loch have been described in connection with the MacGregor Country (Route 6).

TROSSACHS PIER–ABERFOYLE

Returning from Trossachs Pier to the road junction at Loch Achray, the scenic Duke's Pass Road (A821) is joined (R). In the days before the railway reached Aberfoyle, only a steep and rugged bridle-track for horses wound across the Menteith Hills from the Aberfoyle inn, where guides and horses could be procured. The present road was built in 1885 by the Duke of Montrose, to enable tourists arriving at Aberfoyle by the newly-opened railway (many of them Americans) to continue on to The Trossachs in four-in-hand coaches. Bicycles were banned after one frightened the coach-horses and caused an accident. A toll was levied and the old toll-houses still stand at Loch Achray and Aberfoyle. The road was only up-graded to motoring standard in 1932.

The Duke's Road, from Aberfoyle to The Trossachs, in 1932 when newly rebuilt as a motor road (R. D. Campbell Collection)

The Loch Achray Hotel (R) is pleasantly situated on the banks of the Achray Water, facing the loch. A path which begins at the rear of the hotel (parking space) provides access to the summit of

Ben Venue, for fine views over the whole of The Trossachs district (Walk 19) and the walk to the sluices at the southern end of Loch Katrine. A large workmen's camp, erected near the hotel when the Duke's Pass road was being improved in the early 1930s, provided enough large huts to build three Youth Hostels in the Trossachs district. Such is progress that there are now none!

As the road ascends, a grand view of the whole Trossachs country unfolds, extending through the valleys of Lochs Katrine, Achray and Venachar, and including, from west to east, Ben Venue, the Glen Gyle hills, Ben A'an, Glen Finglas, Ben Ledi and the distant town of Callander. There is a car park and viewpoint indicator (R), from which Loch Drunkie can also be seen far below. This loch was dammed and raised by 6m in the 1850s, in order to provide compensation water to the River Teith, in connection with Glasgow's water supply from Loch Katrine. However, when Queen Victoria rode up to the loch while staying at nearby Invertrossachs in 1869, she found this 'Drunkie' was almost dry.

The extensive conifer plantations about here, in the Forestry Commission's Loch Achray Forest, form part of the huge Queen Elizabeth Forest Park. In 1931, when the Montrose estates were being sold off to meet death duties, the Forestry Commission purchased some 8,000 acres of land here, stretching from the Menteith Hills to Loch Achray.

The road attains its 243m-high summit at the Duke's Pass. The road network in the Forest Park is normally closed to public traffic, but the 12km-long Achray Forest Drive which goes off here (signposted L), affords superb views across the forests to The Trossachs. This circular route, which rejoins the Duke's Pass road near Loch Achray, enables visitors to picnic deep in the forest; fish beside Lochan Reoidhte ('Roach'), Loch Drunkie or Loch Achray; walk beside Loch Drunkie, or even glimpse a deer. The drive was opened in 1977 to mark the Silver Jubilee of Queen Elizabeth II. A one-way system operates for cars, but look out for on-coming cyclists. There is a modest charge per car. (Fishing permits available from the Queen Elizabeth Forest Park Visitor Centre, Aberfoyle.)

Extensive slate quarries on the slopes of Craig Innich (reached on foot by a track (R)) were worked from as far back as the mid-eighteenth century, although they were only fully developed after the railway reached Aberfoyle in 1882. By the First World War about four million slates were being produced annually and despatched to the railway station by means of a horse tramway and a self-acting incline which descended about 150m on a gradient as steep as 1 in 3, making it one of the steepest in Scotland. The quarry workers lived on site in a rough and ready sort of village.

As the road begins its winding descent from the Highlands to the Lowlands at Aberfoyle, the Queen Elizabeth Forest Park Visitor Centre at David Marshall Lodge is off to the left. Opened in 1960, the lodge was funded by the Carnegie UK Trust, of which David Marshall was Chairman from 1950–8. Facilities include a cafeteria; toilets; audio-visual show about the local wildlife; way-marked trails; picnic-places; cycleway and pony trails. The Highland Boundary Fault passes through here and the Fault Trail (Walk 14, leaflet from Visitor Centre) explains the geology of the area. The breathtaking views over the Menteith district from the Visitor Centre range from the Menteith Hills, over the huge Loch Ard Forest, to the great flat expanse of Flanders Moss and the wide valley of the Forth. On the southern horizon, the flat-topped Fintry Hills and Campsie Fells are the out-pourings of old volcanoes. Away to the east, Stirling's castle-crag, an old volcanic vent, rises dramatically from the plain. (Access to Park all year. Visitor Centre open Easter to mid-October, 10a.m.–6p.m. and mid-October until Christmas, noon–4 p.m., weather permitting. 01877 382258.)

ABERFOYLE–CALLANDER

Aberfoyle, a bustling tourist centre in the summer months, has already been described in connection with the MacGregor Country (Route 6). Go left here on A821 for the return to Callander, or for Stirling, Glasgow, or Loch Lomondside. Go right on B829 for Loch Ard and Inversnaid on Loch Lomond. Taking the A821, go left on A81 at Braeval, some 2km south of Aberfoyle, for Callander or Stirling. Keep straight ahead on A81 for Glasgow, or for Loch Lomondside via the A811 from the Ballat junction.

Taking the A81 for Callander or Stirling, the Aberfoyle Golf Course is soon passed (L). About a kilometre on, a car park (L) caters for walkers and cyclists in the Queen Elizabeth Forest Park (Walk 16).

The Lake of Menteith soon comes into view (R). Although this pretty reed and waterlily-fringed lake is often claimed to be 'Scotland's only lake', there are in fact a few other minor ones. The lake, which lies only 17m above sea-level, is some 2.5km long and about 1.5km wide, so that its maximum depth of about 22m actually extends below sea-level. Its waters are home to many kinds of birds, including geese, herons, swans and great-crested grebes, as well as providing good fishing for rainbow and brown trout (by permit). Curling matches are held when severe winters make the ice thick enough, and in 1979 the Grand Match between the north and south of Scotland was held here. The loch may look placid enough at most seasons of the year, but it resembles Loch Lomond in that it can be rough and treacherous, particularly when strong westerlies are blowing. There have been several drowning accidents over the years.

The tree-clad islands of Inchmahome (Isle of St Colman or Colmoc), the smaller Inch Talla ('Castle Island') and Inch Cuan ('Dog Island') add interest to the scene. It may seem paradoxical that the loch is called a 'lake', but its three islands are all 'inches' in Scottish style. However, records show that over the years the loch has been called variously – Lake of Inchmahome (in 1485 and 1845); Loch of Inchmahome (1646) and Loch of Monteath (1724). As if to confuse matters further, local folk called it the 'Loch o' Port' in the nineteenth century.

Port of Menteith (R, on B8034) is a tiny hamlet, which owes its name to its having been the landing place for monks who inhabited the island Priory of Inchmahome. In mediaeval times the Port was a larger and more important settlement which was made a Burgh of Barony by James III in 1467. The Lake Hotel dates from 1854, when tourism in the district was on the increase. The hamlet even boasted its own railway station, which was only 6km away, a 1915 guide noting that 'The walk from the station is a very pleasant one'. The adjacent Port of Menteith Parish Church, designed by the Glasgow architect John Honeyman in 1876 to replace an earlier church, has a mausoleum of the Grahams of Gartmore (1817) in the churchyard.

In the summer months a passenger ferry operates between the jetty south of the hotel and Inchmahome, for the Priory of Inchmahome, which is in the care of Historic Scotland. (Ferry operates from the Port, weather permitting, April–September, 9.30 a.m.–6 p.m.; Sun 2 p.m.–6.30 p.m. Closed October –March. Car park at jetty. Descriptive brochure available at office on the island. Historic Scotland 01786 385294.)

In 1238 the Augustinian Priory of Inchmahome was founded by Walter Comyn, the first Comyn Earl of Menteith, and occupied by monks of the Order of St Augustine in connection with the Abbey of Cambuskenneth at Stirling. King Robert the Bruce is known to have visited the Priory on three occasions between 1306 and 1310 and in 1358 Robert, later King Robert

II, also visited. One of his sons, Robert Stewart, became 10th Earl of Menteith upon marriage in 1361.

Inchmahome also holds memories of the ill-fated Mary, Queen of Scots. The four-year-old queen's stay came about in the period following the disastrous Battle of Pinkie in 1547, which caused her guardian, Lord Erskine, to fear that Stirling Castle no longer offered sufficient security. Therefore, Mary and her mother, the Dowager Queen, Mary of Guise, were committed to the safe keeping of the Commendator of Inchmahome. Queen Mary's Garden, a walled enclosure on the south-west side of the island and Queen Mary's Bower, to the west, preserve the memory of her brief visit. In 1548 Mary sailed for France where, in 1558, she married the Dauphin, Francis. Another famous queen, Victoria, visited the lakeside twice in September 1869, while staying at Invertrossachs House.

A number of interesting mediaeval grave-slabs now lie within the Chapter House of the Priory for safe-keeping. Notable among them are a monument to Sir Walter Stewart, the first Stewart Earl of Menteith who died around 1295, and his Countess Mary; Sir John Drummond, in full armour, with sword, spear and shield, who died around 1300; and a legless effigy of a knight in armour. Tradition avers that Sir John Menteith, the betrayer of Wallace, died at his Castle of Rusky near-by and was also buried within the Priory. Various branches of the Graham family are interred here and there are several commemorative plaques and grave-slabs in the Choir. R.B. Cunninghame Graham (1852–1936), the writer, traveller and politician (see Ardoch, near Cardross, in Route 3), lies buried here alongside his wife. The Priory was placed in State care by the 6th Duke of Montrose in 1926.

The mouldering ruins of Inchtalla Castle, the sixteenth/seventeenth-century seat of the Earls of Menteith, stand on the adjacent island of Inch Talla, possibly on the site of an earlier building. The last Earl, whose grandfather had been reduced to the new and lesser Earldom of Airth in 1633 for imprudently claiming that he had a greater right to the throne than Charles I, died without a successor and in poverty in 1694. Nearby Inch Cuan is said to have been the site of the Earls' dog kennels, although it has been suggested that the islet would have been too small for the purpose. A much earlier fortification, a Roman fort built by Agricola's legions around 83AD, was discovered by aerial photography at Malling, on the loch's western shore, in recent years.

PORT OF MENTEITH

Visitor Services
B Ch F PT SA SC

Sport and Leisure
Cy Fi FP HB PB RC SB W

Public Transport
Bus and Coach
A81/B8034 junction for Stirling to Glasgow via Aberfoyle,
Balfron and Strathblane service; the Trossachs Trundler summer
circular service (Callander–Trossachs Pier–Aberfoyle–Callander)
and Aberfoyle–Callander Royal Mail Post Bus service.

Accommodation
Hotel
The Lake, off B8034 01877 385258

Self-Catering
Lochend Chalets, Lochend House, Port of Menteith 01877
385268

Leaving Port of Menteith, the ivy-clad ruins of sixteenth-century
Rednock Tower may be glimpsed (L) about 2km on. Its
successor, the late eighteenth/early nineteenth century mansion
Rednock House, built in more settled times and later greatly
improved by General Graham Stirling, lies to the south. At the
junction here, take A81 (L) for the return to Callander and then
A84 for Stirling.

  Alternatively, take the A873 (R) for Stirling. This goes by way
of the Farm Life Centre at Dunaverig Farm, Ruskie (Open daily
10a.m–6p.m. April–October and limited opening until
Christmas; tearoom and gift shop. 01786 850277) and the
village of Thornhill (population c900), founded as a market
centre in 1696 by local laird Archibald Napier of King's
Boquhapple, a great-grandson of John Napier of Merchiston,
the inventor of logarithms. The Mains Farm Caravan and
Camping Site (01786 850605) is just off A873 (R) on B822.

  Continuing along the Callander road, little Loch Ruskie or Rusky
soon appears (R). It was here that the infamous Sir John Menteith
had an island fortress in the late thirteenth century. The road soon
reaches its summit, before descending past Cock Hill (L). Now
extensively forested, the hill was once the scene of an annual fair,

held in May, which was one of the largest sheep and cattle markets in central Scotland in the days before the railways came.

Sheep and cattle were driven here through the northern passes and from the south by the Carse of Stirling and the Vale of Menteith. At fair time, the nearby town of Callander was always crowded with Highland drovers, English dealers, shepherds, cattlemen and hosts of collie dogs.

At length the town of Callander is entered by way of Bridgend and the 'Red bridge' over the River Teith. The splendid view north from the bridge, towards the soaring slopes of Ben Ledi, provides a fitting climax to this scenic circuit.

ROUTE 8. BONNIE STRATHYRE
AND FAMED BREADALBANE

Callander to Strathyre and Kingshouse (for Balquhidder and Inverlochlarig) by the A84 and on to Killin (A827) and Crianlarich by the A84/A85

Strathyre and Breadalbane by Public Transport

Bus and Coach
An infrequent bus service links Stirling and Callander with Killin, Crianlarich and Tyndrum. The Edinburgh–Fort William coach service also serves intermediate places between Stirling, Crianlarich and Tyndrum. Royal Mail Post Buses operate between Tyndrum–Crianlarich–Killin–Callander and Killin–Ardeonaig–Callander and return.

The scenic high road north from Callander, by the A84, threads a magical landscape of mountains, lochs and glens, whose beauty and historical associations have long been lauded in song, verse and legend. Entering the Highlands by the sylvan Pass of Leny, the route as far as Kingshouse traverses the district where the Fiery Cross was carried to summon Clan Alpine to arms in Scott's *The Lady of the Lake*. Balquhidder, the village where the famous outlaw hero Rob Roy spent his final years and was laid to rest in the little kirkyard, can be easily reached by a by-road that strikes west from Kingshouse.

In Rob Roy's day, the Balquhidder district could be reached only on horseback or on foot by rough mountain tracks, thus making it a reasonably secure refuge, and visitors from the Lowlands were virtually unknown. All that has changed and the district's magnificent scenery now lies within easy reach of most of central Scotland by good roads. Cyclists and walkers can also reach Strathyre and Balquhidder by the Callander–Strathyre Cycling and Walking Path, which starts from Leny Road (A84) at Callander and follows the track-bed of the old Callander to Oban railway. A quiet country road continues from Strathyre, which runs near the west bank of the River Balvag to Balquhidder (Walk 17).

A fine circular day tour, known as 'The Five Lochs', can also be undertaken by this route, taking in Lochs Lubnaig and Earn en route to Crianlarich, by way of Strathyre, Lochearnhead, Glen Ogle and Glen Dochart in the fair district of Breadalbane – the 'famed Breadalbane' extolled by Scotland's national bard, Robert Burns, in the course of his Highland tour. The tour may be extended to include 'The Six Lochs', by making a short side excursion in Glen Dochart to the pretty village of Killin on Loch Tay. From Crianlarich the way lies south by Glen Falloch, Loch Lomond, Loch Long and the Gare Loch to Glasgow, or the route may be reversed. (See also Routes 1 to 3.)

CALLANDER–STRATHYRE–KINGSHOUSE

Leaving Callander by Leny Road (A84, see also Route 7 for points of interest to Kilmahog), the start of the Callander–Strathyre Cycling and Walking Path (Walk 17) is passed (L). Beyond the village of Kilmahog, the gateway to the Highlands is entered by the wooded Pass of Leny, where there is an abrupt change of scenery. Steep hills now close in on either side, while the nearby Garbh-Uisge, the fittingly named 'rough or rugged river', thunders along its rock-strewn course as it issues from Loch Lubnaig.

The forests about here, now administered by Forest Enterprise, form part of the huge Queen Elizabeth Forest Park. A car park (R), about half way through the pass, affords access to the Leny Wood Circular Walks, a short and a longer walk which afford views of Callander and the Menteith Hills.

These ancient oak woods were once managed by 'coppicing', that is, shoots emerging from the stumps of felled trees were regularly cut for tool-handles, fencing-posts and fuel. Bark was processed to 'tan' animal hides and larger stems converted to charcoal or sawn into planks. Traces of charcoal-making sites and 'bloomeries' (ancient iron-smelters fired by charcoal) can also be seen beside the path.

A footpath on the opposite side of the road (care required when crossing) leads to the Falls of Leny, an awe-inspiring sight following heavy rain, when the foaming waters thunder over a narrow rock ledge into the gorge below. Some 0.5km on, a bridge (L) provides access to the Callander–Strathyre Cycling and Walking Path on the west side of the river; to the path leading to the summit of Ben Ledi (879m, Walk 20), where magnificent views are to be had over much of the southern Highlands and central Scotland; and to the Strathyre Forest Cabins of Forest Enterprise.

Emerging from the pass, the scant ruins of the ancient Chapel of St Bride (L), a burial place of Clan MacKinlay, are contained within a walled enclosure. St Bride, or Bridget, was an Irish female saint who had a cell at Kildare in the sixth century. A descendant of the MacKinlays, William MacKinlay, 25th President of the United States, was assassinated at Buffalo in 1901 and American visitors have sometimes been observed searching the hillside on the opposite side of the river for the MacKinlay's original home. In *The Lady of the Lake*, the bridegroom Norman of Armandave was about to be married at the chapel to Mary of Tombea, when he had to leave his bride and wedding party to carry the Fiery Cross north by Balquhidder and Loch Voil to summon Clan Alpine to arms.

Ardnandave Hill (hence 'Armandave') is the prominent 715m-high hill on Loch Lubnaig's western shore at the point where the loch bends westwards.

The mountain-girt waters of Loch Lubnaig, 'loch of the bend', soon appear (L). Lying some 123m above sea level, the loch is some 6.5km long by about 0.5km wide and has a maximum depth of over 30m. In post-glacial times Lochs Lubnaig, Voil and Doine formed a single sheet of water, but the intervening land has been formed over thousands of years by alluvial deposits.

Queen Victoria must have been particularly impressed by Loch Lubnaig, which she described as 'a very fine, wild, grand-looking loch', for she came this way on three occasions in 1869. The loch's wildness had almost been tamed back in 1846, when the Glasgow Water Co. Ltd. obtained an Act of Parliament to raise the loch's level in order to extract 40 million gallons of water a day. However, the project was abandoned when Glasgow Corporation decided to develop Loch Katrine instead. The southern end of the loch was a hive of industry in the eighteenth and nineteenth centuries, when slates were quarried at Anie and Tombea, settlements which have long since vanished.

About halfway along the loch, at the point where it bends to the west, Ardchullarie Mor, a shooting-lodge built in 1910, stands above the road (R). This white-painted house stands on the site of the farmhouse where James ('Abyssinian') Bruce of Kinnaird (1730–1794) completed his massive, five-volume work *Travels to the Source of the Nile*.

Poor Bruce surely deserved Scotland's 'nae luck' award. His first wife died a few months after they married. Then, upon returning to England from his travels in Africa, Syria, Egypt and Abyssinia, many geographers refused to believe his amazing adventures in search of the source of the Nile. Those who did pointed out that he had reached the source of the tributary Blue Nile – and a Portuguese priest had been there long before him. Returning to Scotland, his second wife also died. Ill-fated to the last, his adventurous life ended rather mundanely when his foot slipped on the steps at Kinnaird House while helping a lady into her carriage: he received a blow to his head, and died soon after.

Ardchullarie features in Scott's *A Legend of Montrose* as the place from which the Earl of Menteith rode forth with Dugald Dalgetty to meet the Highland chiefs assembled at the Castle of Darnlinvarach (Ardvoirlich) above Loch Earn. A fine right-of-way path links Ardchullarie with Edinample on the south side of Loch Earn, by way of Glen Ample.

Ardchullarie Mor, Loch Lubnaig, where
James Bruce wrote *Travels to the Source
of the Nile* (© Robert D. Campbell)

When the Callander–Oban railway was under construction on the loch's western shore in the late 1860s, the engineers experienced much difficulty owing to the nature of the sheer, rocky slopes of Ardnandave Hill which rise straight from the water's edge. In order to carry the line round them, stone causeways had to be built in the loch's waters in certain places and, at one place, gangs of 'navvies' tipped rocks into the water for nine months without any obvious results. Then, in order to warn of falling rocks, several wires had to be stretched along the trackside so that in the event of a rock fall, the wires would be broken, the signals set to danger and approaching trains stopped. The old horse-track also followed the far shore and it was in the vicinity of one of these rocky eminences, known as Craig-na-Coillich, that Rob Roy escaped from his captors and fled up the mist-covered hillside, while being taken prisoner to Stirling by the Duke of Atholl's men in September 1717. It was his third daring escape within a period of six months.

STRATHYRE

Entering the village of Strathyre (population c300), the Immervoulin Caravan and Camping Park is passed (L). In the village's Main Street there is a car park (L); a small Forest Enterprise Visitor Centre (T); hotels and a Post Office/shop.

Old Strathyre, once known as 'Nineveh', on account of its numerous ale-houses, comprised but a small farming township for the accommodation of 'cottars' displaced from the land by sheep farms. In those days, the village was situated on the west side of the River Balvag and it was there that William and Dorothy Wordsworth spent the night in a cottage in 1803, following a tiring 32km hike from Loch Katrine by way of the Balquhidder hills. When Queen Victoria passed through in 1869, she found that the village was still 'composed of a row of a few peasants' houses, with very poor people and a nice, well-built little inn'. However, the coming of the railway in 1870 promoted the construction of several houses and villas on the east side of the river, for letting to affluent summer visitors. The railway also consigned to history the droves of Highland black cattle that had passed through the village bound for the cattle trysts at Doune, Falkirk and Cock Hill Fair near Callander.

The Dugald Buchanan Monument (L), in the form of a drinking fountain, was erected at the entrance to the former railway station in 1883 to perpetuate the memory of this revered Gaelic poet, teacher and evangelist (1716–1768). Verses from his writings in Gaelic and English are inscribed on the stone panels. Buchanan was born at Ardoch Mill on the opposite side of the river and was buried at Little Leny, near Callander, after having died of the plague. Yet another 'fountain' monument which stood on the station platform, a graceful heron standing on a base of Cruachan granite, was awarded for being the 'Best Kept Station' on the line in the 1890s. When the station closed in 1965 the heron made a short flight across the road to the garden of the house 'Dunellan'.

Land use around Strathyre would appear to have come full circle over the centuries. In 1802 Alexander Campbell noted that, 'Although the hills on either side appear almost naked, yet it is believed that the higher, and particularly the lower grounds, were covered with wood; as in the mosses, there have been found trunks and fragments of oak, alder and birch'. By 1802 the numerous multiple-tenancy farms in the district, each supporting several families, producing subsistence crops and grazing a few sheep and cattle to pay the rent, had given way over the past half century to a few farms, each occupied by a sole tenant, grazing sheep and cattle. This had brought about large-scale depopulation in the district, as the excess population drifted away to the Lowlands or to the American colonies. Another great change occurred from the 1930s, when the dense conifer forests of larch, spruce and native Scots pine that now clothe the hills replaced the old grazings, so that forestry rather than farming became the predominant activity in the district.

  Some pleasant walks are to be had in the hills and forests around Strathyre, including way-marked Forest Enterprise trails, which start from the car park and the Forest Enterprise Visitor Centre at the southern end of the village and lead to a circular walk in the forests on the west side of the River Balvag and to the fairy-haunted summit of 572m-high Beinn-an-t-Sidhein ('Ben Shean'), 'the mountain of the fairies' (Walk 22). The lovely V-shaped, ice-carved vale of Strathyre, whose beauty is extolled in the old Scots song 'Bonnie Strathyre', may be admired from the Ben's summit.

Strathyre and Beinn-an-t-Sidhein, before conifer forests were planted around the village in the 1930s (R. D. Campbell Collection)

STRATHYRE

Visitor Services
B CC P PO PT SA SC T

Sport and Leisure
Cy Fi FP PB RC S SB VC W

Public Transport

Bus and Coach

Post Office/Ben Sheann Hotel for Stirling–Callander–Killin–Crianlarich–Tyndrum bus service and the Edinburgh–Fort William via Crianlarich coach service. Post Office for the Tyndrum–Crianlarich–Killin–Callander and Killin–Ardeonaig–Callander and return Royal Mail Post Buses.

Accommodation

Hotels

Ardoch Lodge, off A84 01877 384666
Ben Sheann, Main Street 01877 384609
Creagan House, Strathyre 01877 384638
The Inn, Main Street 01877 384224

Self-Catering

Forest Enterprise Strathyre Forest Cabins, off A84 on W side Loch Lubnaig, contact Forest Holidays 0131 334 0066

Caravan and Camping Park

Immervoulin Caravan and Camping Park, off A84, Strathyre 01877 384285

The flood plain of the winding River Balvag is followed through the Strathyre Forest to Kingshouse, where the junction for Balquhidder and Inverlochlarig is opposite the Kingshouse Hotel (R). The hotel, which also has a craft shop, gallery, tea room and information centre, was originally built as a drover's inn as far back as 1747. At that time the Military Road from Stirling to Fort William (completed in 1750) was under construction and a large government store was erected here, hence the hotel's name.

KINGSHOUSE—BALQUHIDDER—INVERLOCHLARIG

Taking the Balquhidder road, the route followed by Norman as he bore the fiery cross westward to summon Clan Alpine to arms in *The Lady of the Lake*, the Rob Roy country is entered by the beautiful valley of the River Balvag, lying in the shadow of the bonnie Braes of Balquhidder, which were extolled by the Paisley weaver-poet Robert Tannahill (1766–1810) in his song of that name:

'Let us go, lassie, go to the braes of Balquhidder,
Where the blaeberries grow 'mang the Highland heather,
Where the deer and the roe lightly bounding together
Sport the lang simmer day on the braes of Balquhidder.'

Some 1.5km from Kingshouse and hidden away in a woodland
setting, the MacGregor Mausoleum (L), built in 1830, is the last
resting-place of Sir John Murray MacGregor of Lanrick, the first
chief of Clan MacGregor to use the clan's name after its
restoration in 1774. Before then, MacGregors in the Balquhidder district had been using the name Murray, as they
resided on the Duke of Atholl's lands. Sir John, a distinguished
Gaelic scholar, was a Colonel in the Army and raised a regiment
called the Clan Alpins which was commanded by his brother,
Colonel Alexander Murray MacGregor, who also lies buried
there.

KIRKTON OF BALQUHIDDER
The Kirkton of Balquhidder (population c200), nestling close
by the eastern end of Loch Voil, is soon entered. Today
Balquhidder cannot boast of a single shop, but in the centuries
before the 1745 Jacobite Rising, the kirk made it a place of
importance and a focal centre for what was then a populous
district.
  The remains of a stone circle below the manse, the nearby
Pudreag Stone and an Iron Age crannog on the loch, all confirm
that the Balquhidder district was inhabited in the pre-historic
era. Roman coins found by Loch Voil suggest that the Roman
legions may also have penetrated this far north, from their fort
at Bochastle. Christianity was introduced to the district in the
eighth or ninth centuries by St Angus, a monk from Dunblane,
who built a stone oratory near the junction of the Balvag and
Kirkton Glen. The house 'Beannachd Aonghais' ('Blessing of
Angus') is said to mark the spot where he first kneeled to bless
the glen.
  MacLarens, MacGregors, Stewarts, Murrays and Fergusons
have all lived in the Balquhidder district at one time or another.
The MacLarens, who acquired their name from Abbot Labhran
of Auchtubhmor, remained predominant until the fourteenth
century. Their gathering-place was the Creag-an-Tuirc ('the
boar's rock'), behind the present Manse (Walk 23).
  The MacGregors, displaced from their lands in Glen Orchy,
Glen Strae and Glen Lyon, settled around Loch Katrine from

1533 and in West Balquhidder from 1542. Rob Roy came here in 1717 and more than 70 years after his death at Inverlochlarig, young Walter Scott, a lawyer's clerk, rode into the glen accompanied by a sergeant and six men from a Highland regiment based in Stirling. Their mission was to sort out a dispute over the property of Invernenty, which was occupied by some MacLarens. On this, Scott's first visit to the district, he was particularly fascinated by the stories about Rob Roy related to him by the Sergeant in charge of the detachment. Some years later, in 1817, Scott's *Rob Roy* was published and achieved immediate success.

The 1745 Jacobite Rising proved disastrous for the parish of Balquhidder, since many of the local clans had supported the ill-fated cause of Prince Charles Edward Stewart. Estates were confiscated, houses burnt, and Highland dress, the carrying of arms and the playing of bagpipes prohibited. The Military Road was built through Strathyre; the old multiple-tenancy farms supporting several families were converted to large sheep farms run by sole tenants and, as the excess population drifted off to America or to the Lowlands, massive depopulation occurred.

In the nineteenth century, Scott's romantic works promoted the development of tourism, particularly following the opening of the railway through Strathyre in 1870. Nevertheless, as late as 1880 Balquhidder was described as, 'consisting chiefly of rude, low-walled thatched cottages'. The twentieth century has witnessed the clothing of the lower hill slopes with conifer plantations, improved road communications and the demise, in 1965, of the railway through Strathyre.

Rob Roy's grave, in a railed-off enclosure near the church car park (R), lies within the site of the first Christian church here, which had been erected around 1250 over the gravestone of St Angus.

In April 1717 the Duke of Montrose captured Rob while he was asleep in a house in Balquhidder and carried him off as a prisoner to Stirling. Then, as the party was crossing the River Forth at the Fords of Frew, Rob threw himself from his horse in mid-stream, floated his plaid to draw fire and escaped. In September that year he was captured yet again, at the house of Monachyle Tuarach, and taken south. At a narrow, rocky part of the track on the shores of Loch Lubnaig, Rob again managed to escape and fled up the hillside. By that time he had become a legendary Robin Hood-like figure throughout the land, owing to his daredevil escapades, impudent pranks and resistance to capture, all the while treating his enemies with forebearance, avoiding bloodshed except where absolutely necessary and taking from the rich to give to the poor.

Rob's final years at Balquhidder were relatively peaceful. His rehabilitation from outlaw to hero had commenced with the publication in 1723 of Daniel Defoe's *Highland Rogue*, which aroused the interest of King George, and he soon became a celebrity. Rob made his peace with Montrose and submitted to the King before his death in 1734 at Inverlochlarig Beag. His death came about following a dispute with one John MacLaren over some land, when a fight was arranged in the field at the east end of Loch Voil, in which it was arranged that young Alisdair Stewart would fight on MacLaren's behalf. Stewart drew first blood and Rob yielded the land to MacLaren. Rob had been wounded in the fray and within the year he was dead.

Beside Rob's grave (centre) are those of his wife Mary (left) and his son Coll (right). Another son, Robin Oig, the black sheep of the family, also lies in Coll's grave. In March 1736 Robin murdered John MacLaren of Invernenty, whom he held responsible for his father's death. MacLaren had also offered to lease Kirkton Farm, where Rob's widow and family resided, and this had further incensed the MacGregor brothers, who perceived the possibility of losing their home if the factor accepted MacLaren's offer. Robin fled the country and fought in France under the Duke of Cumberland.

Rob Roy's grave in the kirkyard at Balquhidder (© Robert D. Campbell)

Returning to Scotland with a pardon, he married the daughter of Graham of Drunkie, but she died three years later. His next adventure was to forcibly abduct Jean Key, a wealthy young widow, from Edinellie Farm near Balfron and marry her at Rowardennan. The lady did not live long. Robin Oig was hunted again and eventually captured in 1757. This time there was to be no escape, for he was taken to Edinburgh for trial and execution. His body was returned to Balquhidder for burial by MacGregor friends.

Rob's eldest son James played an active part in the '45 Rising. With 12 MacGregors, he surprised and burned the barracks at Inversnaid and then fought for Bonnie Prince Charlie at Prestonpans and Culloden with the MacGregor batallion. He suffered imprisonment in Edinburgh Castle for having assisted his brother Robin in the abduction of Jean Key, but he managed to escape and died in poverty in Paris aged 59.

The present Balquhidder Church was built in 1855 to a design by David Bryce, for David Carnegie of Stronvar. The architect designed an almost identical church for Carnegie at Gothenburg in Sweden, where the Carnegies had made their money in brewing and sugar-refining. Interesting artefacts within the church include the St Angus Stone (north wall), which is believed to have lain over the grave of St Angus; a stone font of indeterminate age found when the earlier church was abandoned; and the bell of the old church bearing the date 1684, which was presented by Robert Kirk (author of *The Secret Commonwealth of Elves, Fauns and Fairies*), minister from 1669–1685 before he moved to Aberfoyle (See Route 6). Kirk's first wife, Isabel Campbell, lies buried in the kirkyard at the top of the bank above the west gate.

The ruined church of 1631 which stands near-by, partly on the site of the pre-Reformation church, was built for David Murray, Lord Scone, whose initials appear above the doorway. Robert Kirk was minister of this church and, at a later period, it would also have been well known to Rob Roy and his family. The MacLaren chiefs are commemorated within the church, while the Carnegie family burial place lies to the west.

The pre-Reformation church which stood about here was visited by King James IV on several occasions after 1506. Within its walls in 1589 the chief and clansmen of Clan MacGregor swore before the altar on the decapitated head of Drummond of Earnoch, the King's forester, that they would protect the murderer and share the guilt. This was but one of several incidents that stained the clan's reputation in the eyes of authority and, following the massacre of the Colquhouns at Glen Fruin in 1603, the MacGregor's name and tartan were proscribed; they were hunted down ruthlessly, and a concerted attempt made to eliminate the clan altogether.

Some pleasant walks on the Braes of Balquhidder start from

beside the church, at the information board, west of the church car park (Walk 23).

Many visitors return direct to Kingshouse after the pilgrimage to Rob Roy's grave. Nevertheless, it is worth while continuing westwards to explore the true Rob Roy country and visit the site of the hero's death at Inverlochlarig, thereby tracing the route by which the fiery cross was conveyed to Loch Katrine in *The Lady of the Lake*:

'The signal roused to mortal coil
The sullen margin of Loch Voil,
Waked still Loch Doine, and to the source
Alarm'd Balvaig, thy swampy course.'

Mention of literary associations recalls the fact that the Balquhidder district also features in Robert Louis Stevenson's novels *Kidnapped* and *Catriona*. The splendid scenery has also provided a backdrop for filming on location: films shot here include *Geordie*, starring Bill Travers (1955), *The Thirty Nine Steps*, starring Kenneth More (1960) and the 1960s television series *Doctor Finlay's Casebook*.

A grand view of Loch Voil, 'the loch of the quick or raging flood', with the bonnie Braes of Balquhidder as a backdrop, may be enjoyed from the old humpback bridge over the River Balvag by taking the road on the left just beyond the church. A crannog (a man-made island homestead from the prehistoric era) can sometimes be seen here, depending on the loch level. This by-road also leads to Glen Buckie, for the right-of-way path to Brig o' Turk via Glen Finglas.

Loch Voil, which lies some 126m above sea level, is about 5.5km long, up to 0.5km wide and occupies a 23m-deep glacier-carved trench. Levels remain fairly constant except after heavy snow or rain, when the Balvag's course becomes a flood-plain and Lochs Voil and Doine become one.

A road (R) just beyond the bridge leads to Stronvar House, now a country house hotel. The MacGregors had a tower-house on a nearby islet called Innis Gregor, long before the present house was built. This stronghold, reached by a drawbridge, belonged to the war-like John Dhu MacGregor, 'Black John of the Mail-Coat'. A brother of the MacGregor chief, he was one of the few MacGregors killed at the battle of Glen Fruin in 1603, when the Colquhouns suffered grievously at their hands.

The present house was built for the Stewarts of Glenbuckie in 1825 and named Glen Buckie House. In 1849 the estate was purchased by the aforementioned David Carnegie, who greatly improved and extended the estate, reinstated the ancient name Stronvar, and had the house rebuilt in 1850, to a design by David Bryce. The Carnegies finally disposed of the house and estate in 1952 and Stronvar became a Youth Hostel for some years, before becoming a hotel.

BALQUHIDDER

Visitor Services
B Ch PT SA SC

Sport and Leisure
Cy Fi FP HB PB RC W

Public Transport
Bus and Coach
See Strathyre. All services call at Kingshouse, opposite the hotel, 2.5km away.

Accommodation
Hotels
King's House, on A84 01877 384646
Monachyle Mhor, 3km W of Balquhidder 01877 384622
Stronvar House, Balquhidder 01877 384688

Leaving Balquhidder, the way lies along the northern shore of lovely Loch Voil. About 4km from Balquhidder, Craigruie (R) takes its name from a large stone by the lochside, called Craig-an-Righ, 'the King's rock'. Tradition holds that King Robert the Bruce, when fleeing from his enemies after defeat at the battle of Methven in 1306, kept his pursuers at bay here by wielding his sword to awful effect and it is said that he hid in a cave on the hillside above for a time.

Monachyle Mhor Hotel (R), at the western end of Loch Voil, stands almost opposite Monachyle Tuarach, on the far shore. The old farm which stood there was once occupied by Rob Roy's nephew Donald and it was there, as has been noted, that Rob was captured by the Duke of Atholl's retainers in September 1717.

Loch Doine, 'loch of the black river', a little loch just 1.5km long, lies beyond the head of Loch Voil. William and Dorothy

Wordsworth passed by here in 1803, while completing a marathon day's hike from Loch Katrine to Strathyre. They visited the ancient burial ground of the MacGregors at the head of the loch, which stands as a sad reminder of the days when the glen was home to many more families than it is today. In the years before the old way of life in the Highlands was swept away forever and sheep replaced people in the second half of the eighteenth century, the Braes district to the west of Balquhidder Church supported 50 tenant farmers and their families, with a cottar under every tenant. Yet by 1837, the local minister could count only three tenants and a single cottar. As the road ascends here, there is a glorious prospect backwards towards Ben Vorlich's triangular peak rising above the eastern hills.

A kilometre or so beyond Loch Doine, the Invernenty Burn cascades down through a corrie on the far side of the glen. The farm of Wester Invernenty which stood about there was long tenanted by Rob Roy's cousin Malcolm, who died impoverished. The circumstances surrounding Rob's subsequent dispute with the incoming tenant, John MacLaren, which was to result in the deaths of both men, have already been noted. It was a later dispute over the MacLaren's tenancy of Invernenty that first brought Sir Walter Scott to the district.

The road ends at the car park near Inverlochlarig, which stands in the shadow of Beinn Tulaichean (945m). At this wild and lonely spot, Scotland's most famous outlaw died on 28 December 1734, aged 63. Rob's cousin Malcolm had held the farms of Inverlochlarig and Wester Invernenty for many years, long before he came here with his family around 1717 to spend his final years.

On his death-bed, Rob was visited by MacLaren of Invernenty, the neighbour with whom he had quarrelled, as a gesture of peace. Rob would not be seen helpless in bed and so MacLaren was kept waiting until he had dressed in his Highland garb, complete with dirk and pistol and with his broadsword beside him. He was seated in his chair and then, after the interview, was laid in his bed, exhausted. 'Now,' said he, 'all is over; let the piper play, "Cha teill, cha teill, cha teill mi tuille"' (I'll return, I'll return, I'll return no more). The old outlaw had expired before the dirge was finished.

KINGSHOUSE–KILLIN

Heading north from Kingshouse, the Balquhidder Braes Caravan Park (tentpitches) is passed (R). Edinchip, the seat of the chiefs of Clan MacGregor from 1798 until recent times, stands on the hillside opposite. The present house dates from 1830. The summit of the road here marks the watershed between the catchment areas of two great rivers, the Forth to the south and the Tay to the north.

LOCHEARNHEAD

The road soon descends to Lochearnhead (population c200), pleasantly situated at the western end of beautiful Loch Earn. The village, which owes its origin to the construction of the Military Road from Stirling to Fort William in the mid-eighteenth century, is now Scotland's top watersports centre. Lochearnhead Watersports (01567 830330), which offers water-skiing, canoes, kayaks and sailing dinghies for hire, also has a licensed cafe. Loch Earn Lodges, Lochearnhead Hotel and Clachan Cottage Hotel are all located a short distance along the A85 (Crieff) road (R), (P) (T).

Loch Earn, possibly named 'Ireland's Loch' from the influence of early Irish missionaries, is a typical glacier-carved basin, some 6.5km long, over 1km wide and up to 87m deep. The loch was harnessed at St Fillans in 1957–8 to supply hydro-electric power stations at St Fillans and Dalchonzie, supplemented by water from Loch Lednock Reservoir, which lies in the hills to the north-east.

Looking south from the village, cream-painted Edinample Castle is a prominent feature on the loch's southern shore. It was built in the late sixteenth century by Sir Colin Campbell of Glenorchy, 'the Grey Laird', at a time when the Campbells were consolidating their land holdings and influence throughout the district. There is a crannog in the loch just offshore from the castle. Ben Our and Ben Vorlich (985m) dominate the southern skyline. Ben Vorlich may be ascended from the east gate of Ardvorlich House on the south Loch Earn road. Ardvorlich, long in the possession of the Stewarts of Ardvorlich, was the 'Darnlinvarach' of Scott's *Legend of Montrose.*

LOCHEARNHEAD

Visitor Services
B CC Ch G P PO PS PT SA SC T

Sport and Leisure
Cy Fi HB PB RC S SB W Wa

Public Transport
Bus and Coach
At opposite bus shelter on A85 for Callander–Killin–Crianlarich–Tyndrum bus service and Edinburgh–Callander–Fort William coach service. Post Office, opposite A84/A85 junction, for Tyndrum–Crianlarich–Killin–Callander and Killin–Ardeonaig–Callander Royal Mail Post Buses.

Accommodation
Hotels
Clachan Cottage, on A85 01567 830247
Lochearnhead, on A85 01567 830229
Mansewood Country House, on A85 01567 830213

Self-Catering
Hoseasons Holidays (hotel and chalets) 01502 500500
Loch Earn Lodges, on A85 01567 830211

Caravan and Camping Park
Balquhidder Braes Caravan Park, on A84 3km S of Lochearnhead 01567 830293

Note: There is also accommodation at St Fillans, at the eastern end of Loch Earn.

North of Lochearnhead the A85 is followed. When leaving the village, the Glen Ogle Trail is signposted on either side of the A85, just beyond an old railway bridge abutment. This 6km-long circular walk partly follows the route of the old Military Road of 1750 and the track-bed of the former Callander and Oban Railway. Ascending wild Glen Ogle, the old railway can be seen clinging to the mountainside on the western side of the glen, while the grassy track of the old Military Road can be traced below the present highway. Paragliders can often be spotted soaring above the slopes on the right and you may even be lucky enough to spot one of the region's birds of prey, perhaps a buzzard or peregrine. In fact the glen has a wide range of wildlife, including mink, otters, badgers, foxes, weasels, stoats, rabbits and brown and mountain hares. Red and roe deer may also be seen, particularly in the winter months. When Queen Victoria came this way in 1842 she likened the glen to India's Khyber Pass – which she had never actually visited.

Glen Ogle, looking towards Ben Our and Ben Vorlich
(© Robert D. Campbell)

The 288m-high summit is reached near the pretty little reed-fringed Lochan Lairig Cheile (L) before descending to Lix Toll in Glen Dochart, where the A827 branches off for Killin and Aberfeldy (R). Bovain, a house on the site of the ancient home of the chiefs of Clan MacNab, from at least the early fourteenth century, stands on the far bank of the River Dochart. The wild MacNabs held dominion in Glen Dochart for several centuries, until their power was gradually usurped by the ambitious Campbells of Glenorchy from the sixteenth century.

Robert Burns, Scotland's national bard, penned the classic wayfarer's introduction to this fair district of Breadalbane during a visit to the area in 1787:

'Admiring nature in her wildest grace
These northern scenes with weary feet I trace;
O'er many a winding dale and painful steep,
Th' abodes of covey'd grouse and timid sheep,
My savage journey, curious, I pursue,
Till fam'd Breadalbane opens to my view.'

KILLIN

A short, 7km return excursion from Lix Toll on the A827 leads to Killin (pop. c800), a pretty village situated near the western end of 22km-long Loch Tay at the confluence of the Rivers Dochart and Lochay, and set against a magnificent mountain backdrop formed by the Tarmachan and Ben Lawers ranges.

Killin, the oldest and largest settlement in the district, lies at the heart of Breadalbane, the scenic district which embraces the upper River Tay catchment and extends from Kenmore at the eastern end of Loch Tay, through Glens Lochay and Dochart and westwards by Strath Fillan to the watershed beyond Tyndrum. The geography of the district accounts for its name, which is rendered in Gaelic Braghaid Albain. Alban was the ancient name of Scotland, hence Braghaid Albain, the uplands leading westwards to Druim-Alban, the great dividing range of the country.

Beautifully-fashioned and ornamented stone axes and implements which have been unearthed around Loch Tay from time to time point to Breadalbane having been inhabited from as far back as the Neolithic period of the Stone Age, some 5,000 years ago. Bronze Age peoples who inhabited the district from around 2000BC left cairns, stone circles, cup-marked rocks and boulders, and in 1868 a Killin crofter uncovered a wonderful hoard of bronze weapons and implements. In the succeeding Iron Age, from around 400BC, a Celtic people who had colonised Scotland from the south and could make iron implements, built circular stone forts on hilltops and crannogs in Loch Tay.

The arrival of the Roman legions around 80AD placed on record the first history of the people who inhabited Breadalbane's hill-forts and lake-dwellings, although no significant Roman remains have actually been found in the district. In the mysterious period known as the Dark Ages, which followed the final departure of the Roman legions from Scotland around 410AD, Picts and then (from c500AD) Scots from Ireland overran the Caledonian inhabitants of the region. The Scots had settled initially along the western seaboard in what is now Argyll, but they were a territorially ambitious race and in 843AD they annexed the Pictish kingdom, which lay to the east of Druim-Alban. Early in the eighth century, the Celtic missionary St Fillan arrived from Ireland to spread the gospel in Glen Dochart and the broad strath beyond, which bears his name to this day – Strath Fillan.

The wild Clan MacNab, or Mac-an-Aba, 'children of the Abbot', who trace their descent to the lay Abbots of Glendochart, inhabited Glen Dochart for some 800 years, from at least the latter part of the twelfth century. Their ancient seat was at Bovain in Glen Dochart, but they later built a stronghold at Ellanryne, beside the River Lochay at Killin. When it was burnt down by General Monck's soldiers in 1654 during the Civil War, Kinnell House at Killin became their principal seat.

The MacNabs' power and influence was gradually usurped from the fifteenth century by the territorially ambitious Campbells of Glenorchy. Finally, in 1823, the debt-laden MacNab chief, whose lands were largely mortgaged to the Campbells, emigrated to Canada with many of his clansmen. The remaining MacNab estates were then sold off by his creditors.

The Campbells of Glenorchy did not rest until their fiefdom covered a huge tract of mountainous territory, some 400,000 acres, which extended from Aberfeldy to the Western Isles. A chain of castles was built throughout the district to guard their possessions. As their power increased, the clan chiefs were created Earls of Breadalbane in 1681 and Marquises of Breadalbane in 1831. Their principal seat, originally on the Isle of Loch Tay off Kenmore, was from 1560 at Balloch Castle, Kenmore. In 1801–7 Balloch was demolished and replaced by the magnificent Taymouth Castle.

The MacGregors were another clan who once inhabited the district. Dispossessed of their lands in Argyll by Campbell guile in obtaining legal land charters and resenting the incursion of the Campbells into Breadalbane, they proved a constant thorn in the side for the Campbells of Glenorchy. Alas, their cause was a hopeless one, facing as they did the combined might of the Glenorchy and Argyll Campbells, royal favourites who enjoyed the full backing of the law. Nevertheless, history ordained that it was only the MacGregors who retained their clan seat in the district, at Edinchip on Loch Earnside, until recent times.

As the old clan system was dismantled following the Jacobite Rising of 1745, the people became crofters, tradesmen and later shepherds. In the 1830s and early 1840s, during the time of the 2nd Marquis, widespread depopulation occurred throughout Breadalbane when his factor carried out wholesale eviction of crofters from his estates to make more room for sheep. Many of those evicted emigrated to Canada and the evidence is still to be seen today in the grass-covered ruins of crofter homesteads which litter Glens Lochay and Dochart. The population of Killin parish, which had numbered 2,048 in 1801, had declined to just 1,277 by 1881.

When the branch line from the Oban railway opened in 1886, Killin received a boost as a popular holiday resort and a number of large houses were built for letting in the summer months to wealthy families from the cities. Steamers began sailing on Loch Tay in 1882 and continued until the Second World War. Today, Killin offers a wide range of accommodation, ranging from hotels to bed and breakfast houses, caravan and camping sites and a

The pier at Kenmore. A steamer service operated on Loch Tay from 1882 until the Second World War (R. D. Campbell Collection)

youth hostel, with a good selection of restaurants and cafes.

The spectacularly picturesque entrance to Killin is over a long, narrow bridge erected in 1760, which winds drunkenly over the River Dochart just below the cascading Falls of Dochart. The falls, which are an inspiring spectacle after heavy rain, readily explain the river's Gaelic name – 'Scourer of evil'. Inchbuie, or Innis Buidhe, 'the yellow island', one of three islands in the river at this point and the ancient burial ground of Clan MacNab, lies immediately downstream of the bridge. The key for the burial ground is available from the Tourist Information Centre. When signing for same, it may be observed that MacNabs still come to visit the burial ground from all over the world, notably the United States, Canada, Australia, New Zealand and England, thus proving the adage that, 'Though seas come between us, the heart is Highland'.

Kinnell House, whose main entrance is at the south end of the bridge (private pedestrian access only to the railway walk (Walk 24)), was the seat of the MacNabs from 1654, when their nearby Castle of Ellanryne was burnt down by General Monck during the Civil War. A stone circle dating from the Bronze Age stands in a field to the west of the house, near the road.

The Breadalbane Folklore Centre and Tourist Information Centre, at the north end of the bridge (L) (T), is housed in the old Bridgend Mill by the Falls of Dochart. Built in 1840 as a meal-mill, it later became (along with another mill downstream) a woollen-mill where tweed was woven until 1939. The Folklore Centre offers a fascinating insight into the folklore, clan history and natural history of Breadalbane. St Fillan is said to have founded the meal-mill on this site and to have preached nearby.

Important relics held at the Centre include his healing stones –
used for curing various afflictions. Here you may also learn about
the legendary Celtic war-leader hero Fingal (who is reputedly
buried near-by) and of the remarkable prophecies of the Lady of
Lawers, who lived on Loch Tayside in the seventeenth century.
Parking is available at the Centre only for the disabled. Park some
200m along Main Street (R); at the east end of Main Street beside
the MacLaren Hall (L) or at the end of Station Road (R) (T).
(01567 820254. Open March to October; weekends only
February; closed November to January except between Christmas
and New Year.)

  Heading along Main Street, a short road beside the school (L)
leads to a gate, giving access to a field where a standing stone is
said to mark the last resting place of the Celtic war-leader,
Fingal. Within the adjacent Breadalbane Park, the Killin and
District Recreational Club offers visitors bowling, tennis, five-a-
side football and putting. (Open May–September and by
request at other times.) There is also a children's playpark within
the park. Among other recreational facilities available in Killin,
there are some splendid walks around the village and in the
surrounding hills (Walks 24 and 25), while pony-trekking and
horse-riding are also available. Loch Tay is one of the finest trout
and salmon lochs in Scotland and permits for fishing in the loch
and associated rivers are available locally. Boats and canoes can
be hired from Killin. (Enquire at Tourist Information Centre.)

  Killin Parish Church, at the east end of Main Street (R), was
built in 1744 to replace a pre-Reformation church which stood
in the old churchyard behind the Killin Hotel. The church may
well have given name to the village, for Killin has been held to
mean 'Cill-linn', 'the church by the waterfall' (on the River
Lochy), although some say it comes from 'Cill-Fhinn', 'the burial
place of Fingal'. The baptismal font, an unusual ninth-century
seven-sided stone font, was found in the old churchyard, which
can be entered on the riverside of the hotel. The laird's loft, used
by the Campbells of Breadalbane, still exists and in the vestibule
is a photograph of the church bell, cast in 1632 for the earlier
church and still in use. Outside the church there is a monument
to the Rev. James Stuart, Minister at the time the church was
built and translator of the New Testament into Scottish Gaelic.
(The church is usually open daily during the summer months.)

  Continuing along the Aberfeldy road (A827), Pier Road (R) leads
past (L) Finlarig Castle, now sadly ruinous and obscured by trees.
The castle was built by the Campbells of Glenorchy in the early
sixteenth century. Later in the century, it was one of the castles

occupied by Sir Duncan Campbell, the notorious 'Black Duncan of the Cowl', who financed his castle-building activities by oppressing the poor and conspiring against the rich. 'Black Duncan' was a royal favourite and this may account for the arms of James VI and Queen Anne dated 1609, carved over the main door on the south side. Nearby is the ruinous Breadalbane Mausoleum, once the burial place of the Campbells of Breadalbane, which was erected in 1829 on the site of a chapel built by Sir Colin Campbell around 1523. The castle and mausoleum are now in a dangerous state of repair and visitors approach at their own risk.

The castle's beheading pit on the north side, said to be the only one in existence, was for despatching people of noble birth, while commoners had to make do with being hanged from a branch of a tree on a nearby mound. The stone for holding the head in place over the pit could be seen until recent times, but it was removed for safe-keeping after having been broken in two by potential thieves. (While visiting Killin, the author was much surprised to find that this grisly relic was stored only a few metres from his bedroom and, strange to relate, could not get to sleep thereafter.)

Near the end of Pier Road, Eilean Puttychan by the loch shore is one of the numerous crannogs built in the loch in prehistoric times. Paths lead from a parking area back to the village, either by the loch shore, the banks of the River Lochay and then by the old railway line, or direct by the railway (Walk 24).

Continue along the Aberfeldy road, past the Maragowan Caravan Club Site (R) and Killin Youth Hostel (L). The Bridge of Lochay Hotel (L), which dates from 1765, may seem familiar to cinema buffs, for it featured in the 1960 version of the John Buchan spy thriller *The Thirty-Nine Steps*. Immediately beyond the Bridge of Lochay, Killin Golf Club (L) welcomes visitors on its picturesque course (01567 820312).

Just before reaching the hotel, a short 5km excursion may be made on the south Glen Lochay road (L), passing (R) Moirlanich Longhouse, which dates from the mid-nineteenth century. This is a rare surviving example of the once-common Scottish longhouse, which housed a family and their livestock under one roof. The building is now in the care of the National Trust for Scotland. (Open Easter Sunday, then Wednesday and Sunday 2p.m.–5p.m. May–September. 01567 820988.)

Continuing on, the River Lochay is crossed near the Lochay Hydro-Electric Power Station (L), which opened in 1958 and is supplied with water from the River Lyon in Glen Lyon by means of a 7km-long tunnel through the mountains. The Falls of Lochay are just above the station. At the road junction, go right on the north branch of the Glen Lochay road to return to the A827, passing (R) Boreland House, once a seat of a branch of the Campbells of Breadalbane and later let to wealthy tenants as a shooting-lodge.

The giant pipeline which can be seen descending from the Tarmachan range just beyond Bridge of Lochay, forms part of the Lawers Hydro-Electric Scheme and serves Finlarig Power Station on the loch shore, which opened in 1956. The catchment area, which extends over much of the Tarmachan and Lawers ranges, diverts water to the enlarged Lochan na Lairige near Ben Lawers, from where it descends by a 4km-long tunnel and high-pressure pipeline to Finlarig Power Station.

About 6.5km east of Killin, a road (L) leads to the National Trust for Scotland Nature Reserve and Visitor Centre (open daily 10 a.m.–5 p.m., April to end September. 01567 820397) on the south-eastern slopes of Ben Lawers (1214m). A path leads from the Visitor Centre to the summit of the mountain, from where :

'Yonder Ben Lawers' mighty crest
O'erlooks Breadalbane to the west.'

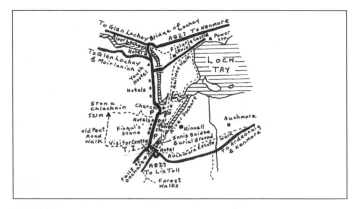

KILLIN

Visitor Services
B Bk CC Ch D G I MR P PO PS PT SA SC T YH

Sport and Leisure
A Bw Cf Cy Fi Go HB L PB Pu RC Ri S SB Sk SL TC VC W

Public Transport

Bus

Post Office, Main Street, for buses to Tyndrum, Callander and Stirling, and Royal Mail Post Buses to Crianlarich, Tyndrum, Callander, Ardeonaig and Aberfeldy.

Accommodation

Hotels

Ardeonaig, South Lochtayside, 11km E of Killin 01567 820400
Bridge of Lochay, Aberfeldy Road (A827) 01567 820272
Clachaig, Falls of Dochart 01567 820270
Dall Lodge Country House, Main Street 01567 820217
Fishers, Main Street 01567 820285
Killin, Main Street 01567 820296
Morenish Lodge Highland House 01567 820258
Tighnabruaich, Main Street 01567 820216

Caravan and Camping Parks

Cruachan Farm Caravan and Camping Park, on Aberfeldy Road (A827) 4km E of Killin (R) 01567 820302
High Creagan Caravan and Camping Park, Killin 01567 820449
Maragowan Caravan Club Site, Aberfeldy Road, just N of village 01567 820245
The Shieling, Aberfeldy Road (tent pitches) 01567 820334

Self-catering

Loch Tay Highland Lodges, Milton Morenish Estate 01567 820323
The Shieling, Aberfeldy Road 01567 820334

Youth Hostel

Killin Youth Hostel, Aberfeldy Road, just N of village 01567 820546

Note: There is also accommodation at Kenmore, at the eastern end of Loch Tay.

Tourist Information

Breadalbane Folklore Centre, Falls of Dochart 01567 820254 (March–November, and weekends in February.)

KILLIN–KENMORE–ABERFELDY

The A827 continues by way of Kenmore and Aberfeldy to join the main Perth–Inverness (A9) road at Ballinluig. Kenmore, a picturesque estate village of whitewashed houses at the eastern end of Loch Tay dates mainly from 1760, when it was formed by the third Earl of Breadalbane, and has a fine bridge over the Tay, erected in 1774. The grand Taymouth Castle, once the seat of the Campbell Earls and Marquises of Breadalbane, stands (L) 1.5km east of the village. Construction commenced in 1799 and the castle had many royal visitors, including Queen Victoria and Prince Albert in 1842.

There are some fine forest walks on Drummond Hill to the north of the village and a golf course. Boats are available for hire and a wide range of watersports are catered for at Croft-na-Caber Watersports and Activities Centre (01877 830588). A new attraction at Croft-na-Caber is the Scottish Crannog Centre, a modern reconstruction of a prehistoric man-made island homestead. They were a feature of many Scottish lochs and river estuaries until as late as the seventeenth century. Loch Tay has yielded evidence of at least 18 crannogs. (Open April–October. 01887 830583.)

KILLIN–CRIANLARICH

Returning to Lix Toll by the A827, the way lies westwards by the A85 through mountain-girt Glen Dochart. The tiny clachan of Luib offers a good selection of accommodation, including the Luib Hotel (01567 820664); the Suie Lodge Hotel (01567 820417); and the Glendochart Caravan Park (01567 820637), which also has tent pitches. It was not always thus. When William and Dorothy Wordsworth passed this way bound for Killin, they stayed at the Luib Inn and were not impressed, for they had a bad supper, the tariff was unreasonable and the servant uncivil. In the days before the railway came, great droves of cattle heading east by the main drove road from Skye and the Western Highlands to the Lowland trysts would often spend the night at Luib's cattle 'stance'.

The slopes of mighty Ben More, 'the great mountain' (1,174m), dominate the southern side of the glen. On its lower slopes the ruined gable of a house called Auchinchisallen stands near the road on the east bank of the Allt Coire Chaorach. It was within an earlier house on this site that Rob Roy and his family were granted refuge in 1712 by the Campbell Earl of Breadalbane, following their eviction from Craigroyston on Loch Lomondside by the Duke of Montrose.

The MacGregors had no good reason to be admirers of the Campbells, but Rob's mother was a sister of the chieftain of the Glen Lyon branch of the Campbells and, since the name

MacGregor was proscribed, he generally went by the name of Robert Campbell. He remained at Auchinchisallen until 1716, during which time he not only continued raiding Montrose's lands, but took part in the 1715 Jacobite Rising. In April 1716 Auchinchisallen was burnt down by Government soldiers, who carried off all Rob's stock and goods, but not before his marksmen had brought down about 15 of their number.

A route for experienced walkers, leading to the summits of Ben More and its neighbour Stobinian (1165m), enters the forest behind the site of Rob's house, just to the east of the bridge over the Allt Coire Chaorach. Parking is available at a lay-by west of the bridge.

West of here, the River Dochart flows through two picturesque lochans, Loch Iubhair and its westerly neighbour Loch Dochart. Lochdochart House, an early nineteenth-century house built by Edward Place, a wealthy landowner from Yorkshire, overlooks Iubhair's western end.

A tree-clad islet on Loch Dochart is crowned by the ruins of Lochdochart Castle, another of the castles built in the late sixteenth century by Sir Duncan Campbell of Glenorchy. As Sir Duncan was determined to extend his power and influence by whatever means necessary – fair or foul – he built no less than seven castles on his estates. Lochdochart's demise came about during the Civil War, when Clan MacNab deserted from the National Covenant to support Montrose, thus placing them in conflict with the Campbells of Glenorchy. The MacNabs held Lochdochart Castle for a time by subterfuge, until 1646 when Montrose swept through Breadalbane killing, burning and driving away cattle. Lochdochart was one of several castles put to the torch at that time.

The village of Crianlarich, an important road and rail junction, is soon reached. For the return to Glasgow and the central Lowlands, head south from here by the A82. To complete the round of 'the Five Lochs', go west from Tarbet on Loch Lomondside by the A83 to Arrochar and then head south by the A814 along the fiord-like shores of Loch Long, the Gare Loch and the Clyde estuary. Alternatively, continue south on the A82 from Tarbet by way of Loch Lomond's bonnie banks and the Vale of Leven to reach the north bank of the Clyde at Dumbarton. The M8 can be gained by crossing the Erskine Bridge. By continuing on up Strath Fillan from Crianlarich, Fort William and Inverness may be gained, or Oban by the A85 which branches west from Tyndrum. (See also Routes 1, 2 and 3.)

SUGGESTED ROAD TOURS

FROM GLASGOW AND CLYDESIDE

1. The Three Lochs (Routes 1, 2 and 3)

Glasgow to Tarbet, Loch Lomond (A82 or M8/M898/A82), returning by way of Arrochar, Loch Long, the Gare Loch, Helensburgh and Clydeside (A83/A814/A82). The circuit of the Rosneath Peninsula may be included from Whistlefield or Garelochhead (B833).

2. Balloch, Glen Fruin and Helensburgh
(Routes 1, 2, 2A and 3)

Take the same outward route as for the Three Lochs, but take the Black Hill road at Arden on Loch Lomondside for Glen Fruin and Helensburgh (B831/B832). Return to Glasgow via Dumbarton (A814/A82). Alternatively, continue up Loch Lomondside on A82 to Arnburn and take the new Glen Fruin road, to emerge on A814 near Garelochhead. Return to Glasgow via Helensburgh and Dumbarton (A814/A82).

3. The Five Lochs/The Six Lochs
(Routes 1, 2, 3, 6 and 8)

Glasgow to Callander via Strath Blane and the Lake of Menteith (A81). Head north via Loch Lubnaig and Strathyre to Balquhidder (by minor road, for Rob Roy's grave) and on to Lochearnhead on Loch Earn (A84). Continue north, through Glen Ogle to Lix Toll (A85). For the Six Lochs, a side excursion can be made from here to Killin on Loch Tay (A827). Returning to Lix Toll, continue west through Glen Dochart to Crianlarich (A85). Head south via Glen Falloch and Loch Lomondside to Tarbet, then west to Arrochar, before turning south for Glasgow via Loch Long, the Gare Loch, Helensburgh and Dumbarton (A82/A83/A814/A82).

4. Loch Lomond's Eastern Shore and Ben Lomond
(Route 5)

Glasgow to Drymen via the Stockiemuir Road (A81/A809 /A811/B858); west to Balmaha (B837) and then north on the scenic single-track road along Loch Lomond's eastern shore to Rowardennan, for the ascent of Ben Lomond. Return to Glasgow by the same route, or from Drymen Bridge, via Balloch (A811/A82).

5. The Round of The Trossachs (Routes 6 and 7)

Glasgow to Callander, via Strath Blane and the Lake of Menteith (A81). Continue to Kilmahog (A84), then head west by lovely Lochs Venachar and Achray to Trossachs Pier for the steamer trip on Loch Katrine (A821). Continue over the scenic Duke's Pass to Aberfoyle, calling at the Queen Elizabeth Forest Park Visitor Centre (A821) before returning to Glasgow (A821/A81).

6. The Rob Roy Country (Route 6)

Glasgow to Aberfoyle, via Strath Blane (A81/A821). Continue west by Lochs Ard, Chon and Arklet to Stronachlachar on Loch Katrine, in the heart of the Rob Roy country (B829). Cross over to Inversnaid on Loch Lomondside. Return by the same route or, from Braeval just beyond Aberfoyle, head east to Stirling via the Lake of Menteith and Thornhill (A81/A873/A84) before returning to Glasgow (M9/M80/A80).

FROM EDINBURGH OR STIRLING

Stirling is reached from Edinburgh city centre by taking the A8 to Newbridge roundabout and joining the M9 there. For a more scenic route, follow the Forth Valley National Tourist Route, which is signposted (white on brown signs) from Junction 1 on the M9 and goes via South Queensferry, Linlithgow, Bo'ness, Grangemouth and Falkirk. (A leaflet may be available from Tourist Information Centres.)

1. The Five Lochs/The Six Lochs (Routes 1, 2, 3 and 8)

Stirling to Callander via Doune (A84). Head north, via Loch Lubnaig and Strathyre to Balquhidder (by minor road, for Rob Roy's grave) and on to Lochearnhead on Loch Earn (A84). Continue north, through Glen Ogle to Lix Toll (A85). For the Six Lochs, a side excursion can be made from here to Killin on Loch Tay (A827). Continue west from Lix Toll through Glen Dochart to Crianlarich (A85). Head south via Glen Falloch and Loch Lomondside to Tarbet, then west to Arrochar, before heading south via Loch Long, the Gare Loch, Helensburgh and Dumbarton (A82/A83/A814/A82). Cross the Erskine Bridge (M898) to join the M8 for Edinburgh. East of Glasgow, take M73/A80/M80/M9 for Stirling.

2. The Round of The Trossachs (Route 7)

Stirling to Callander and Kilmahog via Doune (A84). Go west from Kilmahog by Lochs Venachar and Achray to Trossachs Pier, for the steamer trip on Loch Katrine (A821). Continue over the scenic Duke's Pass road to Aberfoyle, calling at the Queen

Elizabeth Forest Park Visitor Centre (A821). Return to Stirling via the Lake of Menteith and Thornhill (A81/A873/A84).

3. The Rob Roy Country (Route 6)

Stirling to Aberfoyle, via Thornhill and the Lake of Menteith (A84/A873/A81/A821). Continue west by Lochs Ard, Chon and Arklet to Stronachlachar on Loch Katrine (B829). Cross over to Inversnaid on Loch Lomondside. Return by the same route or, from Braeval just beyond Aberfoyle, go via Callander and Doune (A81/A84).

4. Loch Lomond's Eastern Shore and Ben Lomond (Routes 5 and 6)

Stirling to Drymen via the valley of the Forth (A811/B858). Go west to Balmaha (B837) and then north on the scenic single-track road along Loch Lomond's eastern shore to Rowardennan, for the ascent of Ben Lomond. Return by the same route, or from Ballat crossroads east of Drymen, go via Aberfoyle, the Lake of Menteith and Thornhill (A81/A821/A81/A873/A84).

WALKING ROUTES

Walks around Loch Lomond and the Gare Loch

The walks described here represent but a small selection of the many scenic rambles within the district. Certain walks may be subject to closure or diversion and dogs may not be allowed on others. Therefore, if in doubt, it is recommended that a check be made with local countryside Rangers as to the current position before setting out. Addresses and telephone numbers are shown in the section concerning visitor services, etc.

BALLOCH DISTRICT
Balloch and Balloch Castle Country Park*
1 The Stoneymollan Road ('Lennox Heritage Trail')
2 Round 'The Horseshoe'

* See entry for Balloch in Route 1.

LOCH LOMOND, WEST SIDE
3 Firkin Point
4 Cruach Tairbeirt
5 Ben Vorlich and Loch Sloy
6 Glen Falloch

LOCH LOMOND, EAST SIDE
7 Aber Shore
8 Over Conic Hill
9 Sallochy Wood
10 Ben Lomond from Rowardennan
11 Craigroyston and Rob Roy's Prison

HELENSBURGH AND THE GARE LOCH
12 The Highlandman's Road

Note: in the following descriptions, (r) indicates the distance of the outward journey and return.

BALLOCH DISTRICT

I. The Stoneymollan Road (Lennox Heritage Trail)

9.5km to Cardross; 6km (r) to Cross Stone

This historic route was once an important link for travellers between southwest Scotland and the central Highlands, linking with ferries at Cardross and Ardmore on the Clyde and at Balloch on the Leven. Today, it is sometimes known as the Lennox Heritage Trail.

From the south end of Balloch Road go right into Old Luss Road and left into Lower Stoneymollan Road. Cross the A82 by footbridge to Stoneymollan Road, which is a tarmac road on either side of the hill and a rough hill track over its upper, central section.

To the right of the gate at the summit, on the fence-line, the historic Cross Stone appears to have once supported a stone or wooden cross, possibly as a marker for travellers. The extensive view ranges over Loch Lomond to Ben Lomond, and through Strath Endrick and the valley of the Forth towards Stirling, with the Ochil, Fintry, Campsie and Kilpatrick ranges to the south and east.

Emerging from a conifer plantation on the Cardross side, there are views towards the River Clyde and even the distant peaks of Arran. Descending past Blackthird Farm, Darleith House may be glimpsed among the trees (L). This grand mansion was home to the Darleith and then the Yuille family for many years, being built around the sixteenth-century Tower of Darleith over a period of some five centuries. Go left and then right at the junction below the farm.

Approaching Cardross, the historic Chapel of St Mahew (L) was built in 1647, on the site of an earlier pre-Reformation chapel, by local laird Duncan Napier of Kilmahew and restored by the Roman Catholic Church in 1955 after having become ruinous. Cardross is entered by Darleith Road. Go left along Main Street for Station Road (R) and the railway station.

Note: Dogs must be kept under control on the open hill, where livestock grazes.

2. Round 'The Horseshoe'

12km

The walk (or cycle) round 'The Horseshoe', a horseshoe-shaped circuit on quiet country roads through pleasant farmlands with views of the Highland hills, has long been a favourite hike for local folk.

From Balloch Bridge follow the River Leven Towpath (now part of the Glasgow–Loch Lomond Cycleway and the Leven Valley Heritage Trail) downstream. In the late eighteenth and nineteenth centuries the towpath was used by horses towing cargo sailing barges upriver to the textile dye-works in the Vale of Leven and to Loch Lomond. The River Leven Barrage was built in 1971 to control the level of Loch Lomond for the supply of water to a large area of central Scotland. The gates are automatically adjusted and there is a fish ladder to allow migratory fish such as salmon and sea trout to pass upriver.

At Heather Avenue note a 'lade' (L), a channel which supplied water to the Croftengea and Levenfield dyeworks. Before railways, herds of cattle being driven from the Western Highlands to the Falkirk tryst crossed the river here at Balloch ford. Ascend the steps, or go via Heather Avenue, to cross the river on the Leven Viaduct (known locally as 'the Stuckie Bridge'), built in 1876 to replace a timber structure. It once carried the Forth and Clyde Railway (Balloch–Stirling), opened in 1856. Levenbank and Milton dye-works formerly stood on either side at the far end of the bridge.

At Main Street, Jamestown, carry on through a small industrial estate and, from behind the Haldane housing estate, a short path (R) leads up to Auchincarroch Road. Go left here and enjoy the view which ranges from Ben Lomond and the Luss Hills to the Vale of Leven and the Renfrewshire Heights. Continuing on, Mid Auchincarroch Farm once belonged to the MacAlisters, an old Covenanting family who owned much land about here. On Sundays they actually attended kirk at Kilmacolm, south of the Clyde, by walking and boating there and back. They were believed to have given sanctuary in the seventeenth century to the martyred Covenanter Robert Nairn, whose grave is in Bonhill churchyard. This was confirmed when a barn was demolished during the nineteenth century and a double gable wall was found with enough space for a man to hide in and containing items left by Nairn.

At the crossroads near Merkins Farm, go left and descend past Caldarvan, once the railway station for Gartocharn 3km away. The house Auchenlarich (L) was built in 1894 for George Eyre-Todd, well-known historical author and magazine editor, who was visited here by many leading authors and artists of the day. Go straight ahead at the junction here and also at the next one.

Caldarvan House (R), a red sandstone mansion below Duncryne hill, was built in 1905 to replace an earlier house destroyed by fire. For a century and a half after 1802, Caldarvan was the property of the MacKenzies, a family of Glasgow solicitors and local landowners. After the last war, the house was occupied by A.E. Pickard, the colourful Glasgow cinema and property magnate.

Duncryne or Duncruin (142m), 'the round hill', is an igneous plug of volcanic origin which pierces the overlying old red sandstone. The latter type of stone was once quarried locally to make paving stones for the streets of Glasgow and Paisley. Ice Age glaciers bumped over Duncryne leaving behind a typical 'crag and tail' formation. Once owned by the monks of Paisley Abbey, and later by the Dukes of Montrose, the hill was long held to be the haunt of the Lennox fairies or witches.

Caldarvan Loch, a favourite haunt for birdlife, is briefly glimpsed (R) before the road takes a sharp turn right and passes (R) Westerton House. This mansion was the seat of the Alstons and then the Kippens (by marriage with an Alston) from 1790 until 1946. William Kippen, owner of the Glasgow *Express* newspaper in the nineteenth century, did not approve of railways and so he walked or drove in a cart to Dumbarton to catch the Glasgow steamer.

The road soon winds down to Ballagan on the A811 road, a hamlet where the red sandstone flagstones from the Kilmaronock quarries were cut before being shipped down the Leven and the Clyde to Glasgow and Paisley. Take the quiet Ledrish road (R) for Balloch via Balloch Castle Country Park (see Route 1), or follow the footpath beside the A811.

LOCH LOMOND, WEST SIDE

3. Firkin Point

12.5km from Luss; 7.5km from Inverbeg. (See also Route 2)
A footpath beside the A82 road, which affords magnificent views of Ben Lomond, links Luss with Inverbeg. A kilometre north of Inverbeg, an abandoned section of the old A82 provides easy walking along the loch shore, past Firkin Point and on to Hollybank, 2km south of Tarbet, from whence a footpath beside A82 leads to Tarbet. There is also access from a car park and picnic area (open April–October) at Firkin Point, which is ideal for wheelchair users.

On leaving Inverbeg, the course of the old Military Road of 1750 which climbed up and over the great headland known as the Rubha Mor, can still be traced on the hillside. Remnants of the oak woodlands which once clothed the shores of the loch and were harvested commercially, still survive beside the old section of the A82. Beyond Firkin Cottage, an ancient yew tree west of the new A82, known as Robert the Bruce's Tree, marks the spot where the king gathered his men after crossing the loch in 1306 as they fled after defeat at the battle of Dail-righ near Tyndrum. The old Firkin Toll House is a relic of the turnpike (toll) roads of the nineteenth century.

The old road ends 2km south of Tarbet and the footpath continues beside the A82 to Tarbet, passing Stuckgowan House (see Route 2).

4. Cruach Tairbeirt

2.75km (r)

The watchmen of Clan MacFarlane once stood guard on the hill Cruach-Tairbeirt, above Tarbet, ready to signal below so that 'black mail' could be levied on traffic approaching from the main track along Loch Lomondside. On this walk, today's visitor can also enjoy the fine views down Loch Lomond towards Ben Lomond – and you may be lucky enough to spot roe or red deer.

From the car park at Tarbet jetty, walk along the A83 to Arrochar and Tarbet Railway Station. From the station entrance, just beyond the underpass, a path goes right and is soon joined (L) by a branch path which starts from opposite Craigard Stores, Arrochar. Ignoring the return path (R), the path climbs steeply up the slopes of Cruach Tairbeirt, through mainly conifer woods of larch and spruce, with some deciduous species, before descending to rejoin the outward route and complete the circuit.

5. Ben Vorlich and Loch Sloy

12km (r) to Ben Vorlich

From Inveruglas car park go south past the Power Station and then right on the Loch Sloy access road (authorised vehicles only). The road ascends steeply before levelling out beyond a switching station. There are magnificent views of the rugged Arrochar Alps, including Bens Ime, Chorannach, Vane and A' Chrois. For the summit of Ben Vorlich (943m) make an angled ascent (R) on the approach to Loch Sloy Dam and continue along the ridge to the summit.

Bleak Loch Sloy, dammed in 1950 for hydro-electric purposes, provided the war-cry and was the gathering-place of the wild Clan MacFarlane. James Hogg, 'the Ettrick shepherd', spent a most eventful night in a farmhouse there (now submerged) while on a walking tour in 1803. The Loch Sloy Dam, which is some 353m long and 49m high, raised the level of the loch by 47m and doubled its length. A 3km-long tunnel through Ben Vorlich supplies water to Inveruglas Power Station.

Return by the outward route or, alternatively, Arrochar may be reached from the access road to Coiregrogain Farm, by a path which leads over a low pass to Glen Loin and by the east bank of the Loin Water.

6. Glen Falloch

8km (r) to Ardleish; 12.5km to Crianlarich
From Ardlui or Inverarnan, walk north beside the A82 to the bridge over the River Falloch leading to Beinglas Farm. Cross the bridge and go right to join the West Highland Way, following the riverbank and then going left by the Beinglas Burn.

(1) For Ardleish, cross a stile and follow the way marked Way south. The path soon climbs to the Dubh Lochan, passing through the ruined hamlet of Blairstainge, which recalls more populous times in the district. Beyond the lochan, a viewpoint affords a memorable view down Loch Lomond to Ben Lomond. Return by the same route, or by a ferry which operates to Ardlui from just beyond Ardleish Farm in the summer months.

(2) For the Falls of Falloch and/or Crianlarich, pass behind Beinglas Farm and follow the way-marked Way north. Approaching the Falls of Falloch, the Clach nam Breatann, a strange monolith which marked the northern boundary of the British kingdom of Strathclyde in the Dark Ages, is prominent on the hillside on the far side of the glen. The last remnants of the ancient Caledonian Forest which once covered most of Scotland are passed (R) and, after crossing the A82 road north of Derrydaroch Farm, the old Military Road completed around 1760 is followed on the approach to Crianlarich. The return from Crianlarich can be made by train or coach.

Note: Deer-stalking is usually in progress from about mid-August until late October. Please heed notices and keep away from stalking areas, if only for your own safety. No dogs are allowed on these walks.

LOCH LOMOND, EAST SIDE

7. Aber Shore

3.5km (r)
From Gartocharn, a road by the public toilets leads to the Community Centre. A path beside the centre (L) leads across two fields to a bridge over a burn (L), where a path leads out to a road end. Go right to a junction, where the old Mill of Aber (1806, restored as a house in 1992) is a short way to the right. Go left to Townhead of Aber, then right on a private road (no unauthorised vehicles) which leads down to the loch shore. As the road starts to curve towards the loch, an old yew tree (L) is said to mark the site of the ancient Chapel of St Kessog.

Aber was once the hub of the district, when flagstones from the

Kilmaronock quarries were shipped to Glasgow and Paisley. From the shore there is a fine view of Loch Lomond and Ross Priory may be glimpsed, where Sir Walter Scott wrote part of *Rob Roy*. A gate leads to Shore Wood, part of the Loch Lomond National Nature Reserve. For access beyond Shore Wood a permit must be obtained from Scottish Natural Heritage, Mariner Court, 8 South Street, Clydebank Business Park, Clydebank, 0141 951 4488.

Return to Townhead of Aber and go right for Gartocharn, enjoying the extensive views back over the loch and over towards Gartocharn and the distinctive little hill, Duncryne. Ardoch Farm, on the hillside (R), stands near the site of the old seat of the Buchanans of Ardoch from 1683. John Buchanan built Balloch Castle in 1808 and Boturich Castle in 1834.

8. Over Conic Hill

10km Drymen to Balmaha; 17km (r) Garadhban Forest to Balmaha
Leave Drymen by the old Gartmore road, which ascends the hill behind the village, and go left on the waymarked West Highland Way into Garadhban Forest, or drive to Garadhban Forest car park.

The Way traverses the forest and then open moorland, before ascending Conic Hill (361m). From the summit there is a magnificent view over Loch Lomond's island-studded southern reaches, while the Highland Boundary Fault can be clearly traced as it passes through the southernmost islands of the loch before continuing to the Firth of Clyde. Below the summit, the Way goes left and descends steeply through conifers to Balmaha.

Return can be made by the Balmaha–Drymen–Balloch bus. To return to Garadhban Forest, take the bus, or the path beside the B837, to Milton of Buchanan (2.5km), where a track ascends past Creityhall Farm to enter the Forest and join the outward route. (This is an alternative route on the way for use in bad weather conditions.) Go right for the car park.

Note: No dogs are allowed at any time on Conic Hill. The hill is closed for lambing from mid-April to mid-May.

9. Sallochy Wood

3km (r)
Sallochy lies 6km north of Balmaha on the Rowardennan road (Route 5). From the car park, cross the road and follow the waymarked forest trail beyond. The path veers right to pass through the ruined hamlet of Wester Sallochy, now enveloped by conifers, and then goes left to emerge on a forestry road. Go left along the road to the old slate quarry, which is marked by a spoil heap.

Return down the forestry road until the main road is reached. Cross the road and look for the waymarked West Highland Way (R) to return to the starting point.

Note: A new waymarked route based on this walk was due for completion in early 1999.

10. Ben Lomond from Rowardennan

11km (r)

Ben Lomond, easily accessible from most parts of central Scotland and offering magnificent views from its summit, is Scotland's southernmost 'Munro' (mountain over 914m/ 3,000ft) and ranks among the most-often climbed hills in Scotland. (See Route 5.)

The main path starts behind the public toilets at Rowardennan car park and climbs through the woods to a gate. Emerging on the open hillside, the path veers left round the corrie Coire Corrach and ascends the Sron Aonaich ridge.

The final zig-zag to the 974m-high summit is the steepest part of the climb, with an awe-inspiring view down a sheer drop into the north-facing corrie Coire a' Bhathaich. The spectacular vista from the summit embraces a jumble of Highland peaks, ranging from Bens More (Mull), Cruachan, Lui, Nevis, More (Crianlarich), Lawers and Stobinian to Bens Ledi and Venue in The Trossachs; the Paps of Jura and the Arran peaks; Tinto and Merrick in the Southern Uplands; and the Pentland Hills near Edinburgh. (A View Finder map is published by Mercator Marketing Ltd, Kinkell, St Andrews, Fife, KY16 8PN.)

Return by the same route, or by the western Ptarmigan shoulder. The latter route descends steeply and veers left to follow the ridge south. An obvious path leads steeply down to Ardess, near the Youth Hostel.

11. Craigroyston and Rob Roy's Prison

13km (r)

A fine circular forest walk can be made through the heart of Rob Roy's old territory, by following the West Highland Way northwards. A high-level route, on a forestry road, winds under the towering 'rocks of Craigroyston', which are mentioned in Scott's *The Lady of the Lake*, while a low-level route (signposted just north of the gate at the start of the forestry road) follows a switchback path along the loch shore and passes Rob Roy's Prison, a sheer rock-face where Rob is said to have confined his hostages and ducked them in the loch's freezing waters until they saw reason.

The two routes link again just before, and beyond, the abandoned hamlet of Rowchoish (on the lower route) where there is a public shelter. Wild goats which may be encountered on the lower path are a reminder of a time when the long-departed local inhabitants paid much of their rent to the laird in kid and goat's-milk cheese.

HELENSBURGH AND THE GARE LOCH

12. The Highlandman's Road

10km Rhu to Black Bridge and return to Helensburgh via Drumfad and B832

Back in the days when Glen Fruin was the most populous part of Rhu parish, the Highlandman's (or Church) Road was used by the farming folk in the glen to attend the kirk at Rhu on Sundays. (See Routes 2A and 3.)

From Rhu Parish Church go up Manse Brae, second right into Braehead Place and first left into Station Road. Continue uphill, passing near the site of Rhu station on the West Highland Railway (off Lineside Walk and closed in 1964). The Highlandman's Road crosses the railway by a bridge and becomes a farm track opposite Torr Farm. Passing a gate and stile, a magnificent vista of the Firth of Clyde, the Rosneath Peninsula and the Cowal Hills unfolds. The Highlandman's Wood is passed and the track ends at the Glennan Burn.

From here, either: (1) Go right, past a large Bronze Age cup-and-ring marked boulder and descend by a path through the Blackhill Plantation to emerge at the Hill House car park or the top of Sinclair Street, Helensburgh, or: (2) Continue on the Highlandman's Road, now a grassy firebreak through a recent conifer plantation, to emerge on open moorland at a stile. The view here ranges from the Ochil Hills near Stirling to a glimpse of Loch Lomond, the Firth of Clyde and the Arran peaks. The route, now indistinct, passes a small plantation (L) and follows a wall to emerge on the Glen Fruin road near Black Bridge. The old school-house here stands on the site of the ancient Chapel of St Bride and an old stone incised with a cross survives in front of the house.

From here, either: (1) Go right by the road, past Drumfad Farm, to join the B832 road. Turn right on B832 and descend Helensburgh by Sinclair Street, or keep straight ahead, pass through a gate, and descend to Craigendoran by the path known as the Old Luss Road, a section of the old Luss–Craigendoran road which was abandoned in the 1830s, or: (2) go left from Black Bridge, for the pleasant walk through Glen Fruin, before dropping down to Faslane and returning to Rhu or Helensburgh by bus.

Walks around the Trossachs and Breadalbane

ABERFOYLE DISTRICT
13 Doon Hill
14 The Highland Boundary Fault Trail

CALLANDER AND THE TROSSACHS
15 Callander Craig and Bracklinn Falls
16 Callander to Aberfoyle by the Menteith Hills
17 The Callander–Strathyre Cycle and Walking Path
18 Ben A'an (Am Binnein)
19 Ben Venue
20 Ben Ledi

STRONACHLACHAR DISTRICT
21 Royal Cottage and The Aqueducts

STRATHYRE DISTRICT
22 Bailefuil Walk and Beinn An t' Sidhein

BALQUHIDDER DISTRICT
23 Kirkton Glen, Creag an Tuirc and Glen Dochart

KILLIN DISTRICT
24 The Old Killin Railway and Loch Tay
25 Sron a' Chlachain and the Peat Road

ABERFOYLE DISTRICT

13. Doon Hill

6km (r)

The Rev. Robert Kirk, minister of Aberfoyle and author of *The Secret Commonwealth of Elves, Fauns and Fairies,* is said to have been spirited away to fairyland in 1692 while walking on Doon Hill near the village. (See Route 6).

To retrace the Rev. Kirk's steps, take Manse Road from Aberfoyle – crossing the River Forth by the picturesque old humpbacked bridge – or drive by the same route to the Forestry Commission car park at Balleich. Kirk's grave will be found in the ancient kirkyard (L) which surrounds the ruin of the old Aberfoyle Kirk of 1774, near the north-east corner of the building. At Balleich car park, take the road which goes left past Auchinblae (L), the old

Aberfoyle manse, which was built around 1732. It was there that Scott obtained much information for his historical romances from the Rev. Patrick Graham, the local minister, who also wrote the first real travel guide to The Trossachs.

The public road soon ends and continues as a forestry road. A marked path (L) goes off through delightful oak woods to the 82m-high summit of Doon Hill. The large pine tree on the summit is said to contain Kirk's tormented soul, as a lesson to others who might upset the fairies! Continue along the path to complete the circuit or return by the outward route.

14. The Highland Boundary Fault Trail

4.25km

The Highland Boundary Fault, a massive geological fracture in the earth's crust which occurred some 390 million years ago, extends right across Scotland from Stonehaven in the east to the island of Arran in the west, thus forming an obvious boundary between the Highlands and the central Lowlands. Markers along this Queen Elizabeth Forest Park trail in the Menteith Hills explain the geology of the district, as well as giving information regarding points of interest. (A QEFP leaflet is available at the Park Visitor Centre.)

From the Queen Elizabeth Forest Park Visitor Centre, off the Duke's Pass road near Aberfoyle (Route 7), follow the Waterfall Trail, which starts behind and to the left of the Visitor Centre. (The Waterfall Trail has yellow waymarks and the Fault Trail blue.) The path descends to a footbridge below a waterfall. Cross the bridge and go left on a forestry road. Turn left at the first junction by a road which climbs through the conifers and then go right at a crossroads. Just before crossing the actual Boundary Fault (which is marked), a viewpoint (R) offers a wide Lowland vista over Flanders Moss, towards the flat-topped Fintry Hills and Campsie Fells which are of volcanic origin.

At a four-way road and path junction, take the path ahead which ascends steeply to the TV mast on Lime Craig (312m) for views along the Highland edge and over Flanders Moss and the Loch Ard Forest in the Lowland region to the south. Descend again to the junction and take the path (L) which descends steeply from the former Lime Craigs Quarry, which closed around 130 years ago. The path was once a cable-railway incline which conveyed limestone from the quarry down to kilns at the foot, where it was fired to make quicklime for agricultural purposes.

Cross a forest road, keep descending and then turn right into another forest road, passing above the Dounans Residential Camp School for outdoor pursuits. The second path bearing left

crosses a burn by a footbridge and ascends to the Queen
Elizabeth Forest Park Visitor Centre.

CALLANDER AND THE TROSSACHS

15. Callander Craig and Bracklinn Falls

*5km (r) to Main Street, Callander; 6.5km (r) to Bracklinn Road
car park*

From the east end of Main Street, Callander, go up Bracklinn
Road, passing (L) Arden House, a guest house which became
world-famous as the home of Doctors Finlay and Cameron in
Doctor Finlay's Casebook. Alternatively, drive up Bracklinn Road
to the car park at the start of the signposted path to Bracklinn
Falls (R). Walk down to the bridge over the falls (which are
disappointing except after rain) and return. Sir Walter Scott
once rode a pony across a shaky bridge above the falls for a wager
with his horrified friends!

  Back on the road, continue uphill, winding around the eastern
flank of Callander Craig and over Callander Common, where
the townsfolk once grazed their cattle. Just before reaching a
small wood, take the path (L) which ascends to the Queen
Victoria Jubilee Cairn on the summit of Callander Craig
(343m). The vista extends from Ben Vorlich and Stuc a' Chroin
to the Ochil Hills, the Wallace Monument and Stirling Castle;
the Pentland Hills near Edinburgh; the Fintry and Menteith
Hills; and Ben Venue and Ben Ledi.

  The path continues near the edge of the crags, before entering
the woodlands and descending to Tulipan Crescent, off Leny
Road, Callander. The waymarked Upper Woodland Walk leads
from here back to Bracklinn Road car park.

Note: The path to Callander Craig has been closed by the Forestry
authority due to lack of maintenance resources, but it can still be
walked at owner's risk.

16. Callander to Aberfoyle by the Menteith Hills

14km

From Callander cross the River Teith by the 'Red bridge' to
Bridgend and go right on the Invertrossachs road. Alternatively, in
dry conditions, a gate (R) at the end of the bridge gives access to
a riverbank path which joins the Invertrossachs road some 750m
ahead. Continue past Gartchonzie road junction and East Lodge
at the entrance to Invertrossachs Estate on Loch Venachar. About
400m beyond the former farmhouse at West Dullater, the ancient

right-of-way by the Menteith Hills to Aberfoyle is signposted (L).

The path climbs steeply to enter a conifer plantation, then briefly joins a forestry road beside a small lochan, before going left along the shore of the lochan. Looking back, Ben Ledi can be seen, with Ben A'an and the top of Ben Venue to the west. Open moorland is entered beyond the summit of the path and the vista is now towards the Lowlands, with the hump of Dumgoyne conspicuous at the north end of the Campsie Fells. Descending, the path continues as a forestry road through a conifer plantation, before emerging at the Forestry Commission's Braeval car park on the A81.

For Aberfoyle, take a forestry road which goes right just before reaching Braeval car park and enjoy the splendid views towards Ben Lomond before emerging at either the Dounans Residential Camp School, Aberfoyle, or the Queen Elizabeth Forest Park Visitor Centre, just off the A821. A path descends to Aberfoyle from the Visitor Centre.

17. The Callander–Strathyre Cycle and Walking Path

13km (See also Routes 7 and 8)

The trackbed of the old Dunblane–Crianlarich railway, which closed in 1965, now provides a fine, easily graded cycle and walking path from Callander to Strathyre. From there, a quiet country road leads on to Balquhidder, for Rob Roy's grave.

The path (which is signposted and marked by an old railway signal) starts from Leny Road at the west end of Callander. Crossing the Garbh Uisge by a bridge, the ancient, walled burial ground of the Buchanans of Leny can be seen (L) at the junction of the rivers Garbh Uisge and Eas Gobhain, known locally as 'the meeting of the waters'. With the vast bulk of Ben Ledi dominating the skyline ahead, the site of the Roman fort of Bochastle is passed (R) when approaching Bochastle Farm.

At Kilmahog (access from A821) the wooded Pass of Leny is entered. The nearby Falls of Leny provide a dramatic spectacle after heavy rain. The path emerges at the Forestry Commission's Coireachrombie car park near a bridge which provides access from the A84. The main path to the summit of Ben Ledi commences here (L). The forestry road continues past Stank Farm, where another path to Ben Ledi goes off (L), just before reaching the farm. The forestry road soon ends, just beyond the Forestry Commission's Strathyre Forest Cabins, beside lovely Loch Lubnaig.

The road soon narrows to a path, which winds around the precipitous eastern flank of Ardnandave Hill. It was on the old horse-track above here that Rob Roy made a daring escape from his captors in 1717. A century and a half later, the bold Victorian railway engineers encountered serious difficulties about here in trying to negotiate the rugged terrain and had to resort to building a causeway in the loch's waters to accommodate the railway. Ardchullarie More, a white-walled shooting-lodge on the far shore, stands on the site of the farmhouse where the eighteenth-century traveller James ('Abyssinian') Bruce wrote his monumental work *Travels to the Source of the Nile*.

 At length, the path leaves the old railway and a forestry road is followed for some distance, before rejoining the railway approaching Laggan Farm. The path leaves the railway once more near the head of the loch and ascends steeply (L) to a forestry road on the approach to Strathyre. The path goes right at some forestry houses and then left, before finally following the old railway again. The River Balvag is crossed by a bridge and, after passing the site of Strathyre Station (now a modern housing development), the path terminates beside the old bridge over the Balvag. By crossing the bridge and going right, Balquhidder, the final resting place of Rob Roy, can be gained by a quiet country road.

18. Ben A'an (Am Binnein)

3.25km (r)
Take the waymarked path from the Loch Achray car park on A821 (Route 7), 180m west of the Tigh Mor Trossachs (formerly the Trossachs Hotel). The path climbs steeply through mixed woodland. The going becomes steeper on leaving the forest, when approaching the conical summit of Ben A'an (Am Binnein), 'the small mountain' (461m).

 The fine panorama extends westward along almost the whole length of Loch Katrine, towards Glen Gyle and the jumble of 'Munros' around Crianlarich, and south east over Lochs Achray and Venachar. Lowland hills include Dumgoyne at the end of the Campsie Fells, the Fintry and Gargunnock Hills, and Dumyat in the Ochil range. Return by the outward route.

19. Ben Venue

9km (r) from Loch Achray Hotel; 10km (r) from Ledard Farm
Ben Venue may be ascended from (1) the Loch Achray Hotel, or (2) Ledard Farm on Loch Ard.

 (1) The most popular route starts from behind the Loch Achray Hotel (Route 7). Follow the forestry track, go left at the first fork and then straight ahead at a crossroads. The wide track now becomes a path. Rejoin a forestry road for a short distance and look for a waymarked path (R). Go uphill on the path, through forested Gleann Riabhach. At the forest edge a stile leads to open

moorland. Continue towards the lowest point on the skyline, with the burn on the left. The Ledard path joins at a cairn and the path goes right towards the twin summits of Ben Venue (729m and 727m). The splendid vista includes Lochs Katrine, Achray and Venachar, Ben Ledi, Stuc a' Chroin and Ben Vorlich, Ben Lawers, the Crianlarich 'Munros', Ben Lomond, the Arrochar Alps, the Arran peaks and the Lowland Kilpatrick, Campsie, Ochil and Pentland ranges, with Glasgow's high flats appearing beyond Strath Blane.

(2) From Ledard take the track off B829 (Route 6) which leads to Ledard Farm. Cross a stile and a footbridge over the Ledard Burn (R) before reaching the farm and ascend by a path through the woods, with the burn on the right. The path emerges from the woods, crosses to the east side of the burn and veers right towards a high pass. The Loch Achray path joins (R) at a cairn, before continuing towards Ben Venue's twin summits.

20. Ben Ledi

6km (r) direct from Coireachrombie; 9km (r) via Stank
Although it is not a 'Munro', Ben Ledi is a distinctive mountain occupying a prominent location on the Highland edge and can therefore be observed from many parts of the southern Highlands, the central Lowlands and even the Southern Uplands. In former times the local folk climbed the mountain on the first day of May, the old Celtic New Year, to perpetuate the ancient Druidical rite of lighting the Beltane fires in honour of Baal, the Celtic sun god. Indeed, the mountain's name has been held to derive from Beinn le Dia, 'mountain of God or light', although others maintain that it comes from Beinn an Leothaid, 'mountain of the gentle slope'.

There are two popular routes to the summit, both of which can be started from the Forestry Commission car park at Coireachrombie, just off the A84 in the Pass of Leny.

(1) The easiest and most popular route starts opposite Coireachrombie bridge and winds upwards through conifers before emerging on to the open mountain slope, with the Ben's steep eastern crags towering above. The path crosses a burn and winds left under the crags, before going right to ascend the mountain's southern shoulder. In good conditions, it is a relatively easy climb on mountain grasses to the 879m-high summit of Ben Ledi. The splendid panorama of the southern Highlands includes Ben Vorlich and Stuc a' Chroin; the Braes of Balquhidder; the Crianlarich 'Munros', including Cruach Ardrain, Ben More and Stobinian; and Ben Venue, Ben Lomond

and the Arrochar Alps. Closer to hand, Loch Lubnaig lies below the precipitous slopes of Ardnandave Hill, while Glen Finglas Reservoir lies to the west and Loch Venachar to the south.

(2) The alternative, more difficult route, is to walk north from Coireachrombie car park on the forestry road signposted for Strathyre Forest cabins, which provides vehicular access only for cabin patrons and local residents. Just before reaching Stank Farm, a forestry road (L) leads to a path which ascends Stank Glen by the south side of Stank Burn. Beyond the tree-line, the path goes left towards the crest of the ridge at the Bealach nam Corp or 'pass of the dead'. North of here is Lochan nan Corp, said to take its name from a funeral party which was crossing the pass in winter to St Bride's Chapel. They entrusted their weight to the ice, the ice broke, and many drowned. From the Bealach the route veers sharply to the left and fence posts are followed south to the grassy approach to the summit of Ben Ledi.

Routes (1) and (2) can be combined to make a circular walk and Coireachrombie can be reached from Callander or Strathyre by the Callander–Strathyre Cycle and Walking path if desired.

STRONACHLACHAR DISTRICT

21. Royal Cottage and The Aqueducts

8km (r)

From Stronachlachar Pier or car park (just south of the pier), take the tarmac road which goes left from the Inversnaid road, about 200m west of Stronachlachar, and runs along the south side of Loch Katrine. The aqueduct which brings water from Loch Arklet to augment the Loch Katrine supply is soon crossed. Just before reaching Royal Cottage, at a cattle-grid and fence, take the path (R) which goes uphill.

Royal Cottage, now occupied by Water Authority staff and their families, was built in 1859 for the visit of Queen Victoria to open Glasgow Corporation's Loch Katrine Waterworks (see Route 6). The intakes for the twin aqueducts which supply the city of Glasgow with 100 million gallons of water a day are located near the house.

As the path ascends, with fine views north-west towards the head of the loch, stone-built towers erected over the shafts for the aqueduct tunnels mark the course of the tunnels through the hillside. There are fine views from the summit, north to the Balquhidder hills and south-west to Ben Lomond. A stile gives access to a conifer plantation in the Loch Achray Forest, part of the Queen Elizabeth Forest Park, and the path soon drops down to the B829 road (Route 6).

Turn right on to the B829, which climbs to leave the Forest Park before descending to the east end of Loch Arklet, and has been dammed at its west end to augment the Loch Katrine water supply scheme. At the road junction go right for Stronachlachar.

STRATHYRE DISTRICT

22. Bailefuil Walk and Beinn an t' Sidhein

6.5km (r) Bailefuil Walk; 9.5km (r) Beinn an t' Sidhein
The Bailefuil and Beinn an t' Sidhein (Ben Shean) walks start by following the same route. From Strathyre car park take the path which crosses the River Balvag on a footbridge and go right, along a road. Approaching a road junction, take a footpath (L) which climbs steeply through the Forestry Commission's Strathyre Forest. Where the path joins a forestry road, turn right into the road for about 100m and then left on a footpath (green/blue waymarks). Continue uphill, enjoying views towards Loch Lubnaig and Ben Ledi, until the Beinn an t' Sidhein and Bailefuil Walks diverge.

(1) For the Bailefuil Walk, look for a green marker (R) and follow the path to join a forestry road near the Strathyre TV mast. Continue along the hillside, where wild flowers and deer may be observed, enjoying the views over upper Strathyre. At Cameron's Viewpoint (named after Alistair Cameron, the Forestry Commission's head forester when planting commenced in the 1930s) Lochs Earn and Lubnaig both appear. The road descends, curves right and at a junction go right to return to Strathyre (green waymarks).

(2) For Beinn an t' Sidhein, go left by the path (blue waymarks) which eventually emerges on to open moorland (no waymarks). Turn right along the ridge to the summit of Beinn an t' Sidhein (572m) for splendid views which include Lochs Lubnaig and Earn, Ben Lawers, Ben Vorlich, Stuc a' Chroin and Ben Ledi.

Return to Strathyre by the same route, detour via the Bailefuil Walk or descend to Immeroin Farm by the path ahead and return via Balquhidder and the Stroneslaney road.

BALQUHIDDER DISTRICT

23. Kirkton Glen, Creag an Tuirc and Glen Dochart

(1) 2km (r) to Creag an Tuirc; (2) 8km (r) to Lochan an Eireannaich; (3) 8km to Glen Dochart
From either side of Balquhidder Churchyard take one of the paths which go uphill through the forest and soon converge.

(1) For Creag an Tuirc, 'the rock of the boar', or The Manse Rock,

take the path on the right at the public water supply enclosure. The rock, which provides a fine viewpoint, overlooks the gathering ground of Clan MacLaren. Return by the same route.

(2) For the Kirkton Pass and Glen Dochart, go straight ahead at the water supply enclosure, ignoring all junctions to left and right, and following the Kirkton Burn (L) all the way up Kirkton Glen. Nearing the forest edge, take a small path marked 'Glen Dochart Path' which goes straight ahead, goes left of the edge of the woodland and zig-zags up some crags to Lochan an Eireannaich, 'little loch of the Irishman', overlooked by the savage cliffs of Meall an Fhiodhain. Return by the same route or continue to Glen Dochart.

(3) For the descent to Glen Dochart, go through a gate in a fence near the east side of the lochan and follow the steep path ahead (which is faint in places). Angle down to the Ledcharrie Burn, pass through a gap in a fence and go under a disused railway bridge.

The right of way goes through a gate and passes through the yard of Ledcharrie Farm, to emerge on the A85 road 1.25km east of Luib.

KILLIN DISTRICT

24. The Old Killin Railway and Loch Tay

7km (r)

The locally owned Killin branch railway served the district from 1886 until 1965, with stations at Killin (now a car park) and beside the former steamer pier at Loch Tay. The old track-bed now provides a pleasant walking route from Killin to Loch Tay.

From Killin, cross the River Dochart on the quaint old arched bridge to the Clachaig Hotel and go left along the drive of Kinnell Estate, then left again over the Dochart by the railway viaduct, one of the earliest examples in Britain of reinforced concrete-arch construction. Follow the old railway down to Loch Tay, passing a car park (L) at the site of Killin Station where the walk can also be joined.

For a shorter walk, leave the old railway just before reaching the bridge over the River Lochay and return by the south bank of the Lochay and the north bank of the River Dochart to the Dochart railway viaduct, or vice versa.

Return from Loch Tay by going through a 'kissing' gate (R) and follow the path near the loch shore and the north bank of the River Lochay, passing the site of the old MacNab stronghold of Ellanryne, to rejoin the old railway at the Lochay bridge. Alternatively, return by Pier Road which runs parallel with the old railway for 1km. At the ruined Finlarig Castle (R), turn right on to a farm road. Just beyond Finlarig Farm, a path goes left and along the edge of Killin Golf Course before emerging on the A827 road at Bridge of Lochay. The Bridge of Lochay Hotel featured in the film *The Thirty-nine Steps*. Return to Main Street by the footpath beside A827.

Note: Dogs must be on a lead and kept under control on farm property.

25. Sron A' Chlachain and the Peat Road

12km (r)

From Breadalbane Park, Killin, cross the stile behind the park and take the track which climbs through bracken to a stile at the edge of the oak woods. Continue climbing through the woods and then over the open hillside to the summit of Sron a' Chlachain or Stronachlachan (521m). The magnificent view embraces Ben Lawers, Loch Tay and Killin. Return by the same route or by the old Peat Road, used by the local folk in centuries past to bring down peats for fuel, laden on ponies.

 To gain the Peat Road, head south-west and descend until the forest appears below. Head for the west end of the forest, go through the deer fence at the corner and walk down beside it to a stile. The old Peat Road is joined here which soon zig-zags down to Killin, although the exit at the foot is easily missed. Look for some electricity pylons (L), where the track crosses a fence and descends through a meadow to a gate by the houses in Manse Road.

Note: No dogs are permitted on this walk.

Appendix

Note on the Origin of Gaelic Place-Names

Names of Gaelic origin predominate throughout the region. This was the language of the Scots, a Celtic race who migrated from Ireland and established the kingdom of Dalriada on the western seaboard (in what is now Argyll) from c500AD. The Scots gradually supplanted the native Britons to the east, another Celtic race whose language (akin to modern Welsh) is termed Brythonic or Cumbric. Their kingdom of Strathclyde, centred on Dumbarton Rock, once extended all the way from the Clach nam Breatann ('the stone of the Britons') in Glen Falloch, all the way south to Morecambe Bay, and they were also associated with the Britons of what is now Wales. By c843AD, the Scots had also annexed the kingdom of the Picts, a mysterious Celtic people about whom little is known to this day and whose territory lay to the north east of Dalriada.

By the time the Scots King Malcolm died in 1034, Gaelic was being spoken throughout mainland Scotland, apart from the eastern Anglian (or early English-speaking) region which covered the Lowlands and the Borders. Gaelic place-names frequently replaced existing Cumbric, Pictish and other names, to the extent that even Dumbarton Rock, seat of the Britons of Strathclyde, came to be known by its Gaelic name Dun Breatann, 'fortress of the Britons', rather than the Cumbric Alclut (or variations thereof), 'the Rock on the Clyde'.

However, the Gaelic language was progressively pushed back by the advance of English from the early Middle Ages, leaving behind only Gaelic place-names as evidence of its existence. Nevertheless, as late as 1928, John Irving, in the introduction to his book on Dunbartonshire place-names, noted that 'even today [Gaelic] is to be found lingering among the old inhabitants in the glens of Luss and Arrochar'. The language is now virtually extinct throughout the region, although a local newspaper has alleged a revival of interest. Certainly, place-name boards at railway stations where West Highland Line trains stop currently show both anglicised Gaelic place-names and the original Gaelic.

Glossary of Gaelic Words Commonly Occurring in Place-names and Geographical Features

Alternative spellings in common usage are shown in brackets.

Aber mouth or confluence of a river

Abhainn, Abhuinn, Amhainn, Amhuin (Avon) river

Achadh (Ach, Auchen, Auchin) field, plain

Allt (Ald, Alt, Auld, Ault) brook, burn, stream

Aonach ridge, moor

Ard, Aird high point, promontory

Bad clump of woodland

Bail, Baile (Bal, Bali) hamlet, house

Bàn white fair

Barr height, upland

Beag (Beg) little, small

Bealach (Balloch) pass, gap

Beinn (Ben) hill, mountain

Beul mouth

Binnein pinnacle, little mountain

Blar (Blair) plain, field

Bo cow

Bocan hobgoblin or phantom spirit

Both house

Bothan hut, bothy

Braigh (Brae, Bread) top, summit

Breac spotted, speckled

Bruaich (Bruach) bank, brae, steep place

Buidhe yellow, golden

Burn stream

Caisteal (Cashel) castle

Camas (Camis, Camus) bay, bend, channel

Caol, Caolas (Kyle) strait, firth, narrow, kyle

Caer, Cathair (Car, Catter) fort

Carn (Cairn) heap of stones, cairn

Ceann (Ken, Kin) head, headland

Chaorach sheep

Cill (Kil) cell, church

Clach stone

Clachan hamlet, stones

Cladach shore, beach

Cluain field, pasture, green plain, meadow

Cnap knob, hillock

Cnoc (Knock) knoll

Coill, Coille (Cal) wood, forest

Coire (Corrie) cauldron, kettle, circular hollow

Creag (Craig) rock, cliff

Croit (Croft) small-holding

Cruach pile, heap, hump

Cuil (Cul, Coul) the back, a nook, corner

Dail (Dal, Dil) field

Damh bullock, heifer

Dearg red

Doire (Derry) grove, hollow, wood

Druim (Drem, Drom, Drum) ridge, back

Dubh black, dark

Dún (Dum, Dun) fort, castle, small hill (often fortified)

Eaglais church, temple

Eas waterfall

Easg bog, fen, natural ditch
Eilean (Ellan) island
Fada long
Falach (Falloch) hidden, veiled
Fearn (Fern) alder tree
Fionn (Fin) white, clear (see also **Geal**)
Garbh (Garve) rough
Gart, Garradh enclosure, field
Geal white, clear (see also **Fionn**)
Glas grey, pale, green, wan
Gleann (Glen) narrow valley, dale, dell
Gorm blue, azure, green
Inbhir (Inver) confluence, place of meeting of river or sea
Innis (Inch) island
Lag hollow in a hill
Laigh low
Lairig pass, sloping face of a hill
Leathad slope, declivity
Leathan broad
Leiter (Letter) slope, side of a hill
Liath grey
Linne (Linn) pool (often by a waterfall), sound, channel
Loch lake, arm of the sea
Lochan small lake
Machair plain, extensive beach
Mam round, gently rising hill
Maol (Mull) headland, cape, bald top
Meadhon, Meadhonach (Vane) middle, central
Meall knob, lump, rounded hill
Moine moss-land, mossy, peat
Monadh moor, heath, hill, mountain
Mòr, Mhòr (More) great, large, tall
Muileann (Miln) mill
Òb bay, creek, haven
Odhar (Our) dapple, drab, dun-coloured, sallow

Ord round, steep or conical hill
Poll (Pol) stream, pool, pond, pit
Rathad road, way
Riabhach (Reoch, Riach) drab, grey, brindled, grizzled
Righ (Ree, Ry) king
Ros (Ross) point, promontory
Ruadh red, reddish
Rubha, Rudha (Ru, Rhu, Row) promontory
Sean (Shan) old, aged, ancient
Sgeir (Skerry) reef, rock at sea
Sgorr, Sgurr peak, conical sharp rock
Sith fairy
Sithean fairy hillock or knoll
Slochd deep hollow
Srath (Strath) valley, plain beside a river, strath
Sròn (Strome, Stron, Strone) nose, peak, promontory
Sruth (Struan) stream, current
Stac steep rock, conical hill
Stob point, stump, peak
Stuc (Stuck) pinnacle, peak, conical steep rock
Suidhe sitting, resting place
Tairbeirt (Tarbert, Tarbet) isthmus
Tigh (Tay, Ty) house
Tir country, region, land
Tom hillock, mound
Torc boar
Torr mound, heap, hill
Tulach (Tillie, Tilly, Tully, Tullich) knoll, hillock, eminence
Uachdar (Auchter, Ochter) upper land
Uaine green
Uamh cave, grave
Uisge water, rain
Uruisg goblin, wild man of the hills possessing supernatural powers